THE ART OF THE
CANTERBURY TALES

THE ART OF THE
CANTERBURY TALES

PAUL G. RUGGIERS

THE UNIVERSITY OF WISCONSIN PRESS

MADISON AND MILWAUKEE, 1965

Published by
The University of Wisconsin Press
Madison and Milwaukee
P.O. Box 1379, Madison, Wisconsin 53701

Printed in
the United States of America by
Vail-Ballou Press, Inc., Binghamton, New York
Library of Congress Catalog
Number 65–16365

For Ernestine and Christopher

When vigorous writers have reached maturity, we are at liberty to gather from their works some expression of a total view of the world they have been so actively observing. This is the most interesting thing their works offer us. Details are interesting in proportion as they contribute to make it clear.

HENRY JAMES, *French Poets and Novelists*

The beginning of right acquaintance with Chaucer is the conviction that nothing represents him except the whole body of his writings.

W. P. KER, *Essays on Medieval Literature*

PREFACE

I wish to express my gratitude to the J. S. Guggenheim Memorial Foundation for a Fellowship (1956–57) which provided me with the leisure and the freedom to accomplish the initial stages of this book; and the Faculty Research Committee of the University of Oklahoma which made possible two weeks' study at the Huntington Library, San Marino, California. The germ of some of the ideas presented here has previously been stated in "The Form of *The Canterbury Tales: Respice Fines,*" *College English,* XVII (1956), 439–44, and in "Some Philosophical Aspects of *The Knight's Tale,*" *College English,* XIX (1958), 296–302. It goes without saying that many of the virtues which this book may contain are due to others, and that what is wanting in judgment, in critical taste, in decorum, can be imputed only to myself. I acknowledge here a special debt of gratitude to my colleagues Professor John M. Raines and Professor Rudolph C. Bambas who gave substantial assistance in the final stages of the work, and to my friend Professor Roy Vance Ramsay who argued patiently. More than to any other, I am indebted to Professor Edward L. Hirsh of Boston College who worked arduously in the shaping of this book, and without whose patient, intelligent handling of problems of presentation it might well never have reached its final form.

In the period during which this book was being written, my labors have been immeasurably abetted, challenged, and fortified by Ralph Baldwin, *The Unity of the Canterbury Tales,* Anglistica, Vol. V (Copenhagen, 1955); Charles Muscatine, *Chaucer and the French Tradition: A Study in Style and Meaning* (University of California Press, 1957); E. Talbot Donaldson, *Chaucer's Poetry: An Anthology for the Modern Reader* (New York, 1958); Paull F. Baum, *Chaucer: A Critical Appreciation* (Duke University Press, 1958); Bertrand H. Bronson, *In Search of Chaucer* (University of Toronto Press, 1960); the signal researches of D. W. Robertson, Jr., *A Preface to Chaucer:*

Studies in Medieval Perspectives (Princeton University Press, 1962); and Robert O. Payne, *The Key of Remembrance: A Study of Chaucer's Poetics* (Yale University Press, 1963). All references to the works of Chaucer are to the second edition of F. N. Robinson, *The Works of Geoffrey Chaucer* (Boston, 1957).

An earlier version of this manuscript contained, under a heading "Didactic Tales," the tales of the Physician, the Manciple, the Monk, and the Parson. In the interest of brevity, they have been removed from the book.

P. G. R.

Norman, Oklahoma
November, 1964

CONTENTS

INTRODUCTION

Everyone who comes seriously to the study of the *Canterbury Tales* must face the problem of its structure: is it merely a series of fragments held loosely together by one device or another, or is it a complete structure? When the questions are put this way, it becomes clear that we are dealing with the question of plot or *mythos* in the Aristotelian sense, and that in particular we have raised the subject of the relation of the parts to the whole.

If we work diligently at these matters in an attempt to define the degree of completeness in terms of the continuity or progression of events, we shall find that Chaucer fails entirely to put together a unified plot in any conventional sense. And we shall further discover that the agents do not always exist, so far as we can tell, for the sake of the tale or speech they are to be assigned. We can then to our profit shift our attention from an insistence upon such matters as linear structure or a moving, evolving plot to a consideration of the larger theme or themes of the *Canterbury Tales;* to be brief, we shift our attention to what the work is about. Although it may seem that in so doing we shirk certain scholarly concerns about order, we rely upon the conviction that the individual tales may thus be seen as manifestations of theme. Our attention, not primarily concerned with "what comes next?" is focused upon centers of interest suspended between two poles: a fictive representation of mankind in all its variety governed simultaneously by the spirit of penance and of festivity; and at the close, a non-fictive examination of the vices to be avoided and the virtues to be pursued as the means of attaining the heavenly city.

Though technical considerations dictated a three-part division of this book, what follows is essentially bipartite: an examination of the form of the *Canterbury Tales* and an examination of the more interesting tales which it comprises. The examination of the whole structure stems from much the same conviction that led Lowes to aver that the idea of the pilgrimage is a greater conception than that of any of the individual parts of which it is composed.

It should be made clear that Part I is devoted entirely to considerations of form in the Aristotelian sense; it is a treatment of the *Canterbury Tales* in terms of structure and idea, an attempt to establish the relationship of the large, distributed middle to the beginning and end, and thus to move one step further towards stating the degree of completeness in the whole poem. The outer poles of a departure from an inn at Southwark and an arrival at the outskirts of Canterbury constitute Chaucer's own design for a fixed beginning and end. The development of such a plan for the *Canterbury Tales* has provided problems enough; yet, to my mind, the larger problem has been that of the middle. This may be seen as the imposition of an encyclopaedic form upon the romance quest of pilgrimage; or to put it another way, as the suspension of a variety of points of view between the termini of departure and arrival. These points of view, however varied, take on a cast of the serious from the tales of Knight and Parson which enclose the others. It has thus seemed possible to make meaningful in a new way the relation of the middle to the outer form and to bring about some degree of reconciliation between the unity implied by the beginning and end, and an explicable division of the great middle into its fragments.

That the qualities of the encyclopaedic farrago are to be found in the *Canterbury Tales* seems clear: the tales themselves we may see as the episodes of the larger structure; we may note the mixture of prose treatises with tales in verse; we may note the variety of verse and stanza patterns, the intrusion of various voices. These tales, so variously offered, obviously, may give the surface impression of discontinuity. They may, however, be seen as a series of intellectual discoveries, involving the audience's passage from ignorance to knowledge. This knowledge is itself born out of witnessing the discursive as well as spatial movement of a community of pilgrims from the inn in Southwark towards the promise of a Celestial Jerusalem implied by the spires of Canterbury Cathedral.

The metaphor of pilgrimage becomes a greater reality at the close in the *Parson's Prologue;* it is the ending that Chaucer invented for the structure, an ending implied by it, and we need not miss its obvious implications. The relinquishment of the group to the priest is noteworthy in this context and enables us to see the great middle as the examination of the choices available to man; in the relation of beginning to end, we discern a crisis of springtime aspiration and gratitude finding its resolution in the reconciliation of redeemed man, through penance, with God.

It is fairly clear that Chaucer never brought about a final resolution of the various plans for his pilgrimage. Our impression is that of a gradually modified design.[1] There are gaps between the groups, inconsistencies in pronominal reference, sometimes puzzling assignments of tales to tellers. Because it is composed of fragments, the completeness of the *Canterbury Tales* as a continuous structure is not demonstrable. Having weighed the suggestions of completeness which the form contains, we turn to a matter which provides a clue to the kind of poem we are dealing with: the role of the narrator and the degree of his participation in the social and spiritual journey. Thereafter our concern will be to define the nature of the great middle of the *Canterbury Tales* from principally two points of view: the range of literary types, and more important, the burden of theme or commentary which the various types are made to support. There is an attempt here to describe the kinds of statement which the literary types will tolerate. The criticism here is both intrinsic and extrinsic, and its primary aim is the definition of the thematic range of Chaucer's comic and romantic narratives.

Against the background of this discussion of the broader form and interests of the *Canterbury Tales*, we examine at length in Parts II and III the individual elements of the encyclopaedic middle, the tales themselves. The critical focus is chiefly thematic, but the method varies to include matters historical, generic, and rhetorical. In keeping with the suggestions of Part I that the episodes yield a thematic unity, the tales are examined as movements of discovery and illumination, or as what Frye calls "points of expanding apprehension."[2] The difference in tone which some will note arises out of a difference in the objective. The first considerations of form are those which treat literature as a product, as a total construct in which the congregation of parts somehow yields an effect greater than the sum of the parts. This kind of criticism is, it will be recognized, mainly Aristotelian, extrinsic, formal. In the light of existing difficulties in the text, it is

---

[1] Cf. R. M. Lumiansky, "Chaucer's Retraction and the Degree of Completeness of the *Canterbury Tales*," *TSE*, V (1956), 5-13.

[2] Northrop Frye, *Anatomy of Criticism* (Princeton University Press, 1957), p. 326.

necessary here to be theoretical and hypothetical. However, in dealing with the tales individually, in a somewhat Longinian manner, we
no longer consider the literary performance merely as a product, but
rather as a process carried out before our very eyes by an author who
diverts our attention from the product to the means by which he
accomplishes the literary act. We are here "practical" rather than
theoretical (some may even say banal), and the recitation of familiar
details may seem to be unnecessarily patient. However, the principal
concern here has been to keep in view the poet's conscious construction of plot, manipulation of the agents, handling of language, since it
is virtually impossible to deal sympathetically with Chaucer as a poet
without recognizing that his intrusion into the poetic illusion is one of
the chief means by which he invites our participation in his art.

Attention to the tales, one by one, and to the fragments of which
they are a part, has rightly been the concern of scholars and critics.
Yet, it has seemed to me that the passage back and forth between the
examination of the whole structure and the individual parts of it is an
obligation upon the student of the poet. As we examine the tales individually the moments of amusement or of a specially focused insight
have their particular and rewarding value; but to emphasize the genre,
the mood, the diction of a part without reference to the evolving
design is to miss the special joy of recreating, in so far as it lies within
our power, the work of art.

Everyone who has been in the process of doing precisely this will
find in both parts of this book discussions that strike him as naive, and
others that seem unnecessarily sophisticated or refined. He will have
the impression of dogmatic assertion or an excessive enthusiasm on
matters which do not merit such reponses, or will feel that the over-
balance of particularity or generalization in one place or another is
perilous and misleading. These charges the writer will have to bear
alone, exonerating from collusion or responsibility those generations
of scholars everywhere to whose trail-blazing efforts this essay is but
an appendage. Looking at the *Canterbury Tales* first as a total form
and then as a collection of fragments and tales may seem to some to
be confusing; nonetheless it has seemed valuable as a means of getting
at Chaucer both as a serious commentator upon the human comedy
and as a poet who refined his forms to provide the apt vehicle for a
moral statement.

For Chaucer the substance of the moral vision is built upon the traditional associations of the Holy City and the Divine Order. In his maturity, the vision included good and evil as literary materials; it embraced accident and chance, moral freedom and determinism. As a moral being he was concerned with *what is said;* but as poet he was concerned with *how it is said.* Out of the one grows the interest in prudence; out of the other emerges a liberating artistry.

Any such consideration of the relationship of Christian moral vision to structure and art invites us to consider both literary type and meaning, form and function, on all levels of fiction: the tale, its relation to the frame, the frame itself, and the work as a whole. The romantic form of the pilgrimage, as an enveloping structure for Chaucer's vision, is the ideal form to convey such meanings as grow out of a theocratic view of the universe. The encyclopaedia of narrative types in the middle of the total poem, now given new use within the frame, provides the means of depicting man not only as he ought to be, but as he is, and even as worse than he is. Their very variety reflects in the poet the appetite for materials of every sort, beyond any casual ordering principle.

The two factors of moral vision and art—an older generation might have used the terms "thought and invention"—are but two of the points of view from which the form and function of the *Canterbury Tales* can be assessed. Whether there is a comfortable relation between their spheres of influence the poet himself suggests throughout the poem: sometimes overtly in the frame, often indirectly in the subtle interplay of theme and form, in the degree of rhetorical flourish, in the amount and kind of moral and philosophical comment, in the mixture of styles, and in the various shadings of comedy, irony, and romance.

I do not intend by the terms to put undue emphasis upon the distinction between the edifying and the pleasurable. We need not belabor the point that Chaucer knew the difference, whether from the Donatan tradition or from native genius, between quiet and noisy comedy, and that he knew how to combine the edification of the one with the pleasurable of the other. Our concern is larger, with the patterns of thought and their effect upon form, both of the parts and of the whole.

By maintaining a focus upon the relation between the parts and the whole, and upon the shaping of the structure towards a thematic unity, we may in some small way offset the view that the *Canterbury*

Tales is only a collection of poems and not a single work with an intended design. This view, the result of a comparison with the very different structure and plan of the *Troilus*, carries more than a faint suggestion of failure. These matters we assess below, but we may note here that the *Tales* attempts to render, on an entirely different scale, the complexity of human experience. This complexity, in all its diversity, is given a body and a unity. It moves, in the form of a social group, concertedly towards a goal, and is so persuasively realistic as to force the reader to accept the tales as utterances of the various pilgrims. The tales themselves, we continue to discover, are joined to each other in accordance with some principle of contrast or debate. The whole work has a beginning, a middle *of its own kind*, and an end.

We can only state, finally, what we think we see when we draw back from the poem as a whole: what is disjointed and fragmentary in Chaucer's view of life as pilgrimage is given anchorage within the completer vision which the beginning and end morally imply. By such drawing back we come to see how thought has somehow been modulated and defined by that other order of the poem.

I
FORM

SOME PRELIMINARY
CONSIDERATIONS

The Canterbury Tales and
Troilus and Criseyde

Chaucer's reputation rests securely on the foundations of his two major works, *Troilus and Criseyde* and *The Canterbury Tales*. In both of them we see everywhere a comprehensive and sane view of the human condition built upon a keen but sympathetic interest in human psychology. Criseyde and her uncle Pandarus in the one poem, Nicholas, Alison, the Wife of Bath, Harry Bailly in the other, transcend the accidents of time and place, and shine through the years with a permanent lustre of life itself. Beyond their common interest in living men and women, the two poems have a kinship in the degree to which the author's irony pervades his relationship with his audience, enabling him to maintain that rare detachment that goes with a mastered art. To these similarities we may add, with Lowes,[1] the mastery of dialogue, the handling of dramatic construction, and the energy and control of individual scenes.

More recently scholars have noted other common grounds which the palinode of *Troilus* and the Retraction of the *Canterbury Tales* share,[2] notably the paradox of a simultaneous affirmation and rejection of the world and the experience it offers, remarked in the smaller vision poems as well, principally the *Parliament of Fowls*.[3]

The similarities between the *Canterbury Tales* and the *Troilus* are instructive. Their differences, however obvious, are important and equally instructive. The literary form of the *Tales*, for example, having to do with a quest and a pilgrimage, posits a departure at one end and an arrival or return at the other. In the medieval view this narrative form involves a passage from misery to happiness or the opposite. Between these two poles we are concerned both with the larger

---

[1] John L. Lowes, "The Prologue to the *Legend of Good Women* Considered in Its Chronological Relations," *PMLA*, XX (1905), 749–864.
[2] E.g. Kemp Malone, *Chapters on Chaucer* (The Johns Hopkins Press, 1951), p. 139.
[3] Charles Muscatine, *Chaucer and the French Tradition: A Study in Style and Meaning* (University of California Press, 1957), pp. 123, 132.

effects of eliciting through the episodes a variety of emotional and intellectual responses like pity and fear or anger and envy, and with dissipating these emotional forces within and without the literary form, among the pilgrims and among the listening audience. In the relationship of the agents to each other we are concerned with their sympathies and antipathies, their conflicts and debates, with the statements of their dearest wishes and of their most rueful admissions. For the poet's audience there are not merely one or two crises as the outcome of foregoing acts (as might be expected in a less complex structure), but rather a series of recognitions. These are brought into effective resolution, in the last performance of the *Canterbury Tales,* by means of a new metaphor and by means of a shift from the mood of festivity to one of great sobriety.

By contrast with the *Troilus,* the looser structure and potentially endless form of the *Tales* admit into its design many more persons than Chaucer has involved in actions heretofore. Their presence implies not necessarily finer shades of feeling and opinion than we encounter in the *Troilus,* but surely a greater variety of human response and points of view than can be handled in a more controlled form with fewer characters. This very variety in the *Tales* provides the motivation for the shorter narratives which, within the larger compass, become utterances from the individual pilgrims.

The looser pattern of the *Tales,* then, sustains two levels of fiction: an outer frame in which the predominantly linear movement of pilgrimage is carried on, and a succession of smaller narratives which function within the frame as utterances from the individual pilgrims. In both levels of fiction, but principally in the framing structure, one feels that not all of the timbers have been set in place. Even with the substantial scaffolding of the opening exhibition of portraits and the opening group of tales as a beginning and with the final tale and the Retraction as an end, we are left to wonder about the spaces still uncompleted within the existing structure. We see immediately the importance of the linking materials which function not merely as a bare framework but rather as the larger and more important fiction. If we are disappointed with them it is largely because we sense their importance and lament the failure to fulfill their promise. The frame does, however, provide us with a progression of panels or pageants. Before each we pause and listen. When we encounter the uncompleted spaces which baffle and excite the imagination, we assume that what we witness is a work in process, not a final result, and that the energies of the poet are bringing into existence before our very eyes the occasionally successful union of the larger and smaller fictions. Arnold Hauser offers us an analogy:

...a Gothic building is not merely itself a mass of movement; it mobilizes the spectator, too, and turns an act of enjoyment into a process with a definite direction and gradual accomplishment. Such a building cannot be taken in all at once from any possible view-point; from no quarter does it present a complete, restful view, disclosing the structure of the whole. On the contrary, it compels the spectator to be constantly changing his view-point and permits him to gain a picture of the whole only through his own movement, action and power of reconstruction.[4]

And another which is germane:

The man of the late medieval middle-class epoch looks out on the world with different eyes and from a different standpoint than his forefathers whose interests were confined to the next world. He stands, as it were, on the edge of a road on which colourful, inexhaustible, relentlessly onward-flowing life unfolds itself, and he not only finds everything that happens there extremely interesting, but he also feels himself involved in all this life and activity. The "travel landscape" is the most typical pictorial theme of the age and the pilgrim procession of the Ghent altar is to a certain extent the basic form of its world-view.... The pictures pass in front of the beholder like the scenes of a constantly moving procession—and the beholder is spectator and participant at the same time.[5]

The Relation of the
Tales to the Frame

As we have said, the *Canterbury Tales* contains within its larger narrative form a variety of smaller tales and integrates them within the metaphor of the pilgrimage. The outer formal pattern is spatial and geographically linear, and its "plot" is sketched out in rapid strokes in the links by means of the time and place references as well as by its inner life of quarrel and debate and the general pattern of instigation

[4] Arnold Hauser, *The Social History of Art*, trans. Stanley Godman (New York, 1951), I, 242. I have no intention here of raising the question of Chaucer and the Gothic. I wish only to point out the degree to which the frame becomes a clue to meaning, the device by which our participation is assured.

[5] *Ibid.*, p. 262. See the instructive application of the principles of the Gothic to the framework of the *Canterbury Tales* in D. W. Robertson, Jr., *A Preface to Chaucer: Studies in Medieval Perspectives* (Princeton University Press, 1962), pp. 257–58.

and response. The links themselves give the impression of a consistently sustained tone; the dialogue within them is lively, realistic, and comic. The voices of the individual narrators in confession, protestation, or simple opinion are thereafter heard exerting their special nuances within the tales they tell. The persistent realism of the frame, with its great variety of men and women from all classes, is an artistic corroboration of the interest in human nature in complex situations which arose out of Chaucer's own life as civil servant. The comic, dissentient, and realistic world which he depicts and which his men and women inhabit provides a tart counterpoint to the otherworldly goal implied by the journey.

The vitality of the framing structure is one of the special beauties of the *Canterbury Tales* and is of considerable importance in our appreciation of the artistry of the work as a whole. Each pilgrim is involved in the personal task of his own salvation, the singularity and loneliness of which we may assess for ourselves from the private or public allegiances of individual pilgrims as well as from the unremitting moral honesty of the Retraction. Yet within the world man is involved with others, and in the literature which represents him the processes of enlightenment, of recognition or discovery, of catharsis are worked out socially. The links, along with the *General Prologue*, offer us the opportunity to see human beings first in their private selves with their dominant passion or passions suggested or described, and in the greater or less degree of implication with the community. That is to say, the whole body of society suffers, acts, laughs; and the Host himself for example, no mere impersonal and detached referee, is able to demonstrate his own chagrined participation in the comic, but nonetheless purgatorial experience of marriage. At the same time he affords a kind of focus and reflection of middle range opinion, concurring on one occasion with the opinion of the Knight on the relation between literature and life, quarreling with Chaucer on somewhat the same matter, and yielding to the Parson finally on such matters as transcend the merely social scene.

The tales contained within the framework narrative are of varying degrees of excellence; Chaucer obviously thought well enough of them to preserve them within the frame. To put it another way, he found the framing structure, with its variety of participants, sufficiently broad and democratic to accommodate varying degrees of— to our critical taste—literary worth. We better assess the value of the individual tales when we see that Chaucer was not writing in accordance with a rigid scheme (as Boccaccio did in the *Decameron,* where stories of a particular kind or subject matter are related on successive days). His purpose was more psychologically realistic and dramatic, that is to say, motivated by clearly stated connections between situation, character, and utterance. That he is not uniformly successful is obvious. Yet the failure to collate perfectly the two levels of his fiction is a gauge of the difficulties inherent in so complex an undertaking.

To be sure, a writer will tell a tale as well as he knows how; but to adjust a tale to a particular teller, within particular situations, poses problems of a serious order. The tales individually do have an artistic, assessable value, aside from their context, but that multifaceted view of experience which collectively they supply (and this view implies the inadequacy of any one taken singly) must be seen as the meaning of the Canterbury pilgrimage as a total work of art.

This difficult-to-verbalize totality necessarily involves the grand dialogue which is the soul of the *Canterbury Tales:* it is the links principally which constitute the matrix for the individual tales. It is the links which, through the agents, call into being the disparate aspects and extremes of divine comedy and parodic human comedy. In a special sense the links are, to use a Latin phrase, the *occasiones;* the tales, the *rationes.* The intimate relationship which the frame bears to the smaller narratives is the means by which the comic, realistic world envelops and conditions the terms on which we accept the smaller structures, the means by which both the transcendent and the odious are held in balance.

It is this balance between the vitality of the outer structure and that of the individual tales, this struggle between formal architectonics and the tendency towards fragmentation which forces us to assess the ambivalences of the whole construct. The pilgrimage quest with its departure and arrival is the most characteristic element of medieval romance and marks it generally as belonging to the type. Its tendency, however, towards a dramatic form dominated by dialogue, with a markedly casual and loose-jointed structure, and an apparently easy shift of topic in accordance with the ethos and intellect of the speaker; its generally free mixture of tales moral in intention with others marked by obscenity, jesting, and even abuse; the general air of jocularity and mild satire—all point to the medley or miscellany which has had a more or less continuous history in Western culture from the days of Varro, and before him of Menippus, and which has influenced such writers as Petronius, Apuleius, Voltaire, Swift, Rabelais, and Sterne. We note, too, the absence of a hero around whom the action evolves (with a concomitant rise in the importance of the nagging shrew); the parody either of attitudes, as in the Knight-Miller-Reeve complex, or literary types as in Chaucer's *Sir Thopas* and the *Nun's Priest's Tale;* the confrontation of worlds of social behavior in the Manciple's interpolations. These arise naturally out of the tendency of satire to allow the most diverse social attitudes to prosper without the constant threat of judgment from the author.

Whether, in the *Canterbury Tales,* the subject is marriage, or successful duping, or self-control, or the mystery of fate and fortune, or free will and predestination, or reason and appetite, the variety of subjects adds up to a broad examination of the worlds of social, moral, and religious experience, presented as a series of loosely joined episodes, as separated illuminations of experience. Their very separateness however prevents our seeing the thought relationship between the individual groups, and scholars have groped with only limited, varying degrees of success towards defining the essential structure of the groups, one by one.[6]

Type and Theme

As we move into the great middle of the *Canterbury Tales,* the fragments tend to take on an interest in isolation from each other (although we have fallen into the habit of welding Groups D, E, and F together and Groups H and I); chronology within the spatial movement along the road, owing to the fragmentary nature of this collection, loses some of its importance.[7] If we lose sight of the larger

---

[6] G. L. Kittredge, "Chaucer's Discussion of Marriage," *MP,* IX (1911–12), 435–67; Paull F. Baum, *Chaucer: A Critical Appreciation* (Duke University Press, 1958), pp. 74 ff.; Marie Neville, "The Function of the *Squire's Tale* in the Canterbury Scheme," *JEGP,* L (1951), 167–79; William C. Stokoe, Jr., "Structure and Intention in the First Fragment of the *Canterbury Tales,*" *UTQ,* XXI (1951–52), 120–27; Wayne Shumaker, "Chaucer's *Manciple's Tale* as a Part of the Canterbury Group," *UTQ,* XXII (1953), 147–56.

[7] See the discussion of the Man of Law in Paul G. Ruggiers, "The Form of the *Canterbury Tales: Respice Fines,*" *CE,* XVII (1956), 439 ff.; and E. Talbot Donaldson,

design and approach the individual fragments as discrete episodes (the order of which admits much discussion) we can still savor the rich contrast of various levels of literary experience: in the first fragment the opposition of romance and fabliaux and the opposing views of professions and estates; thereafter, the calculated naïveté of the *Man of Law's Tale*, the thoroughgoing worldliness of the Shipman and the otherworldliness of the Prioress, the nice balance between old tragedy in the Monk's performance and new comedy in the Nun's Priest's, the confession of the Host (a vignette that deserves our careful consideration), the implied range of Chaucer's own "tales," the psychological and theological richness of suggestion in the Friar-Summoner altercation, the varying focus of the so-called marriage group, the bitterness and toughness of the Merchant, the softer yet equally authoritative implications of the Franklin, the difference between old law and new in the Physician-Pardoner pair, the contrast between the annealing fire of the Second Nun and the hell-fire implied by the Canon's Yeoman. We can savor the centers of interest, seeing them as disconnected, except for the steady implications of the pilgrimage narrative form and its linear movement, the presence of the Host as the chief moderator of the social group in action and interaction, and the attitude of the in-the-main detached author who refrains from passing judgment upon the worth of the various points of view.

The range of Chaucer's interest in literary types disposes him towards the larger and more comprehensive form, inasmuch as it allows for variation in genre and style and for the use of prose as well as verse. The articulation of romance and parodies of romance, tragedies and fabliaux, saints' lives and quasi-allegories, moral treatises and beast fables, the Breton lai and the preacher's anecdote into a single long structure invites comparison with other encyclopaedic poems available to him: alongside the closely woven moral system of the *Divine Comedy*, the *Canterbury Tales* seems unwieldy, unfocused; alongside the digressiveness of the *Romance of the Rose* or the refined but banal schematism of the *Confessio Amantis*, it seems precise and controlled.

Such poems as these have much in common: the absorption of moral and philosophical matters into poetry; the juxtaposing of

---

Chaucer's Poetry: An Anthology for the Modern Reader (New York, 1958), pp. 947 ff., where the discussion of the *Parson's Tale* and the Retraction takes into account the relation between spatial movement and meaning.

erotic and spiritual experience; the presence of certain conventional
attitudes towards "good" and "bad" women, towards "good" churchmen and "bad" churchmen; concern with the philosophy underlying
the concept of love; interest in Nature as the vicar of God and in man
as a fallen creature. These are proof of a common intellectual inheritance in matters religious, philosophical, and literary. They are, too,
the very materials which, given the comprehensive interests of the
poet, find their natural expression in the larger encyclopaedic form.
Somewhere between the diffuseness of the *Romance of the Rose* and
the concentration of the *Divine Comedy*, the *Canterbury Tales* provides a multileveled view of experience growing out of the character
and intelligence of the speakers, and providing a broad range of
opinion between the two poles of secular and religious sentiment.

We may tend to see the stories either of the seculars or of the
religious as defining purely secular or religious points of view, but we
must not oversimplify the degree of opposition between them. Eight
of the church's pilgrims tell tales as against fourteen of the "lewed"
folk, and throughout we must take into account the inroads of the
secular world upon the religious world. The intrusion or incorpora-
tion of moral, philosophical, and religious thought into the various
tales is an indication of the involvement of these two worlds with
each other as well as an indication of Chaucer's interest in the range
and limits of the various literary types. It is noteworthy for our appreciation of the total form that the opening and closing tales, the
function of which has been assessed in a variety of places,[8] are both
serious, one secular, the other religious.

The *Knight's Tale* and *Parson's Tale* are Chaucer's own established
poles of thought, philosophico-chivalric and religious, implying the
ideals by which the community lives and prospers. Both of them are
tinctured by various shades of thoughtful irony which we detect in
Chaucer from his apprentice days, and which he found corroborated
by the *Consolatio* of Boethius as well as by the work of Boccaccio.
Taken as a pair, these two tales offer, first, stoic resignation to the
chain of being in which all creatures have a place, and finally a more
dogmatic capstone response cutting across the prior pagan mystery,
which asserts the responsibility every man must assume. Both are patterns of consolation, one sober, resigned, pagan, the other cheerful

[8] Ralph Baldwin, *The Unity of the Canterbury Tales*, Anglistica, Vol. V (Copenhagen, 1955); and Ruggiers, in *CE*, XVII, 439–44.

amidst its threats, confident amidst its gloom, and Christian. Between them are strewn at intervals other religious tales exploring various states of the spiritual experience. Across these falls the delightful counterpoise of profane and secular tales of men and women "as they are." It is this double vision which invests the outermost point, the *General Prologue* outside the *Knight's Tale,* pointing up through ironical portraiture the double allegiance of all men to God and to the world. It is this same double vision which comes to the full bloom of irony in Chaucer's denial of the profane works for which posterity has come to revere him.

We may sense, then, in the opening and closing tales, first, the unifying pressure from two kinds of seriousness. And in the *General Prologue* and the Retraction, which stand as the outermost terminals, we may discern a more ironical unifying pressure exerted by the poet's interest in both the profane and spiritual life of men. There are attempts to bring about some happy resolutions of the opposed worlds in the wish-fulfillment tales of the Wife of Bath and of the Franklin, in which what is best in the social and spiritual life of men is affirmed. Nevertheless the *General Prologue* with its mingling of joy with the spirit of penance, and the Retraction, with its moral judgment of much of the world of literary art, hold in balance from one point of view or another the two sides of the debate.

Thought and Character

From the outset in the *General Prologue,* Chaucer is interested in character in the broadest sense of combining outward and inward qualities. The game arranged by the Host becomes, and remains, the means by which the agents are released into intellectual action. What each says, in the links and in the tales, is revelation of character and a corroboration or extension of it. The human nature of each agent expresses itself both by the kind of story he or she is presumed to choose to tell, and by the presence in it of all those data of opinion, *sententiae,* arguments and commentaries which reveal their powers of thought as well as their ethical bias. In a sense, as each speaks, he is in the process of explaining himself: we see this most intimately in the Miller's bold remarks about cuckoldry, in the Reeve's bitter ruminations about old age, in the Host's complaint about his wife, in the confessions of the Merchant, the Pardoner, the Wife of Bath, and the Canon's Yeoman, and in the pilgrim Chaucer's own scrupulosity, on at least three occasions, about accurate reporting.

What is said in the links reveals the inner life of the agent and prepares the occasion for some outward expression. The agent nurses some private grievance which finds expression in oaths, curses, forceful argument, or he finds himself engaged in an actual quarrel with an enemy. Hence the feeling of an intimate relationship between the inner and outer life, an intimate coalescence of inner conviction and outward expression in intellectual reflection, with stories offered as proofs of one's own, or retaliation upon another's views; hence, too, a generous sprinkling of gnomic and proverbial elements arising out of the particular point of view of the speaker.

Of tremendous importance for the whole structure is the assessment of the "thought" arising out of the individual performances. What the agents of the links say, particularly in the tales they tell, and how they say it (that is, with what intellectual means) together offer us a comprehensive vision of man as a social and a spiritual creature, asserting himself, acting, suffering, laughing. Everywhere is implied that delicate balance between man as a free agent, his emotional life hardening into will, and will into act of pilgrimage; and man as the slave of appetite, or of fate, or of fortune. Each agent reveals in his tale something of his own limited view of the human condition, a view necessarily shaped by his status, his profession, his personal bias. In this regard, it is somewhat useless to debate whether Chaucer as man and poet believed in the will, or in fortune, or in fate except insofar as the agents themselves whom he has created reveal something of the paradox of making choices within the limiting factors of their own characters. Perplexity towards the human condition is a literary enrichment, a part of Chaucerian irony. Throughout the great middle of the *Canterbury Tales* there is no conscious attempt to reduce experience to any set of excessively simple moral maxims (the *Tale of Melibee* invites discussion on this point), and it is futile to look for that didactic confidence and conviction which invests the Dantean pilgrimage at every point.

Thought, as the expression of character, is the heart of Chaucer's pilgrimage: the participation of the human agents in the activities of life through the rational faculty of speech, a faculty revealing itself by the way in which the agents argue and express their views. Placed in dramatic situations and given proper motivations they reveal through their words in the links and through their choice of tales their personal bias and predilections, their habits of response, in short their emotional and intellectual natures.[9] The very concreteness of each and the anchoring of tales to dramatic situations make us see even the most philosophical statements as the ethos of the speaking agent and not primarily as the belief of the poet. On the basis of the characterization provided by the *General Prologue*, we may, within the framework of the *Canterbury Tales*, assess the moral as well as the intellectual elements of character and come to some judgment as to the relationship between them, using the tales as the fullest expression of their moral and intellectual life. The attempt to see a meaningful and intimate relation between tale and teller is fraught with problems and has given rise to much speculation as to the suitability of one to the other.[10] Yet inasmuch as each tale, by virtue of being an utterance of a human being, implies character and thought, and these imply moral quality, the quest for meaning in these terms is a necessary outgrowth of the dramatic form.

The appeal of the individual tales and the power of each to elicit our approval has its source in the special pleasure of literature, a pleasure not merely that of the intellect or of the emotions, but that of our combined faculties responding to a poetical structure the truth of which we prove and test, through which our responses can be channeled and through which we corroborate, however vicariously, the experience of reality. In the varieties of thought which we assess from tale to tale—if only in what Coleridge called the willing suspension of disbelief—in the succession of correspondences which we feel between our own lives and those carried on by the imitation, in our evaluation of the way in which these poems are, in Aristotle's sense, more philosophical than history and tied in with the ethical principles by which man lives, we may descry dimly the poet's controlling

[9] George Lyman Kittredge, perhaps more than any other scholar, stimulated thought about the dramatic validity of the tales, with particular attention to a possible marriage group. See "Chaucer's Discussion of Marriage," *MP*, IX, 435–67, and the later version in *Chaucer and His Poetry* (Harvard University Press, 1915), pp. 185–210. More recently the subject has been considerably expanded in R. M. Lumiansky, *Of Sondry Folk: The Dramatic Principle in the Canterbury Tales* (University of Texas Press, 1955).

[10] For example, J. R. Hulbert, "*The Canterbury Tales* and their Narrators," *SP*, XLV (1948), 565–77.

voice. It operates those other voices of pilgrimage without intrusive agreement or dissent. It expresses itself through the tales by which it will be represented before an audience, through the manner of presentation, and through the management of all the data which the poet's keen eye and mind encompass. There are, too, his own beliefs and opinions, surmises and suppositions about mankind, and his own convictions about the art which contains them. There is, further, his own tempered apprehension of a body of beliefs concerning the relation of this world to the next, beliefs which his audience corroborates.

We can, of course, never assess Chaucer's whole intention with regard to this aspect of character. We can, however, get at it through the relation of form to content in the analysis of the individual tales, and through the examination of those elements of thought which are to be found in them. In this matter we must proceed with caution, taking into account the pervasive irony which characterizes Chaucer's relationship with his audience. This Chaucerian irony extends from the creation of an agent with his own name to vastly more refined matters of imagery, from the sly juxtaposition of the crass with the beautiful to the mixture of styles within single tales.

When we consider Chaucer's tolerance, as an artist, of much that the conscience morally rejects, his faint skepticism about human illusions, his fascination with man as fallen yet redeemed, we can appreciate how the literary form of a pilgrimage should have been ideal for his purposes. By shaping the structure morally from alehouse to temple, and by including between them so great a variety of "ideas, feelings, views, reasonings, and other operations of the human mind," [11] he accomplishes a task of a vastly different order from that of the *Troilus*.

That the pilgrims should have their own vitality, that the author should participate only in his specially withdrawn way, involves us with them directly on the levels of character and of our common humanity. In the capaciousness of the vision which they embody we discover our own attitudes and wishes about the life of man. Even though we know that Chaucer is creating a fiction we are led back from the tales to the links, and from the links back into life itself, so much do the pilgrims strike us as the very stuff of life. In fine, the detailed vision of man's perpetually divided nature which shines through the characters makes the *Canterbury Tales* for posterity a

[11] John Henry Newman, "Literature," *The Idea of a University*, sec. 9.

work of the most elusive art. For some it ranks, I suppose mainly on formal grounds, below the *Troilus*. Its vision of experience, however, is not less comprehensive, but on the contrary more varied, and it is entirely possible that the very complexity of its thematic form prevents our seeing it whole.

I have raised some issues which are important to the assessment of the formal structure of the *Canterbury Tales*. It should be remarked that while in general the term "formal structure" suggests that a poem has a demonstrable unity, it has been useful here only for the sake of showing that the *Canterbury Tales* cannot be subjected to the same formal criteria as the *Troilus*, and for moving on to the view that whatever unity the *Tales* may evince must be appraised thematically. Thus we have noted the relation of linear movement (from Southwark to the outskirts of Canterbury) to a newly defined unity of the poem. We have offered some suggestions that the great middle of the work yields, through the technique of the medley, a variety of points of view suspended between the secular and spiritual interests of man. We have commented upon the dynamic relation of the tales to their framework, and upon the centrality of thought in the links and tales. At this point we can explore with profit one problem of the long poem, the degree to which Chaucer becomes a part of his own structure.

THE NARRATOR

The Pilgrim as Poet

One of the problems in estimating whether the *Canterbury Tales* is or is not a continuous and unified work is that of assessing the role of the narrator and the degree to which he participates in the poem. To decide whether the narrator of the tales is Chaucer, the poet, or a literary creation who speaks in his person, and if the latter, then to decide whether he has a consistently definable ethos and intellect, constitutes a problem so intriguing as to have led to a number of visions and revisions. Sensitive readers of Chaucer have, I dare say, always been conscious of an elusive author who is both in and out of his narrative as it suited his purposes, but scholarship in our time has become more engrossed in the possibilities inherent in the issue and has devoted considerable energy to it.[1]

---

[1] In the three sections of this chapter I have tried to give attention to three facets of the complex personality of the narrator: the character of the man who, as simultaneously poet and pilgrim, is making a contribution to the literary structure of which he becomes an agent; the character of the pilgrim who, though a poet, is a responsible citizen within the Christian city; and lastly, the character of the pilgrim who, as moral agent and artist, must bring ethic and aesthetic into reasonable union. If one "Geffrey" is on pilgrimage as one of the "wel nyne and twenty," it should be possible to define the range of his double nature, no less than that of his fellows on the journey. The doubleness on which I have chosen to focus here is that of the man, conscious of the salvation of his soul, and that of the artist, concerned about the integrity of his poem. Other studies have given their attention primarily to the secular ironist commenting upon the social, human scene. The emphasis here is upon those factors in the personality of the narrator which polarize the moral and spiritual dimensions of the poem. Cf. E. Talbot Donaldson, "Chaucer the Pilgrim," *PMLA*, LXIX (1954), 928–36; John M. Major, "The Personality of Chaucer the Pilgrim," *PMLA*, LXXV (1960), 160–62. See too Ben Kimpel, "The Narrator of the *Canterbury Tales*," *ELH*, XX (1953), 77–86; and Edgar Hill Duncan, "Narrator's Point of View in the Portrait-Sketches, *Prologue* to the *Canterbury Tales*," in *Essays in Honor of Walter Clyde Curry*, ed. Richmond C. Beatty and others (Vanderbilt University Press, 1955), pp. 77–101. Bertrand H. Bronson, *In Search of Chaucer* (University of Toronto Press, 1960), pp. 26–28, offers hard correction: "I have little hesitation in saying that nine-tenths of this talk [about Chaucer's persona] is wrong because it was conceived in and of a world of printed books, and bases its premises and assumptions on conditions that could not obtain in any other.... Chaucer wrote for oral

The critical loci of the *Canterbury Tales* which must come under consideration are the *General Prologue,* with its literary apology and protestations of little wit (ll. 715–24), the *Man of Law's Introduction,* the conclusion of the *Miller's Prologue* (ll. 3167–86), the links fore and aft of *Sir Thopas,* and of necessity the Retraction. There are others, but these are the important ones from which we may deduce something about the character of the pilgrim-poet Chaucer.

For a variety of reasons uniformity of opinion cannot be reached, one factor being the long evolution of tales, links, and *General Prologue:* perhaps limited freedom for writing spread composition out over a period of years. The work lacks a single hero steadily in the foreground who interprets experience. Chaucer himself seems to be content with letting others dominate the scene, and with letting their experiences pass before us without that formal control which other perhaps greater architects like Dante have achieved. It seems to have been enough to continue the jest, so rich in irony for oral presentation, in which the narrator disavows intelligence of a particular situation and presents himself from time to time to his audience as dull and obtuse, lacking knowledge and insight. We have seen Chaucer create such a persona in the vision poems, and it is possible to trace out a further development of the persona in the paradox of the *Troilus* where the poet's sophistication is contrasted with the narrator's limited knowledge of love.

The device is useful in the *General Prologue* when the persistent innocence of the narrator leads to a simpleton's appreciation of the pilgrims without regard to a common standard of morality, a yielding to the essential humanity of his companions, a sense of being overwhelmed by their worth, and success, and obvious talents. Praise and appreciation fall easily from his lips, sometimes for reasons we can ourselves corroborate, but often with the feeling that the narrator's personality has led him to equate their worth with their capacity to arouse interest in him. The candor with which the characters of the pilgrims are presented allows Chaucer the artist the leeway even of satire, but Chaucer the persona or pilgrim seems untouched by satiri-

---

delivery, but this primary fact is continually lost sight of or ignored by those who write on the *persona,* and its implications are seldom fully realized.... The schizoid notion of two Chaucers, so named, presented simultaneously, one a puppet, the other the living, speaking poet, with attitudes and intelligences radically different from each other's, could only have arisen in a time when authors would habitually think of themselves as completely separable from their books, and from their audiences."

cal intention and is, so to speak, removed from direct attack. Signs of apparent approval, different in tone from those used to describe the Knight, Parson, and Plowman are evident in his praise of the Summoner's good comradeship, of the Pardoner's powers of oratory, of the Shipman's seamanship, of the Physician's professional skill, of the Friar's persuasiveness, and of the Monk's prowess as a hunter. Indeed in such passages as these it is difficult to distinguish in the point of view of the narrator what is praiseworthy from what is reprehensible. The effect is one of the most subtle irony in which we can only with great refinement of thought define the whole range of response: a charitable appreciation of what is god-like and what is human in men, a purely secular delight in the great variety within the cooperative society—these combined in an unusually alert observer of life and in an unusually astute creator of character. The remarkable reporter whom the poet has created as Chaucer the pilgrim, without a shred of malice, has turned out to be his slyest joke.

One can make out a better case for a consistently maintained persona in the *General Prologue* (though not a thoroughly convincing one) than one can for the narrator in the remainder of the *Canterbury Tales*. The apology or defense of literary decorum transcending moral propriety at the end of the *General Prologue*, with its echo in the *Miller's Prologue* where the narrator calls attention to tales dealing with subjects of morality, religion, and the like, has the knowing air of containing allusion to the total range of the materials of the *Canterbury Tales*, a foresight that can only be the poet's. There is a sharp point to the line, "Blameth nat me if that ye chese amys," which is surely an ironical aside of the author inviting us to note what is technically admirable, and not merely a naive remark by a simple narrator.

The Man of Law comments upon Chaucer as a kind of literary glutton who has used up all the available stories of lovers. He provides for us a kind of master plan for the *Legend of Good Women* (including some that never materialize), and exonerates him of writing stories of incest. Here we have a daring conflation of the real world in which Chaucer wrote and recited his verses with the world of fiction in which the pilgrims he has created are able to comment upon that other world for the sake of some ironic effect which, it is possible, is largely lost to us now. In this passage of the *Canterbury*

Tales fraught with problems, what does emerge is Chaucer's own joke upon himself, imputing to himself, as poet, clumsiness in rhyme and meter (but implying the opposite), and averring a sense of propriety in subject matter that may have been placed in doubt by tales already in circulation.

There is more to be assessed in the rich contrast of the two tales "Chaucer" tells. In *Sir Thopas* and the *Tale of Melibee* we have a successful and extremely delicate balance between the author in control of the situation and the narrator with a definite kind of personality, size, and shape who interacts with the other members of the pilgrimage. There is delicacy too in the jest of offering a bad romance with such seriousness, a romance which Wells calls a "scrap of burlesque." In the pilgrim-poet's insistence that this is the only tale in rhyme that he knows, we are a far cry from that Chaucer of the *Man of Law's Introduction* who has apparently had access to many good stories and has used some of them. Somewhat offended by the Host's scurrilous judgment of it (it was the best one he knew), he offers his prose treatise on prudence with apparently the same seriousness of effort, if not of intention, as *Sir Thopas*. Here, more than in the *General Prologue*, we have a convincing and definable personality attributed to the narrator, even when we are not able to recreate the special relationship of poet and audience and the sense of a joke commonly shared. But it is a more subtle jest on a larger scale than that of the *Man of Law's Introduction*, where the enumeration of works accomplished suggests, among other things, a progress report. The difference that we discern may be the result, as we suggested above, of different times of composition.

The problem is further complicated by the emergence of Chaucer's own voice in the Retraction, a voice which must be reckoned with in any estimate of the total effect of the *Canterbury Tales*. In a sense this is the final test of the consistency of the persona-narrator and a gauge of his participation. Some suggestions of this matter I explore later on. Suffice it to say at this time that when the Retraction is spoken, the purely personal moral judgment threatens to shatter the artistry and momentarily to dislocate our values, precisely because it is so personal and unexpected. There are of course other examples of the use of a first person narrator with a character created for him by the author, in *Piers Plowman, Pearl*, the *Confessio Amantis*, and in

Dante's *Divine Comedy*, perhaps the most perfect example of them all. Dante's handling of the special problem of a persona who bears the author's name,[2] inasmuch as it is done with a controlled identity of the created persona with himself on the one hand and with a more universal condition of man on the other, may serve as a kind of model by which to assess the difference in Chaucer's own manipulation of his experience of pilgrimage.

In Dante's treatment there is little perplexity about the heart and soul of man. Clear distinctions exist between emotional and rational responses. We are always aware of the poet's conscious control and manipulation of his materials. The moral system and the allocation of the sinners within it are set out for us schematically with correspondences between sinner and locale. The handling of the responses of the pilgrim and the remonstrances of the voice of reason are all the work of the poet. We are conscious of a steady progress towards a goal in the Empyrean, and we come to see, point by point, that Virgil and then Beatrice represent aspects of man's capacity to act as created in the image of God, that is to say, as a rational, and then as an angelic intelligence. At a point in the Garden of Eden on the top of the mount of Purgatory, Dante the Pilgrim and Dante the Poet coalesce; thereafter the two sides of the metaphorical relationship of mankind to poet are indistinguishable from each other. Beyond lies the schooling in the virtues, the prayer of Bernard and the intercession of Mary, and finally the Ineffable. In the intensely personal experience which Dante reports and records, the discoveries along the way become the audience's precisely because, in this poem, Dante himself has made them and relives them for us. Even the intensely personal experience of God can be shared vicariously by the reader. This farthest range of experience is of course not for Chaucer. The Chaucerian religious experience closes, as we can see from the Retraction, at that point similar to Dante's in the *Purgatorio* where the necessary acts of repentance are performed. We may go further to say that the range of experience here is in fact purgatorial.

There are of course resemblances between the two performances, indeed resemblances with the theme of pilgrimage and the use of the

---

[2] See the interesting suggestion of A. L. Kellogg, "Chaucer's Self-Portrait and Dante's," *Medium Aevum*, XXIX (1960), 119-20, that the function of the "gregarious Chaucer of the *General Prologue*" is "to live in the moment and see only the moment," while the function of the "elvyssh" man of *Sir Thopas*, is that of the artist, "the withdrawn intelligence which ... encompasses the whole fabric of its work."

first person narrator wherever they appear in medieval literature. But the differences are more remarkable: the difference between a continuous, complete, moral structure and a discontinuous, incomplete, fragmentary structure, the difference between a perfect balance of the artist and the pilgrim-narrator steadily in the foreground and a variable intermittent relationship between poet and persona; the difference between poet as everyman-hero and the poet as non-hero; the difference between man experiencing and reporting and man observing and reporting. Dante participates seriously, and in participating brings more and more of his real life data to bear upon the hero of his poem, even including prophecies for the future; Chaucer participates in a series of subtle jests in varying degrees of irony and remains in spite of his participation somewhat depersonalized, detached, withdrawn. In the *Parson's Prologue* towards the close of his work he has disappeared into the group, to reappear with a provoking self-centeredness in the Retraction.

Chaucer chooses to reveal himself mainly as a critic of a literary form in *Sir Thopas* and as a counselor of prudence in the *Tale of Melibee,* functions which tend to establish distance between himself and his audience on pilgrimage. The Chaucer of the *Canterbury Tales* does not contain multitudes like Dante. He is not to be equated with everyman or mankind. His moral judgment in the Retraction is, to be sure, precise and personal, as the enumeration of his various poems indicates; throughout the poem, it is not he that is important and hence more and more embodied forth, more defined, more and more historical. It is rather the society which he is depicting of which he is but the observing, momentarily counseling part, and with which in God's good charity he is involved in pilgrimage.

Chaucer's own *Melibee,* however much it is the utterance of a simple man of apparently poor literary taste, is as close as we come to the overt counsel of reason within the body of the *Canterbury Tales.* The Host is something of a guide, something of a referee, something of a master of revels, worse than the best of the pilgrims and better than the worst, but he is not a guide in any spiritual sense, nor is he the voice of reason, the monitor of grace. It is significant that in his turn he gives up his role in the end to the good Parson, from whose lips flow the counsels of truth as Chaucer knew them.

We may see, then, something of the ironical commentator upon the human scene in these few loci in which Chaucer actually participates in pilgrimage. By comparison with Dante we may estimate the degree to which Chaucer is out of, rather than in, his poem. The two tales he assigns himself as poet have something ultimately quite scathing to say about extravagance and stupidity in either literary form or in human affairs. This fictional role, in the *Sir Thopas* part, looks back through the role described in the *Introduction to the Man of Law's Tale*, where Chaucer is praised as a crafty rhymer; but the scrupulosity which is a part of the character of the teller of the *Tale of Melibee* looks forward to a similar scrupulosity on the part of the speaker of the Retraction.

One concludes, then, in dealing with the problem of the narrator of the *Canterbury Tales*, that the very character of the medley works against the poet as hero and demands his withdrawal from, rather than his inclusion in, the poem. What we recognize is the absence of the narrator instead of his presence. When he is present he becomes at one extreme a wise simpleton who admires his fellow-man and pleads for the right to describe him honestly, and at the other, an artist concerned with prudence and morality. Indeed, wherever "Chaucer" appears in his poem, his attitude is that of ironical distance between himself and his audience.

The absence of Chaucer, the persona and poet, as hero of the pilgrimage,[3] obviates the necessity, too, of the personal teacher or guide through whom he gradually achieves God-likeness. Such teachers and guides are to be found, as we have said, in *Pearl*, in the *Confessio Amantis*, and in the *Divine Comedy*. He is, if not the learning hero, the observer and recorder, and through this role we may account for much in the form of the *Canterbury Tales* that provokes and excites us: the discreteness of the fragments, for example, each an island of creative energy with its own cast of characters and inner law; the absence of a single agent on the pilgrimage who interprets each, a deliberate deficiency which enjoins upon the reader the obligation of adding or providing his own experience as the final comment; the generally equitable balance between religious and worldly interests; the implication that the structure of the *Canterbury Tales* could be proliferated at will to include many aspects of experience— these may be taken to corroborate our suggestion that the great

---

[3] On the absence of the heroic in late medieval style, see D. W. Robertson, Jr., *A Preface to Chaucer*, p. 285.

middle of the *Canterbury Tales* may successfully be approached as a discursive, even a disjointed, encyclopaedia.

Nonetheless, in terms of its beginning and end, the structure of the *Canterbury Tales* is complete. The fact that the narrator is a withdrawing ironist, not a hero, does not prevent our seeing finally that the society of which he is a part is delivered from its tensions and debates. The pilgrimage theme, with its clear beginning and end, draws even the ironist-narrator into the final "we" of the audience addressed by the Parson in his attempt to draw together the whole of human society into a pattern of sins and virtues, into confession and repentance. The Retraction offers a final judgment. Its attempt to state the terms of the moral contract in which even artists are involved points to a view of life as well as a literary structure which, by virtue of the hope of redemption with which it closes, must be called Christian and comedic in ultimate intention.

In discussing the role of the narrator we have raised the question of prudence and morality, inevitable concerns of the student of the Retraction. Some of the issues which emanate from the question we now assess from the point of view of the pilgrim-poet first as moralist, and then as artist.

The Pilgrim as Moralist

Upon the serenity of the close of the *Parson's Tale* falls the shadow of Chaucer's Retraction, the rejection of the very means—literary art—by which the visible world has been defined. Totally without the arrogance which occasionally attends rejection, the solicitude for the state of his soul as a conclusion to the *Canterbury Tales* has given rise over several hundred years of Chaucer scholarship to a great variety of speculation. Chaucer arrives in the end, so to speak, at a spiritual beginning. He reaches this point without the trembling suffusions of romantic love and without any special mystique. He has looked with a kind of wise self-restraint upon humanity, and now comes finally to confess to his role and obligations as artist and human being at once in it. That he should have, for this, short-circuited the promise of a jolly feast has caused more than a little confusion and doubt as to authenticity of the Retraction, largely owing to something within us which cannot reconcile its indifference to the artistic worth of the poems. It has been damned by J. W. Hales as a "morbid passage," which we must suppose was written by Chaucer in "an hour of reaction and weakness." [4] This judgment is representative of its kind, medial between an outright rejection of the piece,[5] and a confident acceptance of it as "certainly genuine." [6] A substantial part of contemporary scholarship is fairly concerted in accepting the Retraction not merely as genuine, but as intimately affecting the meaning of the *Canterbury Tales* as a whole poem.[7]

The burden has not been easy on those who would defend the Retraction as genuine, as is clear from Hales's remark, in which we detect a real need to dismiss the Retraction as a concession to a lapse of nerve; nor has it been easy to dismiss the Retraction as a mere literary convention. Nonetheless the Retraction has the advantage of being in the "parent" manuscript of the *Parson's Tale*, and the problem at hand, at least from a literary point of view, is not that of authenticity or even of conventionality per se, but the effect such a Retraction would exert upon the foregoing literary structure by functioning as a part of it. Inevitably in such considerations we find ourselves imputing certain sentiments to the artist or to the man and in the process we inevitably raise the problems of hypocrisy and duplicity.[8] I do not feel at this point concerned to defend Chaucer's

---

[4] Quoted by Eleanor Prescott Hammond, *Chaucer: A Bibliographical Manual* (New York, 1908), p. 322.

[5] J. M. Manly and Edith Rickert, *A Text of the Canterbury Tales*, 8 vols. (University of Chicago Press, 1940), offer the view that, among others, "some priests may be responsible for the language and the inaccurate detail" (II, 472), and that "one may, therefore, be allowed to doubt whether Chaucer himself was responsible for the choice of the two prose treatises which are put together to form PsT and for the melancholy Retraction which, instead of the promised celebration at the Tabard, closes the collection of tales" (IV, 527).

[6] J. S. P. Tatlock, *The Development and Chronology of Chaucer's Works*, Chaucer Society, 2d Series, No. 37 (London, 1907), p. 25.

[7] W. W. Lawrence, *Chaucer and the Canterbury Tales* (Columbia University Press, 1950), pp. 157 ff.; Sister M. Madeleva, *A Lost Language and Other Essays on Chaucer* (New York, 1951), pp. 105 ff.; Wayne Shumaker, "Chaucer's *Manciple's Tale* as Part of the Canterbury Group," *UTQ*, XXII (1953), 147–56; Ralph Baldwin, *Unity of the Canterbury Tales*, pp. 105 ff.; and Donaldson, *Chaucer's Poetry*, pp. 949 ff.

[8] Howard R. Patch, *On Rereading Chaucer* (Harvard University Press, 1939), p. 243; Patch writes, "...we have no right at all to say that anyone in the fourteenth century who accepted Christian morality and saints' legends was naif. Even in the *Retraction*, Chaucer was not that. Perhaps he was frightened there, and he was probably sick. He may have had a momentary flash of insight into the values of purity

honesty or his integrity either as an artist or as a man. I have indeed no quarrel with those scholars who account for the Retraction on grounds of spiritual repentance, although the details of the reconstructions of Chaucer's last hours—if they were his last hours—are at best fanciful.

We do well to keep in mind the dictum of Sister Madeleva, "The *Retraction* is strictly a moral evaluation, having nothing at all to say of literary qualities or excellencies." [9] Her view of the Retraction as "a grim determined stride to a heavenly Jerusalem" is felicitous and apt, but my concern is not with these matters which have been well discussed by others in other places. I am concerned rather with the function of such a judgment within the total compass of a literary form, and with the possibility that the ironist-author, by capitalizing upon his spiritual compunction and by making it a part of the total literary form, has made the best use possible at this stage of his moral convictions by applying somewhat the same ironical plastic stress to the *Canterbury Tales* as that which we have encountered at the close of *Troilus and Criseyde*. The palinode to the *Troilus*, we may say, establishes a pattern.

I am of necessity making assumptions: that while the moral recantation may well indeed be a convention, it was not merely genuine, but sincere; that the moral man in the artist finds an opportunity here, not simply to deny those pieces of which he had reason to be proud, the *Troilus* and the fabliaux, among others, but rather, since they could not be withdrawn from circulation, to provide for them the perspective of the interior life of the spirit; in short to set before us more palpably than ever before the tension which we have noted

---

and holiness, one that threw his sense of proportion out of joint. Far from being simple at this time he is more nearly subject to the charge of duplicity. But moderns will find it hard to understand how he undoubtedly escaped that." See too the remarks of William A. Madden in defense of Chaucer, "Chaucer's Retraction and Mediaeval Canons of Seemliness," *MS*, XVII (1955), 182: "Here is Chaucer's problem: whether to let his art act autonomously or to border it by prudence.... I would argue... that the resort to external literary sources to explain these elements in his work is to misunderstand Chaucer's problem and his deepest convictions. It casts doubt on his originality as well as on the genuineness of his moral compunction and on his sincerity.... In the end, Chaucer, like his age, gave precedence to spiritual considerations, and whatever the original motivation behind his poetic activity he ultimately came to see certain values as likely to do more harm than their entertainment or instructional value could justify. To accuse him of mockery at this point is, in effect, to make him a more radical heretic than the most radical contemporary, and worse, it makes him a hypocrite."

[9] Sister Madeleva, *A Lost Language*, p. 110.

throughout the *Canterbury Tales* between denial and affirmation and to put a final period to that tension by rejection. From the rejection, however, from the point of view of meaning, flow some affirmations which must be discussed.

It is the ultimate act of the ironist to pass judgment upon his own work; the emergence, at the close, of his personal voice, with much the same private conviction as we noted at the close of *Troilus*, confronts the audience with a judgment which stands at the end of all the previous action and, in repudiating certain parts of it, brings into sharp relief that religious voice which has been as much a part of the *Canterbury Tales* as the secular one. This new judgment takes into account all of those depictions of man as a creature of a fallen world erecting, however sympathetically, a variety of false gods. In bringing the fictive and the real world face to face there is a confrontation of the now prudentially ordered soul of the author with the disordered society which he has created; the confrontation marks his withdrawal from the game of art which, while it could have been proliferated indefinitely in the great middle of the *Canterbury Tales*, must sometime have a stop. Here we are able to detect degrees of kinship between the pilgrim-protagonist who spoke the *Melibee* and who earlier in the *Man of Law's Introduction* wished to be exonerated of the charge of writing one kind of indecency, and the writer of the Retraction.

Chaucer here accepts the knowledge provided by the previous tale. The theological challenge which has been raised he now answers in a thoroughly personal way, lifting the sense of the pilgrimage permanently beyond that of any merely social meaning. Earlier he has set side by side religious and purely secular attitudes, contrasting the values of both worlds and balancing the two allegiances within the ironist's purview. The presence of one in the very midst of the other, resulting in the subtle conditioning of any purely naturalistic or romantic or religious point of view, is the source of the perennially provocative interest which posterity has found in Chaucer's mature poetry.

Particularly perplexing is the fact that the quest which is implied by the pilgrimage is not demonstrated as finally achieved or resolved, either by the whole community which seeks it, or even by one of its created characters. The closing lines of the *Parson's Tale* provide us with a divine vision of what the achieved Paradise will be for all and state the terms on which it may be achieved. The final emphasis, however, is not social but private, a withdrawal from the "we" of the *Parson's Prologue* to the "I" of the Retraction in a final individualized *exemplum* of the method by which salvation and the kingdom may be attained.

The Parson's long illustrations of the vices and virtues provide a catalogue of man's sinfulness side by side with what he may achieve in the way of God-like virtue. The confession occurring between repentance and satisfaction for sin, indeed the sacrament of penance, is for both the individual Chaucer, whether poet-protagonist or poet-man, and for the body of society, a necessary part of the scheme of the divine comedy, the bridge between God and Man and within the literary frame the necessary instrument of return. A pattern of reconciliation operates to bring the pilgrimage to its close, a pattern not vastly different in meaning from that which governed the close of the tales of Constance and Griselda. There as here, the intention is the same, the restoration of loved ones to each other, of children to parents. The "I" confession of guilt and a seeking of forgiveness through repentance becomes, as I have suggested, the model for the "we." In the silences that eddy out from the conclusion of the Parson's performance we must take what consolation we can from the metaphorical promise of the celestial Jerusalem suggested by the spires of Canterbury Cathedral and assume the imposition of that Celestial City's values upon the social, moral, and civil relationships of the social groups on pilgrimage.

The geographical movement from the suburb of London, promised at first as a cycle the farthest point of which was to be Canterbury, now is settled upon as purely linear in spatial as well as temporal terms; the closing image has to do with the termination of the natural day. The Host as self-appointed moderator has given way to a necessarily spiritual umpire who urges upon all men an improvement of the self as the necessary ground for resolving any quarrel between God and man. The Chaucer whom we have met throughout the poem has spoken for the most part in the voice of innocence uttering wisdom. Although he is a member of the pilgrimage he has relegated to himself mainly the role of observer and reporter. When he has spoken, his jests have been so subtle as to be lost upon the fictive group and have found their natural mark in that listening audience and that reading audience which we all form. It is we who detect the sanity behind the parody of romance, and we who must see the censure behind the precepts of moderation.

That Chaucer should not have urged these intellectual platitudes passionately is not unusual; the quieter irony is more his typical métier. The rejections of the *Clerk's Tale*, of the *Prioress's* and *Second Nun's Tales* prepare us for Chaucer's response to the spiritual encouragement of the Parson, and indicate a final decision between the opposing claims of those poems affirming the life of natural man untrammeled by morality and those affirming the life of the spirit. The spirit of repentance implicit in the theme of pilgrimage from the very beginning now has its final statement. The moral law, we see in retrospect, has been woven into it tale by tale, and the discordances of the human community of the *General Prologue* have steadily implied that law.

It must ever be noted that Chaucer does not offer any of his pilgrims in attitudes of repentance at the close of the Parson's sermon. This may distress our sense of what the form should achieve. For the pilgrims the conclusion is apparently the knitting up of the festivities in the sermon delivered by the Parson on the way to Canterbury. They fade off into the surmise of arrival at Canterbury. The other conclusion of the Canterbury Pilgrimage which Chaucer has chosen is the assumption of the attitudes of repentance for himself. He resolves the terms of the debate as suggested by the Parson in that pattern of reconciliation which we have been able to observe at work from time to time within the poem and which seems to be the point of most of the religious and romantic structures within it.

Perhaps Dorothy Sayers, with the aid of her master Charles Williams, has offered a clue to what is implied by the artistry of the Retraction. Writing about Dante, she notes "that simultaneous rejection and affirmation of the visible world which runs all through the poem." She goes on, "If the world is not known as the vehicle and the image of the Glory, then it is a substitute and an idol; it must be renounced as an idol before it can be received as an image." [10] In these terms the Retraction, which is the fruit of repentance, is an

---

[10] Dorothy L. Sayers, *Introductory Papers on Dante* (London, 1954), p. 208. She quotes from the tremendously suggestive introduction by Charles Williams to *The Figure of Beatrice* (London, 1943), pp. 10–11, a passage which is sufficiently provocative to be reproduced in full here: "The tangle of affirmation and rejection which is in each of us has to be drawn into some kind of pattern and has so been drawn by all men who have ever lived. The records of Christian sanctity have on the whole

admission of an irresoluble conflict between the world as image and the world as idol. It does not pretend that the delight in the world of men and women did not exist—it rather throws it into sharp relief—but asserts the sense of another pressing reality which the form now allows Chaucer finally to admit: the rueful confession from an artist who looks back upon his achievement that the most interesting materials of poetry are the signatures of fallen man. But oh! we add, the joy of having been capable of recording them!

Certain conclusions become clear: it is we, the reading and listening audience, who participate in the quest; we who, to the extent that we read sympathetically, achieve the goal. It is we who come to see even the incompleteness of the middle as an ironical and wintry comment upon the springtime promise of a controlled and ordered form of some one hundred and twenty tales. It is we who, accepting the pilgrimage as a metaphor of life, weigh the relation of the profane to the spiritual, and with the poet allow the penitential impulse to cleave finally through the secular form. It is clear, too, that the outer romantic structure implies a learning process in the course of the journey; what is demonstrated is offered to us not in a systematic progression through the ranks and degrees of moral experience in the Dantean fashion,[11] but in an eclectic mélange freely constructed upon the

---

stressed the rejection. This indeed can hardly be avoided in any religion—nor perhaps outside all religion; the mere necessities of human life—change, misadventure, folly, age, and death—everywhere involve it. But even more within religion the discipline of the soul, ordinary or extraordinary, enforces it. The general praise of ascetic life and even the formal preference of one good (such as virginity) to another good (such as marriage) have themselves imaged that enforcement. On the other hand such great doctrines as the Resurrection of the Body and the Life Everlasting have continually recalled the Affirmation; with every act of charity towards others, every courtesy towards others, and even permissibly towards ourselves. The very equalling of ourselves with others and of others with ourselves is a declaration of the republic of images. No doubt these doctrines, metaphysical or moral, are to be understood after a great manner and towards God. But no doubt also every way of understanding leaves them exact in themselves. After the affirmations we may have to discover the rejections, but we must still believe that after the rejections the greater affirmations are to return."

[11] The problem of the degree and kind of influence exerted upon Chaucer by Dante remains a challenging one. For various aspects of scholarship on the subject the student would do well to consult F. N. Robinson, "Chaucer and Dante," *Jour. of Comp. Lit.*, I (1903), 292–97, his review of Cino Chiarini's *Di Una Imitazione della Divina Commedia: La Casa di Fama di G. Chaucer* (Bari, 1902); John Livingston Lowes, "Chaucer and Dante's *Convivio*," *MP*, XIII (1915), 19–33, and "Chaucer and Dante," *MP*, XIV (1917), 705–35; J. P. Bethel, "The Influence of Dante on Chaucer's Thought and Expression" (unpublished dissertation, Harvard University, 1927); and the consideration of Lowes's thesis by Howard Schless, "Chaucer and Dante," in *Critical Approaches to Medieval Literature*, ed. Dorothy Bethurum (Columbia Uni-

notion of bickering and casual arbitration by a referee. The scope is
purgatorial, the method dianoetic. The goal, in Chaucer's amended
plan, is the hope of a spiritual rebirth, through penance, built upon
the knowledge acquired along the way. Thus the two concepts of
form, romance and miscellany, each with a proper inner law, make
their contribution to our appreciation of what the whole poem is
about.

The Pilgrim as Artist

The admission on any terms at all of the fabliaux [12] into the structure
of the *Canterbury Tales* raises several problems simultaneously, problems which Chaucer himself finds matters of a mingled artistic and
moral concern. For the critic it raises the question of Chaucer's respect for the uses of literary types with their capacity to carry the
burden of certain kinds of statement; it also raises the question of
decorum. These both remained for Chaucer primary cares through-

versity Press, 1960), pp. 134–54. Older materials are well surveyed by Hammond,
Manual, pp. 81–83, 374–76, and 487. Much that is critically profitable can come out of
an intelligent confrontation of these two incomparable poets of medieval culture.
We do well to remember, with Eliot, that the past is what we know, and Dante was
a part of Chaucer's past. To be sure, Chaucer did not have total recall, and what he
knew of Italian language and literature was not always precise. Yet Dante serves,
with his highly structured moral system and encyclopaedic range, as a referent, even
a touchstone, for much in Chaucer that is merely glancing or oblique. And we learn
much from their respective handling of conventions, from their self-conscious interest
in the shaping of experience, and from the conversion of their vision of life to the
substance of literature.

[12] The fabliaux continue to stimulate and to challenge scholarship, partly on the
impulse set in motion by Per Nykrog's *Les Fabliaux, Étude d'histoire littéraire et de
stylistique médiévale* (Copenhagen, 1957). Nykrog's thesis is itself a response to the
older views of Joseph Bédier, *Les Fabliaux*, 5th ed. (Paris, 1925), in its assertion that
the fabliau is not a bourgeois literary type, as Bédier would have it, but courtly in
origin, "créé pour la noblesse et exprimant sa vision du monde." To this set of opposed
attitudes we may still offer, on the suggestion of Knud Togeby, in his review of
Nykrog's thesis ("Les Fabliaux," *Orbis Litterarum*, XII [1957], 85–98), the opinion of
Faral that "les fabliaux ne sont ni la création ni la propriété d'une classe sociale parti-
culière, mais représentent plutôt une tendance d'esprit qui a été celle d'une époque
entière." Nykrog is rich in bibliography, and there are some good suggestions in
Richard F. O'Gorman's review of T. B. W. Reid's *Twelve Fabliaux*, in *Symposium*,
XVI (1962), 312–15. There is an analysis of fabliau style in Erich Auerbach, *Mimesis:
The Representation of Reality in Western Literature*, trans. Willard R. Trask
(Princeton University Press, 1953), pp. 208–16. No one should neglect Muscatine's
chapter "The Bourgeois Tradition," *Chaucer and the French Tradition*, pp. 58–97, or
the old article of Walter Morris Hart, "The Narrative Art of the Old French Fabli-

out the structure, especially with regard to those poems which he considered secular and profane. On these grounds, the two defenses of the necessary relation between speaker's style and literary form are linked to the mingled spirit of rejection and affirmation which we note from time to time in the canon of Chaucer's work and which has its most awesome statement in the Retraction.

The old opposition of Plato to Aristotle on the matter of morality and literature is one which, I suppose, will never completely be resolved: the best form of government, they would both agree, given perfect men, is no form of government. But once men are acknowledged to be imperfect, their passions and the arts which depict or reflect them become matters of grave interest. What are the uses and functions of poetry? Is it the means by which the disordered passions of men are further disordered, and the souls of men diverted from the right knowledge of God, and as such a danger to the state? Does poetry in particular have a use beyond that of delight?

Aristotle's answers to these Platonic questions in the *Poetics*, the *Ethics*, and the *Politics* aim at a statement both of the utility and of the moral value of the arts, particularly of poetry. Recognizing that poets imitate the actions of men, and that the imitation is not itself reality, Aristotle distinguishes the kinds of imitation: things as they are, or as better or worse than they are; as they should be; or as they are said or thought to be. He also recognizes that a poem considered as a structure is not a thing apart from the effect it creates in its audience. He sees, further, that the special pleasure it affords is that of cognition, inasmuch as poetry, among the other arts, gratifies man's desire to know. On the moral, rather than the purely aesthetic side, the pleasure of knowing and the purgation of untoward emotions

aux," in *Anniversary Papers* [for] *George Lyman Kittredge* (Boston, 1913), pp. 209–16.

We have become increasingly sensitive to the degrees of seriousness implied by Chaucerian fabliaux, but scholarship has a tendency to overstate the case. Bronson's remarks in *In Search of Chaucer*, p. 115, are salutary: "It is no accident that it is the fabliaux that are the most drenched of all his pieces in naturalistic detail. They are the most *earthy* of his writings, and by the same token—apart from morality in the narrower sense—in his eyes the most limited and least valuable. We may prize them the more, and justify our judgment by claims of superior artistry and by appeals to the higher criticism that might have amazed him. When he came to total up, towards the end of his life, 'the book of the tales of Caunterbury, compiled by Geffrey Chaucer,' no ripe artistic judgment admonished him to leave out the Man of Law's Tale, the Physician's Tale, the Second Nun's Tale; and to the two weightiest members of the pilgrimage, himself and the Parson, he paid the compliment of assigning the most abstract pieces of all."

which are aroused by the drama are precisely the blessings that flow from poetry. Its function is to amuse, but the amusement is useful in that it provides the relaxation necessary to life through the essentially harmless pleasure attendant upon dissipating disordered passions. That which law itself is unable to accomplish in the control of disordered passions poetry manages to do through the process of purgation.

Certain matters of discussion offer themselves immediately, principally the view of art within Christian culture and a suggestion of the role that art may perform within that culture. The view that Chaucer holds is not unlike that of Dante, particularly in the Casella episode in Purgatory. In it Casella the musician sings one of Dante's own songs, during which the purgatorial process which should be begun is temporarily delayed in order that the beauty of the moment may be savored. But beauty here is not truth in any ultimate sense, and the stern-voiced Cato rebukes the laggard souls who, suspended for a moment of contemplation, neglect their real goal, which is finally to know God face to face. That is to say, poetry and music have their uses and role; the cognitive pleasures art affords are essential to life, and these have some bearing upon the reasons for which man was created,[13] but these fleeting revelations cannot be construed as the ends, but only the means by which the ends come into view. Poetry may be a means of grace, not the grace itself. The perceptions which are possible within the world of art, the ecstasies, the ravishments out of the world, the thought-inspiring in it, may be affirmed in a wellnigh endless succession of moments, provided that the illuminations themselves bear upon the highest illumination, and do not in any way prevent the flight up the mountain and the stripping off of the slough standing between the soul and knowledge.

In no way need we see art as excluding either the ugly or even the depraved, or the darker aspects of the soul. It is clearly impossible, in Newman's words, to have a sinless literature dealing with sinful man. The fallen world, with its diverted will and its moral evil, is precisely the world which literature takes as its natural province, the world of comedy as well as the world of tragedy, of the bleakest realism as well as the most ardent romanticism. The world of any one of these is not more or less true than the world of any other. Indeed, no one taken

[13] Jacques Maritain, *Art and Scholasticism*, trans. J. F. Scanlan (New York, 1954), pp. 79–80.

by itself, or any number of them in combination, can provide more than a single aspect of experience for contemplation at a particular time.

The Christian view, with its basic concern for the salvation of the soul, is apprehensive about a world which may divert man from his ultimate goal, and wary about the pleasures afforded by art. Writers of comic realism in the Middle Ages were forced to solve the problem, or to sidestep it, by a variety of defenses. Boccaccio, with his own long medley of tales held together by a frame, serves to illustrate the general concern of poets of a naturalistic bent not only to employ the full range of experience as the materials for their poetry, but to defend their practice. By the time he was forty, it will be remembered, Boccaccio had finished the *Decameron*, and if we can trust the opinion of Sacchetti, it enjoyed a fame beyond the confines of Italy. With all its range and versatility and skill, it is not the work Boccaccio wished to have as his monument. But it has captured the imagination of posterity, and its attitudes have proved to be more enduring than their author wished. They are considerably more provocative than his later ideas about the power of poetry.

The defense of the *Decameron* is spread out in three places: the Introduction to the collection, the Introduction to the Fourth Day, and the Epilogue. The views may be summarized as follows: Cured of lovesickness by discussions with a friend, the poet turns his talents to the service of the servants of love. His tales offer useful counsel as well as pleasure. Women are his worthy audience, and he a worthy poet nurtured by the muses on Parnassus. He is faithful to the originals of his tales; faithfulness to one's materials dictates the level of diction and is of greater concern to the artist than the strictures of prudes who are more conscious of the word than the deed, of the appearance of goodness rather than the reality. The writer's freedom to depict the truth should be not less than that of the painter of the naked body.

Furthermore his tales are written not for the churches or schools but for mature society, at a time when morality has somewhat been set aside by the mere need to survive. The writer cannot be concerned about the disposition of his readers, some of whom may be adversely affected by these tales. Literature, like fire, wine, the weapons of war, and even Scripture, may be badly used. These tales will give good or bad counsel according to the character of the reader.

Since each tale is preceded by a rubric or argument, the reader has the
responsibility for making his own choices, according to the varying
qualities and subjects. If some of the tales are overly long, they were
meant to be read by persons of leisure; if they contain the lighter
devices of comedy (imitated from the sermons of the friars), that is
because they are meant for pleasure.

Boccaccio's own attitudes towards the tales changed. Some twenty
years after the *Decameron* he reproached a friend for allowing his
womenfolk to read the tales. They were, he maintained, trifles something less than decent and calculated to arouse the passions. He did
not wish to be thought a pimp, a dirty-mouthed and lecherous old
man. These sentiments, generalized to encompass and reject virtually
all poems that will not support a higher, allegorical meaning, are to be
found in the last two books of the *Genealogy of the Gentile Gods.*[14]
Poetry, like the other arts, contains dregs, he writes. These dregs are,
more often than not, comic writing, although he would except
Plautus and Terence who, even if they did not intend anything beyond the literal, yet managed by their genius to describe universal
manners of mankind. The others, including Ovid, defiled the bright
glory of poetry. They prompted by their dirty stories, "lascivious
men to crime, unsettled those who were established in virtue, and
weakened the moral order of the whole state. . . . It is such poets that
paganism no less than Christianity abhors, and such it is that Plato
would banish. Indeed I think they ought to be not expelled but
exterminated" (XIV.xix).

These two attitudes, first of defense and then of rejection of the
more naturalistic tales, are to be found, obviously, in Chaucer as well
as in Boccaccio. To be sure, Chaucer shares with Boccaccio that other
view that "serious" poets shape materials—other than comic—and
employ myths, images, and figures for the sake of larger truths to be
conveyed. He is even willing, as is Boccaccio in the tale of Griselda,
to work at a patent allegorism in the so-called "serious" tales. But this
kind of work he does not feel called upon to defend. His common
ground with Boccaccio in the defense of the secular and comic tradition is the belief that poems in this tradition are capable of teaching
the reader and putting him on his guard. And with Boccaccio he
believes in the power of these to persuade for good or ill according to

[14] See Charles G. Osgood, *Boccaccio on Poetry* (Princeton University Press, 1930),
pp. 87–94.

the temper of the reader. With him he maintains that the reader has some responsibility for what he chooses to read. With him he recognizes that the diction in which a tale is couched is determined by the level of the subject matter, and that fidelity to one's sources is the guiding artistic principle in the writing of fiction.

Chaucer, when he gives opinion on the function of literature, freely acknowledges its power to teach as well as to please. But there comes a point at which, if one asks the question about the teaching power of the more profane tales Chaucer is defending, one must also go on to ask what is being taught. Here, in fact, is the point at which Chaucer feels impelled to offer, not another statement of the range of his materials from the point of view of an artist, but a statement of their limitations from the point of view of a moral man. How subversive are poems which do not teach primarily the love of God? How much do they excite a purely sensual pleasure?

The fact that Chaucer's long poem contains both the affirmation of the poet's right to depict the compass of human experience and the rejection of those works that conduce to sin marks the great difference between him and Boccaccio. The latter can be excused, as Petrarch excused him in 1373, on the grounds of his youth, the frivolity of the subject matter, and the intended audience. But Chaucer cannot be excused, nor excuse himself on these grounds. He chooses to make the secular (and secularized) tales a part of his large structure, and, as I see it, to give them the function of providing one extreme of human behavior and experience, of presenting various aspects of evil as a foil to the good; the actions of youth as a foil to those of age; the vision of society disintegrating under the pressures of selfish interests. In short being guided on the one hand by artistic considerations of the relation of subject matter to literary form and on the other by the moral grasp of the inner law of pilgrimage: penitent regeneration through self-knowledge. Comedy thus is made to serve the larger demand of the romantic form, and the poet's task is to offer the objectionable tales in such a way as to take into account our own demurrals but at the same time to urge our interest and participation in them. Accepting the apology for the latitudes of expression and for the suiting of the tale to the ethos and station of the speaker, we accept too the varying mixtures of sacred and profane, and come to see that the so-called non-serious tales imply the moral norms of the whole poem.

The passages in which Chaucer "takes us in" merit our interest at this point. The first defense spoken by the narrator, in the *General Prologue*, assumes the familiar attitude of guileless innocence before the task of imitation.

> But first I pray yow, of youre curteisye,
> That ye n'arette it nat my vileynye,
> Thogh that I pleynly speke in this mateere,
> To telle yow hir wordes and hir cheere,
> Ne thogh I speke hir wordes proprely.
> But this ye knowen al so wel as I,
> Whoso shal telle a tale after a man,
> He moot reherce as ny as evere he kan
> Everich a word, if it be in his charge,
> Al speke he never so rudeliche and large,
> Or ellis he moot telle his tale untrewe,
> Or feyne thyng, or fynde wordes newe.
> He may nat spare, althogh he were his brother;
> He moot as wel seye o word as another.
> Crist spak hymself ful brode in hooly writ,
> And wel ye woot no vileynye is it.
> Eek Plato seith, whoso that kan hym rede,
> The wordes moote be cosyn to the dede.   (ll. 725-42)

The defense seems entirely conventional; it prevents the view that he is writing these tales as a reflection of his own base attitudes. In the light of the *General Prologue*, in which he sets out all the grades of society and involves them in a game, it is clear that the kinds of stories will be drawn from every conceivable sphere, from every genre, from every class of men. The various classes of men will produce different views of experience, the elevated as well as the debased, the happy as well as the sad. If the mind of the artist is sufficiently comprehensive, it will represent all of the various grades of experience in the interest of "truth." Within the limits of prudence, even the basely comic is admissible.

What Chaucer is defending is the realism [15] upon which he is em-

---

[15] Robertson, *Preface*, pp. 206-7, 276-77, and elsewhere, makes a target of realism in Chaucer. But if we abandon a useful, even though slippery term, we shall be forced to find another to describe what elsewhere Robertson approaches by such terms as "striking verisimilitude" and "greater immediacy" (p. 185). Is it possible, in discussing painting in Italy, for example, not to use the term at some time or other to describe what was coming about in the work of the Giotteschi? And can one read the sermon literature of the period, both on the Continent and in England, without being struck by its close reading of the social scene, by its hard literality? Robertson calls attention to the keenness of Chaucer's intellect, praising it for its ability to grasp abstract

barked. He does not need to defend the exploration of the ideal or the romantic in which his age abounded. What he is defending is his delight in the range of human experience, even when the methods of getting at its essential beauty are those which depict its ugliness or folly. Chaucer lacks vigorous contempt, holy indignation, and in some writers this may look like softness or tolerance for evil, but in Chaucer, the absence of fulminating scorn is his special strength. As a Christian, not given, for all we know, to mystical ecstasies, he knows what it is to be human, sensual, and greedy as well as intelligent, and in all honesty he depicts the whole scale of behavior, leaving out only the most depraved. There is in Chaucer no appetite for the purely salacious, no loss of a sense of what is right or good or true: the Monk's bridle jingling in the whistling wind has its special meaning only with reference to the chapel bell; the world of the fabliaux has its friars in the chancel and its monks reading their breviary, and these remind us of the other—or at any rate another—range of human experience without which the whole story of a varied humanity is incomplete.

The risk that Chaucer is taking is that of any Christian artist who creates a beautiful form. How well he will carry it off, he does not know; he knows only that the task is to be done as best he can, with as much honesty as he can muster. In view of the range of personality

---

concepts and for "perceiving the significance of concrete materials as manifestations of those concepts" (p. 279). But surely this may be said of great poets in any age, that they anchored their universal truths to the data of experience. What we treasure, among other things in Chaucer, is precisely a perennial freshness in an extremely close reading and observation of life itself. It is entirely possible that I fail to follow Professor Robertson on this point; yet it seems to me that to render Chaucer, whether consciously or unconsciously, a creator of iconographical types and an adherent of so particularized an aesthetic limits severely the character of his genius. For how shall we account for or name the kind of examination of the mind and heart of literary agents, not only in *Troilus and Criseyde* and in its original, but in Boccaccio's *Fiammetta?* And how shall we account for the attitudes and persons, surely non-figural, portrayed everywhere in the *Decameron?* or in the tales of Sacchetti?

Perhaps what is needed is a study of the traditions of comedy, irony, and satire in Latin and in the vernacular literatures up to the time of Chaucer, employing the techniques of Ernst Robert Curtius, *European Literature and the Latin Middle Ages*, trans. Willard R. Trask, Bollingen Series, XXXVI (New York, 1953). The Boccaccio of the *Decameron* could urbanely defend the naturalistic, the bawdy, the realistic in a manner strikingly at variance with the Boccaccio of the *Genealogy of the Gentile Gods*. And with Petrarch he admitted the possibility that poets may have no allegorical intentions at all, in a sense allowing, for Plautus and Terence at least, that they were not merely contemporary with their own age, but also contemporary with his own. Surely we can admit the same possibility for Chaucer with regard to his time and ours.

which he is in process of depicting, the vulgar and the profane are inevitable.

His words have a ring of seriousness: Christ and Plato are his authorities in the matter of speaking truthfully of human nature. In essence they are his defense, justifying the freedom of art to tell the truth as the writer sees it. Even so serious a matter, however, as the relation of artist to his materials must be seen within the context of his simple nature as narrator, guileless and innocent. His lack of guile conveys a certain air of wide-eyed innocence, an unassuming simplicity in the assertion that in imitating the truth of reality there can be no evil, as Christ [16] by example and Plato before Him by precept make clear.

The apologetic or defensive note is taken up again in the *Miller's Prologue* with much the same point about truth to "my mateere" (l. 3175), and with a re-emergence of an old concern about the division of his work into the profane and the holy. Now that the tale is at hand, he is more forthright, more ironical in tone: "Turn the page and find something more suited to your tastes. Do not blame me if the one you choose is a bad choice." And then, in much the same words as he puts into the mouth of the Wife of Bath (ll. 189–92): Do not take as serious what is meant as play. In the injunction we detect the conscience of the artist who knows that he is taking the risk [17] for the sake of something else.

I make no apologies for human nature, and I cannot pretend that students of the Chaucerian comedies will find them uniformly elevating or uniformly happy. They were not meant to be. Within the framework of a pilgrimage, and given the discontinuous fragments, the statement ethically or intellectually which we may derive from the *Canterbury Tales* must in all fairness be assessed from the whole structure and not from its individual fragments, or least of all, from tales within any fragment. That is to say, given the variety of persons speaking and the variety of literary types uttered, the pattern of contrast and quarrel, of debate and discussion, prevents in advance the

---

[16] If Chaucer is remembering Christ's words recorded in Matthew 15:17–20, then we may add that the artist's intention determines the morality of his work.

[17] See the startling insight offered by Jacques Maritain, *The Responsibility of the Artist* (New York, 1960), p. 33: "What the artist, insofar as he is an artist, loves over and above all is Beauty in which to engender a work, not God as supreme ruler of human life nor as diffusing his own charity in us. If the artist loves Him over and above all, he does so insofar as he is a man, not insofar as he is an artist."

ascendance of one view over another within the great middle and assures that the whole truth, whatever it may be, can arise only out of the juxtaposition of the various views with each other. This pattern of juxtaposed views, if it may be called a pattern, derives its shape or form, as I have urged elsewhere, precisely from the notion of a pilgrimage-departure from an inn and a pilgrimage-arrival at a goal typified by cathedral spires, and from the statement of both social and moral or religious values in the first and last tales.

The motive of the pilgrimage is gratitude and repentance, a natural rise in spirit which mysteriously duplicates the burgeoning of nature. But repentance itself is based upon knowledge, or at least an acknowledgement of foolish pride, or mere cleverness, or stupidity, or jealousy which stand as obstacles along the way. Beneath the stupidity, the sham, the hypocrisy, if they can be stripped away, lies the essentially human which the comic serves to bring into view. It is the essentially human creature with as little folly as possible who presents himself *in patria*. Laughter, even the bitter rueful admission of certain unpalatable social truths in tales like that of the Shipman and that of the Merchant, serves no less than the happy wish for the community expressed by the *Franklin's Tale*, to free us from the obstacles along the way.[18] And in the use of pilgrimage, Chaucer's wisdom makes, for the moment, peace between the needs of art and the demands of prudence.

If such a reconciliation of art with prudence is possible, how then can we accommodate the Retraction, the final statement of prudence, with the earlier justification of art? The puzzling rejection of the very means by which experience has been given definition, by which the

---

[18] Charles G. Osgood, in *Poetry as a Means of Grace* (Princeton University Press, 1941), puts Chaucer in the company of Euripides, Spenser, Dante, Shakespeare, Milton, and Browning in the matter of serious commentary upon one important phase of the human condition: "...the drama of the temptation and fall, and Adam and Eve in their unhappy disillusioned maturity, the Eternal Masculine and the Eternal Feminine, at first unreconciled, but at last brought in repentance and suffering to full understanding of each other. There is much in this for men to learn about women, and for women to learn about men. And lest there still be those who contend that Milton's judgment of such matters is untrustworthy because it is warped by Puritan prejudice and his domestic mistakes, let us observe that men of the world like Euripides and Chaucer and Spenser and Dante and Shakespeare and Browning agree with him. For they all observe that the basis and germinal element of evil in men is their egoism, in women their love of social power and preeminence; that when man comes to tragic grief it is usually through some weakness or perversion of his sense of the influence of women; but if regeneration comes to pass, it is woman who goes ahead of him and points the way..." (pp. 100–101).

sanctity of the human reality has been sung, has seemed to many an unnecessary and a harsh judgment. Nonetheless the Christian poet posits a right use for art: life depicted as good, or as implying order beyond its disorder even when most profane. Chaucer *seems* to shrink from assessing his own comedy as moral, even though we recall throughout the structure, both by juxtaposition and by infusion, the presence of moral norms within tales. But what the Retraction spells out in its oblique way is a statement of the limits of artistic experience and of the great burden which the lying art of literature imposes upon its practitioner.

The confrontation of the world of literature with that of religion is the last stroke of the pen before the end of service; his poetry has provided delight and joy, even elevation. Nonetheless the final service which art can perform is to speak ill of itself. St. Thomas, approaching death, could say of his *Summa*, "It seems to me rubbish." Chaucer, at the end of pilgrimage in which he has participated, can say, in effect: "Poetry is insufficient."

The logical end of pilgrimage is the meeting of the soul with its Creator. For Chaucer the end is the moment of confession and appraisal, the oblation of the artist bewailing the failure, so essentially a part of the artistic endeavor, adequately to depict what is ultimately inimitable. At the final point at which art becomes thrall to the spiritual, the pilgrim passes from the road into the vestibule of the Most High; thereafter poetry retreats, and the poet as man and artist awaits the final assessment.

From this point of view we err in finding Chaucer's final statement appalling; rather we have missed the point. The poet's voice at the close is no mere plastering-on of a gratuitous religious sentiment, an ugly ornament upon the structure. It is, in fact, a judgment of the relation between the moral and the artistic life, and a statement—if we can read it in the whole structure—of the limits of poetical experience.[19] Within the pilgrimage of this life, the statement does no dis-

---

[19] Cf. Robert M. Jordan, "Chaucer's Sense of Illusion: Roadside Drama Reconsidered," *ELH*, XXIX (1962), 33: "The 'Retraction' is . . . a . . . more explicit statement of Chaucer's sense of the difference between real and nominal truth, that is, between truth and illusion. . . . In invoking the Pauline mandate that 'Al that is writen is writen for oure doctrine' Chaucer is praying that his depiction of the many faces of the nominal might be acceptable as a sign of the changeless truth of the real.

"The continual shifting of the perspective that characterizes Chaucer's poem is indicative of the uneasy adjustment which holds the poet's two worlds in precarious

service to poetry. After the vision in the mirror which it provides must come the desire to satisfy the greater hunger which the vision has created. Whatever our personal beliefs, within the structure of pilgrimage it can be no other way.

Our appreciation of the artistry and the thematic intention of the *Canterbury Tales* as an integral poem depends upon our recognition of affirmation and rejection as informing principles of the same structure. The judgments of the Retraction are a part of what the whole poem says. Just how much art shapes the moral rejections and conversely how much moral rigor underlies the comic affirmations remain highly discussible questions to be confronted by each reader. This much seems clear: the palinode at the conclusion of *Troilus* establishes a pattern in which the moral vision is heightened, underscored, placed in bold relief as a means of providing the only valid and sane perspective by which to assess the foregoing action. In the Retraction the pattern is expanded to allow Chaucer to place his whole literary career in a moral perspective. But the artist could not resist making the moral assessment a part of his whole poem, thereby making himself, in the widest extension of his art, a character in God's book, the plot of which the Parson has provided, and giving himself as persona a version of the *confessio* for his dramatic utterance. The use of such a pattern, as much as any other datum, encourages us to see the extent to which the comic and the realistic can be made contributing parts of a serious statement about the range of human experience within the compass of pilgrimage. As for the effect upon us, insofar as the form is successful, it is we now who should affirm and we who should reject, at least for the time we read, and this after all is poetic faith.

---

equilibrium. The humor which accompanies Chaucer's disavowals of responsibility for the narratives he recounts is the outward sign of a deeply divided spirit. In this inverted way Chaucer articulates his awareness that the world he has created poetically . . . is but an illusion. . . . But the seriousness of the 'Retraction'—like the seriousness of the ending of Troilus—makes it clear that levity is a form of protection against the terror that lurks in art. Chaucer had to find a way of living with the impossible paradox that to be true to his art was to be false to his convictions. He was caught between artistic vanity, which embraced the truth of his creation, and Christian piety, which rejected it. The record of his struggle is the 'multiple unity' of the *Canterbury Tales:* illusion and disillusion stand incongruously together."

THE RANGE OF THE
MIDDLE

In retrospect we can see that the ironical detachment of the persona-poet and his withdrawal from functions other than critical and prudential do not prevent the depiction of his Christian world. On the contrary his detachment enables the world to be spread out before us in all its multiplicity and complexity in the great middle of the *Canterbury Tales*. This middle we now proceed to examine in terms of literary types, of the modes of experience underlying them, and the themes which subtly shape their final form. From the vantage of literary genre we may determine the limitations which are inherent in genre; from the vantage of theme we may determine the shaping power of thought over type.

Chaucer himself not only gives evidence of his awareness of the range of literary forms, but also, in terms of content, makes the distinction between serious and non-serious literature. The reading from the dream of Scipio in the *Parliament of Fowls* hints at the subject. The *Prologue to the Legend of Good Women* (F 414 ff.) makes a precise distinction between entertainment and edification. The *Miller's Prologue* distinguishes low comedy ("cherles tale") from "storial thyng that toucheth gentillesse, / And eek moralitee and hoolynesse" (ll. 3179–80). This familiar distinction between works dealing with the love of this world and those directing our eyes beyond it has its final statement in the Retraction itself.

In the links on either side of the *Monk's Tale* Chaucer displays both theoretical and practical knowledge of comedy and tragedy, dealing both with the "shape" of these forms and with the effect upon the audience. He is equally cognizant of varieties of romance: stories of love, battle, chivalry, of elf-queens and enchantments, and of virtue achieved. He knows these by name as well as by subject, and the effects of his intimate acquaintance are to be seen everywhere in the *Tales*, even to the extent of parody or burlesque.

If we needed further proof of Chaucer's precise knowledge of the range of types, we see it in the casual ease with which he conflates the attributes of comedy, romance, and tragedy in the *Nun's Priest's Tale*, leavens the moral romance with comedy in the *Wife of Bath's Tale*, and deepens the tone of comedy towards satire in the *Merchant's Tale*.

We may go so far as to say that Chaucer is a plastic poet who exploits all the genres which provide vehicles for his themes. His proclivity is in the main for ironic comedy and romance; they prevail at the heart of his genius. Each is involved with the other, deepened or widened to make way for the more serious and elevated or for the more farcial and satiric attitudes. The same commingling of romance and comedy which we note in the *Troilus* we remark in the *Canterbury Tales*. Even in the predominantly sober *Knight's Tale* or the *Man of Law's Tale*, realism intrudes to deflate the tone and subtly change the point of view.

This special apposition of religio-romantic and comic attitudes to each other is the goal upon which much of Chaucer's intelligence finally bears. The delicate balance between man as God-created yet self-asserting, as God-seeking yet self-loving provides him with his essential materials; the antagonism between the poles of man's nature he spells out from the very beginning in the mixture of springtime joy and penitence and works out in the opposition between the goal of Canterbury / Jerusalem and the desire to reach the goal on terms wilfully defined.

The two terms which we have now isolated to describe the classes into which the tales fall need definition. When we use the term romance to describe the secular literary type, we mean a long form, usually of French origin, in which the hero ideally passes through a succession of adventures, conquers his enemy or enemies, frees a woman, attains her love, and achieves some measure of virtue and acceptance in the process. The most usual form assumed is that of the quest-pilgrimage, with a departure and an arrival at a goal, with the strong possibility of a return. The subject matter is the familiar triad of love, adventure, religion. The hero, by his bravery or daring, and by his ability to overcome obstacles, is raised above the level of ordinary men, and tends by his example to bring about in the audience some idealized vision of experience or a confirmation of their hopes. The most serious and elevated form of romance in the Christian tradition has been hagiographic: the saint is shown attesting, in the life of grace, an endurance and perseverance beyond that of other mortals and reaching through suffering the goal of reconciliation with his God. The demonstration of the hero's more-than-human qualities necessitates, in the more naive secular and religious treatments, a world of marvels in which there is assistance (or hindrance) from otherworldly creatures and a beneficent nature.

In its most systematic form, romance is best exemplified by the purgatorial process in the *Divine Comedy*, where life is viewed as a meaningful progress towards an attainable goal and where the *débat* between the vices and virtues is carried out point by point by various devices like the bridle and the whip, the beatitudes, and the loss of the sign of the purged sin. In its serener aspects it sees art as serving the useful function of pointing the way to truth, and of bringing into clear focus a restored natural perfection in which man is crowned priest and emperor over himself. In the Dantean view the total meaning of romance in this sense has to do with learning about charity, or about dealing charitably with others, or with transforming eroticism into something else; in short with setting the soul in order.

Below the purgatorial world of aspiration and hope lies Dante's frozen center of Hell representing the paralysis of the best human motives; and above the center he locates varying degrees of overt and conscious resistance to the good of others and to that of the self, up to the least offensive carnal appetites. The horror of non-commitment to the good in the situation of the trimmers and neutrals indicates something of the medieval fondness for polarity: whoever is not with me is against me. In Chaucer the range of tone is from playful, even joyful, to satirical and serious; humanity is viewed from the vantage of the all-too-human at one extreme, as in the *Miller's Tale* and that of the Reeve, where the audience is apt to see the sexual fulfillment serving as a valid retribution to stupidity or pride, and at the other a whole-hearted allegiance to evil, as in the *Pardoner's Tale* in which the upside-down values of the protagonists test or deny order and law. The tragic tends to be an aspect of this range of experience, as the pathetic tends to be an aspect of romance; noise, confusion, and riot are apt to be its dominant note, as a note of hopeful and serene expectation is apt to be that of romance.

As Aristotle pointed out in the opening chapters of the *Poetics*—with acuteness, I feel—literary types are preceded by attitudes towards experience which the poet holds by personal disposition, and we may add, by convention. Chaucer's views include the notions that man is a significant part of creation, that suffering is meaningful, that life is a process, that aspiration is the inner life of achievement, that the soul has an ultimate destiny, that the upper air is, so to speak, peopled with guardian spirits, and that in the mysterious "below" lie forces of destruction. We need not wonder that Chaucer's specialty is romance.

Aristotle also pointed out what was for him the great dichotomy of classes into which men fall: men better or worse than average. If we add to the first the suggestion of men as they ought to be and to the second men as they are or as they are thought to be, we do not change the division, but rather begin to account for the great variety of experience and types of plot available to the poet. The division was for Aristotle a matter of the broadest kind of morality, and is in the Greek terms a division into the serious and the laughable or absurd. This consideration of the degree of seriousness in the subject matter and in the disposition of the poet we confront in Chaucer, in whom the word "worthy," for example, used in a variety of contexts, points up the distinction in clearly moral contexts between persons striving after virtue and those indifferent to it. For the moral Christian poet, for Dante and for Chaucer to be specific, the view of men as better or worse than the average yields the familiar purgatorial and infernal levels of human actions where the agents are depicted on the one hand as seriously involved in the process of making themselves acceptable to God, and on the other, as arrested at some chosen level less than the Good.

The polarity I am suggesting of two classes of literary experiences was noted long ago by Saintsbury, who recognized that the opposition between them was nearly as sharp as that of Greek tragedy to Greek comedy or satiric play, and who suggested that in Chaucer it may have been studied. The question that is immediately raised is that of tragedy. Chaucer's distinction, made on the basis of a somewhat shadowy literary tradition, has to do with a sad end to the affairs of men. But Chaucer's disposition is sunny alongside Dante's, and he does not specialize in the unhappy tale. Even those which deal with the destruction of the agents are carefully contrived to corroborate the values of the audience; they assume a stance of righteousness and become moral tales; in particular they become what Northrop Frye calls comedies without humor in which the audience does not have to take the villainy seriously.[1]

The *Monk's Tale*, with its series of vignettes, is in the view I have been offering, an anomaly in the *Canterbury Tales*.[2] (Even in the series the tale of Nebuchadnezzar must be seen as a tragedy with a happy ending.) But the anomaly has a function within the larger thematic frame, serving by juxtaposition with the *Nun's Priest's Tale* to point up beyond the fall of princes, beyond an empty contempt of the world, the power of men to escape the operations of mere destiny and to control, up to a point, their progress through the world of accident and chance. Like the good ironist, Chaucer recognizes the role of luck, of canniness, of expedience, but like the good moralist he seriously ponders the mystery of responsibility and the working of the human will. Governance, self-possession, self-control become for him central considerations in both the serious and the non-serious tales. For Chaucer the distinction between a happy or a sad ending becomes a matter of the retention or loss of these. It is instructive to look to Dante where the so-called tragic or sad end of the agent does not preclude his ultimate salvation unless the end is couched in terms of an incorrigible use of the self and others without regard to the larger concerns of human responsibility. If the agent has not lost sight of his eternal goals, nor of the value of hope and repentance, his suffering becomes meaningful and his so-called tragic end is of no consequence in the larger pattern of Divine Comedy, but is rather merely an episode in it. Even in Chaucer's *Troilus*, where it is perhaps useless to talk of grace and perdition, the action ends with a laugh in a Neo-Platonic heaven.

There are other ways by which to classify the tales, and there have been many attempts to classify them.[3] Taxonomy of the tales would, of course, be in a vastly better plight if Chaucer had written the full quota promised in his first plan. With the twenty-four performances

[1] *Anatomy of Criticism* (Princeton University Press, 1957), p. 40.

[2] A theory of Chaucerian tragedy is coming more and more into being. Cf. D. W. Robertson, Jr., "Chaucerian Tragedy," *ELH*, XIX (1952), 1–37; R. E. Kaske, "The Knight's Interruption of the *Monk's Tale*," *ELH*, XXIV (1957), 249–68; Robert A. Pratt, "'Joye after Wo' in the *Knight's Tale*," *JEGP*, LVII (1958), 416–23; John F. Mahoney, "Chaucerian Tragedy and the Christian Tradition," *Annuale Mediaevale*, III (1962), 81–99; and George B. Pace, "Adam's Hell," *PMLA*, LXXVIII (1963), 25–35. See too D. W. Robertson, Jr., *A Preface to Chaucer*, pp. 346, 473.

[3] Cf. the attempts at classification in Robert O. Payne, *The Key of Remembrance: A Study of Chaucer's Poetics* (Yale University Press, 1963), pp. 147–70, with which I am in substantial agreement on the matter of types, and in which the author is fully aware of the limitations in any system of categories.

of the pilgrimage one always feels strong demurrals about *any* system because of Chaucer's own eclectic handling of the literary types, and because of the small number of examples from which to generalize. One such classification which does not go quite beyond the consideration of types, but which indicates the difficulties of classification is as follows:

1. *Tales mainly realistic:* Miller, Reeve, Cook, Shipman. (Shall we add Friar, Summoner, Pardoner, Canon's Yeoman, Part II? What of the fabliau tone in the *Wife of Bath's Tale* and that of the Merchant?)
2. *Tales of chivalry:* Knight and Squire. (Shall we include Chaucer's parody here? Shall we include here the tales of the Wife of Bath and the Franklin?)
3. *Religious tales about saints:* the Prioress's miracle, and the tale of the Second Nun. (Shall we include the Clerk and the Man of Law in this general classification?)
4. *Pious tales about saintly persons:* Clerk and Man of Law. (Shall we consider these allegories? What about the *Physician's Tale?*)
5. *Moral treatises: Melibee,* Parson. (Shall we call them both treatises? Is the *Melibee* also a poem? an allegory? a sermon buried in an artificially contrived frame?)
6. *Fables with moral comment*: Manciple. (Shall we group the *Physician's Tale* here as a legend with moral comment? What of the beast fable in the *Nun's Priest's Tale?*)
7. *Confessions: Wife of Bath's Prologue, Pardoner's Introduction* and conclusion to his sermon (moral tale? exemplum? fabliau?), the *Canon's Yeoman's Tale,* Part I.
8. *Preacher's exempla:* Friar's Tale, Pardoner's Tale, Nun's Priest's Tale?
9. *Breton lai:* Franklin, and Wife of Bath?
10. *Tales of whatever sort with added didactic elements:* Merchant, Wife of Bath, Nun's Priest, Franklin. (Also Manciple, Physician, Man of Law, Pardoner, Canon's Yeoman, Summoner, Monk? Is the *Merchant's Tale* a parody of romance? Should it be included with Group 1?)
11. *Tragedy:* Monk's tales. (Are they, like the *Physician's Tale,* merely history in a moral context?)

It is not a classification I should care to defend at length, but it does point up a number of difficulties which confront the classifier. One conclusion that is possible from any attempt at grouping is that Chaucer was an experimenter and that the tales individually reflect a constant concern with the forms of art as well as an indifference to their built-in limitations.

In classifying the tales as either comedies or romances I have kept in mind, within the two main categories, the broadest possible correspondence to Chaucer's own distinction between literature for edification and literature for pleasure, recognizing that the tales within each group span the range from serious to non-serious, and attempting to assess the degree to which the tales function as serious statements in the total theme. Such a division is based upon human character as capable or incapable of regeneration and yields the familiar poles of comedy and romance.

Wherever the tales deal with the unwillingness of the agents to surrender their instinctual incorrigibility, with the determined assertion of their appetites over social convention, they belong to the world of comedy, ironic, melodramatic, even exemplary. With such agents we can never feel more than a sneaking and even despairing admiration for their invincible folly. This group includes the tales of the Miller, Reeve, Shipman, Friar, Summoner, Merchant, Pardoner, and Canon's Yeoman.

Wherever the agents manifest powers of growth, submit themselves to a learning process, are in some way regenerated, they belong to the world of romance. We pin our hopes upon these heroes and heroines because they corroborate our inner convictions about human freedom. When they err and fall, in a sense we err and fall with them, but with them we also rise. I see the tales of the Knight, Man of Law, Prioress, Nun's Priest, Wife of Bath, Clerk, and Franklin as romances.

This dichotomy between despair and hope, between corrigibility and incorrigibility, tends to make clear Chaucer's own recognition of the spiritual death that lurks in the one camp and the spiritual life that thrives in the other, and marks him yet again, as he chose once to be remembered, a religious as well as a comic poet. The purgatorial basis of romance and the infernal basis of comedy are not, after all, different for him from what they were for Dante.

The division suggested can lend itself to oversimplification; yet it by-passes the temptation to see the tales of the secular agents and those of the religious as providing a workable scheme of classification.[4] It is not simple for the reason that Chaucer's attitudes and intentions are not simple, either as artist or as a moral commentator. Both the comedies and the romances show variety of treatment, variety of mood. In some the form is freighted with *exempla*, overt statement; in others theme is subtly linked with style, implication, oblique suggestion. The multileveled view of experience which comprises the great middle of the *Canterbury Tales* is not, obviously, any simple alternation of one overt view with another. It is an interaction of worlds in the mind of the poet, presented to us in particular manipulations of literary forms, the manipulations themselves being the result of the thought or meaning each form supports and conveys. Thus the focus of what follows is the thematic range of the comic and romantic forms, the deepening and widening of their scope to allow for the bitter and sardonic as well as the lyrical and spiritual. By such an examination we come to see how, in the most ancient sense, Chaucer reveals himself as the plastic poet in his grasp of the whole range of experience, the world of wish-and-wonder as well as the world of the all-too-real.

Aside from the varying degrees of success and failure in the artistic endeavor which we all feel, there lies over the great bulk of the *Canterbury Tales* what someone has called an incorruptible sincerity of expression reflecting the concern of the poet for the truth of experience.[5] It is this which, more than any other factor, justifies the patient examination of their thematic statement.

[4] The decision to omit certain of the tales reflects my own taste and judgment. Much of the *Canterbury Tales* is of varying quality; two tales (Manciple and Physician) are successful on terms other than purely artistic and I recognize the possibility that Chaucer's intention may have included the overt didactic utterances. The Cook's and Squire's fragments cannot yield in their incomplete state a coherent interpretation until we know that Chaucer intended them to be fragments. The *Monk's Tale* belongs, properly, in an appendix, unless we care to place the tale of Nebuchadnezzar in one camp and the others on the opposing side.

For the function of the *Monk's Tale*, see pp. 184–85; for the *Manciple's Tale*, p. 247, *n*. 1.

[5] In 1936, C. S. Lewis, in *The Allegory of Love: A Study in Medieval Tradition* (Oxford University Press, 1936), pp. 163–64, offered the view that Chaucer is mainly a poet of courtly love, that his fourteenth-century audience thought of him as the poet of the dream-allegory and romance written in the high style and imbued with doctrine. To shift emphasis from such matters, Mr. Lewis writes, is to deal falsely, in a sense, with his work. "We have heard a little too much of the 'mocking' Chaucer. Not many will agree with the critic who supposed that the laughter of Troilus in heaven was 'ironical'; but I am afraid that many of us now read into Chaucer all manner of ironies, slynesses, and archnesses, which are not there, and praise him for his humour where he is really writing with 'ful devout corage.'"

In 1948, George R. Coffman, in a footnote to his essay "Chaucer and Courtly

Love Once More—The *Wife of Bath's Tale*," *Speculum*, XX (1948), 49–50, defended by way of answer a "prevailing Comic Spirit" in Chaucer and called for not only an interpretation of his "prevailing intent," but also a comprehensive review of the whole problem of terminology as an essential part of repeated attempts "to probe the heart of Chaucer's philosophic and aesthetic concept." Relying upon Lowell's dictum that the main consideration in Dante is the saving of the soul, and in Chaucer, the conduct of life, he offers a prefatory definition of satire drawn from W. F. Thrall and Addison Hibbard, *A Handbook to Literature* (New York, 1936), p. 386: "A literary manner which blends a critical attitude with wit and humor to the end that human institutions may be improved."

Both points of view have their value. The first has been deepened to the point where we have been persuaded to see Chaucer as an allegorist par excellence, using courtly love as an instrument of doctrine, carrying a somewhat wearying freight of Biblical exegesis and Augustinian aesthetic. The other has been widened to include a range of experience that is deeply serious, even "tragic," "psychological," and the like. We have become conscious of stringent attitudes in fabliaux and romances alike, of criticisms implied of the aristocratic milieu, of a sensitivity to profoundly important human problems. We have come to recognize that the Chaucerian manner can be extremely detached, objective, that the audience can, with the poet, have the sense of "looking down" like Troilus from an exalted vantage upon agents vastly inferior in power of action, we feel, to ourselves. The two points of view do not cancel each other out, as both the Bible and Boethius attest, but it should be stated that the term satire for the distancing of poet and audience from subject represents only one face of the coin; as the subject increases in seriousness, the term irony serves us better.

II
FUNCTION: COMEDY AND IRONY

THE MILLER'S TALE

*In great comedy ... there is tension between the
normative past as the ideals of the aristocracy, and
the norms of present life as the life of the
bourgeois.*

ALBERT COOK,
The Dark Voyage and the Golden Mean

*Men's future upon earth does not attract [the
Comic Spirit]; their honesty and shapeliness in the
present does; and whenever they wax out of
proportion, overblown, affected, pretentious,
bombastical, hypocritical, pedantic, fantastically
delicate; whenever it sees them self-deceived or
hoodwinked, given to run riot in idolatries,
drifting into vanities, congregating in absurdities,
planning short-sightedly, plotting dementedly;
whenever they are at variance with their professions, and violate the unwritten but perceptible
laws binding them in consideration one to another; whenever they offend sound reason, fair
justice; are false in humility or mined with conceit,
individually, or in the bulk; the Spirit overhead
will look humanely malign, and cast an oblique
light on them.*

GEORGE MEREDITH,
The Idea of Comedy

After the romance, the pageantry, and the philosophical tone of
the *Knight's Tale*, the *Miller's Tale* comes as a radical change of pace,
of literary type, of intellectual attitude. To be sure, Chaucer has
prepared us in the *General Prologue* for the depiction of the basely
comic (in the familiar lines already quoted, p. 36). The Miller's own
prologue, after its drunken outburst and the quarrel with the Reeve,
establishing a certain baseness of intellect and ethos in both agents,
closes once again on the plea of accurate reporting and the absence of
any "yvel entente" in the poet. In essence the two apologetic passages

are a defense by the poet of all comedy—with all that is implied in the difference of tone, level of diction, intellectual attitudes, and morality —outside the domain

> Of storial thyng that toucheth gentillesse,
> And eek moralitee and hoolynesse,　　　　　　　　(ll. 3179–80)

and of the right to admit to the realms of art even the lowly popular French fabliau; in short, notwithstanding the strictures of prudence, to admit to the larger structure of the *Canterbury Tales* those aspects of man's experience usually denied as material for polite literature, but which now may be offered as no less serious a commentary than the previous tale has been.

Employing the device of contrast, Chaucer sets side by side two views of love: that which finds support in both philosophy and theology and that vastly less rationalized variety which is the action of the "natural" man. The one leans heavily upon justification of the ways of God with his creatures; the other relies mainly upon instincts and abandons any religious ties except those that allow the story to take place within a familiar ambience. The one is a characteristic of the gentry and the knightly class; the other involves the actions of common men and women. The one necessitates the more elevated style suited to serious subject matter; the other the lower style befitting the agents. The one is dominantly romantic and thought-provoking; the other dominantly realistic and laugh-provoking. But each of the antithetical elements borrows from its opposite and intermingles with it to create that unique style and subtle commentary which so many students note and which Tillyard has happily termed "oblique."

The shifts which one can so easily define in passing from the *Knight's Tale* to that of the Miller are intimately tied in with the literary form. Man's physical prowess on the field of battle, the control exerted by moral codes over the amatory appetite, the acquisition of some virtuous resignation to the will of God (I am recalling here Dante's perceptive remarks about the subject matter of romance), make the *Knight's Tale* a well-nigh perfect illustration of the type. That worthy's tale, furthermore, is vested with a faintly, though clearly, definable didactic tone which gives it, by comparison with the *Miller's Tale*, the slight flavor of a mild corrective, as though reason here might throw a yoke over natural inclination. The view that is explored within his tale constitutes, however, but one attitude towards love. That of the fabliau provides another, one which has the virtue of offering variety of invention and freshness to the patterns of pilgrimage.

Thus, when we come to the tale told by the Miller, we have been prepared for a change in style as well as for the change in subject matter. The *Knight's Tale*, after all, is a leisurely tale intended for a court audience; the philosophy that lends the story its tone also gives the tale its careful four-part structure. In the end, the agents act as they ought within the limits of God's law; their struggle to realize the law of love informs the action at every point and is itself, in a sense, the plot. But now we leave the world of the court for the freer air of the world of contrivance and deception, of situations and actions generating their own special kind of morality and their own justice. In Tillyard's words, "We have to do with the way of the world, not the ways of God." [1]

The basic similarities between the tale of the Knight and that of the Miller have been admirably explored. [2] The wooing of a young woman by two young men, seen from widely divergent points of view to be sure, is the situation common to both. In the courtly romance, the amatory instinct is seen ultimately as the means by which man accommodates himself to the Divine, and this accommodation is itself, within the framework of the story, a virtuous one wrung from the necessary and inevitable destinal order. In the *Miller's Tale*, there is a shift from perfecting or correcting the appetites within the imposed terms of the grand contract to the more immediate and limited goal of gratification of appetite as an end in itself, the "highest good," so to speak, within the comic frame. A further change in plot, more usual in traditional comedy of this sort, provides a blocking agent in the form of the old husband, a situation which opens the way for later closer examinations of marriages and the threatening adulterous third.

The shifts of emphasis that we note are, too, an accommodation of the character of the Miller to the tale he is assigned. This earthy, vigorous, ribald, tactless cheat is admirably suited to the tale of decep-

[1] Eustace M. W. Tillyard, *Poetry Direct and Oblique* (London, 1948), p. 88.
[2] William C. Stokoe, Jr., "Structure and Intention in the First Fragment of the *Canterbury Tales*," *UTQ*, XXI (1952), 120–27; Charles A. Owen, Jr., "Chaucer's *Canterbury Tales*: Aesthetic Design in Stories of the First Day," *ES*, XXV (1955), 49–56.

tion, except for—we note—its polished cleverness, which is beyond his capacity. Nonetheless, what he has heard in the *Knight's Tale*, we deduce, has filled him with impatience and incredulity; the philosophical justifications, the appearance of complexity in what must have seemed a very simple problem, the elevation itself of the theme as stated by Theseus—all have made him champ a little. The Knight has no sooner finished than there bursts from his tongue loosened by spirits the outcry:

> "By armes, and by blood and bones,
> I kan a noble tale for the nones,
> With which I wol now quite the Knyghtes tale."
>
> (ll. 3125-27)

What he intends is a kind of reprisal, and in a subtle and misguided way, a kind of reprise. Whatever the parallels that one may wish to see in the two pairs of young men in their respective tales—one wishes to see in Nicholas the direct and vigorous action of Arcite and in Absalom the softer nature of Palamon—the Miller has chosen to give the major victory to the man of action. Needless to say, his tale is an answer, a requital, told from the point of view of one who has missed the point of the story he has just heard. But he *thinks* he sees the point, and to that point he makes his answer. It has come down to us as one of the choicest samples of the literary art of an age and stands as a kind of monument to comedy of the purer sort. Unfettered by morality of the obvious kind, technically perfect, it stands first among the fabliaux, and from the point of view of narrative skill, perhaps first in the whole canon of the *Tales*. By exonerating himself of evil intention at the outset of the tale, Chaucer seeks to escape the charge of unseemliness; more important for the artist, he reserves to himself the greater freedom of disassociating himself from what his agents may be given to say or do in accordance with their stations, their ethical bias, and their intellectual limitations.

Once attuned to the world of the fabliau the astute reader detects in the *Miller's Tale* a sense of exhilaration in the writing of the tale itself. It is written with such perfect control of the nuances of character and the intricacies of situation that on the surface it seems an end in itself, pure play and diversion for the poet. Yet it is not a thing apart from the structure implied by framing links nor from the dramatic interplay of character among the pilgrims themselves. As I have suggested above, it constitutes an answer to the preceding story by setting up its two agents as parodies of a romantic and a realist and making them pursue the same girl. Needless to say, this is not the plot of the *Knight's Tale,* which places its emphasis not upon character development but upon the accommodation of the two agents to the plan of the universe according to the law of love. But it is what the gross Miller is capable of seeing in it, or what Chaucer, for his own purposes, allows him to see in it. The answer the Miller offers arises out of the whole story rather than out of a particular personal enmity between himself and the Knight. In this sense the tale he tells is no mere joyful perfection written for its own sake, but rather for the sake of a function it must perform in the first group of tales. It differs from the role performed by the *Reeve's Tale* in that the *Reeve's Tale* strikes us not so much as a response to the content of the previous tale as a response of the teller's personality to that of an adversary who has provoked him beyond endurance.

Thus Chaucer achieves two varieties of articulation, one a subtle debate of issues seen from differing points of view, the other the friction of two personalities acting in the framework of the pilgrimage, and these are two devices which may be noted in other parts of the *Canterbury Tales.* There is a perceptible intellectual movement in the passage from the treatment of high romantic matter, of the schooled responses of the knightly code, of love as the pattern of the universe, to the low comic treatment of unmoral matter and undisguised and unrationalized appetite. There is too a perceptible freedom in yielding to the demands of the literary form; Chaucer is free of that faint doubt as to the freedom of his agents which makes for so much poignancy in the *Knight's Tale.* He grasps at once, on both the literary and psychological levels, the problem of the relationship of the framework to the tales, and solves that problem, not without a certain risk to verisimilitude, by entrusting to the Miller's coarse and obtuse personality the brilliant ironies of his tale.[3]

[3] The ironies of the tale have been assessed from a variety of points of view. E. Talbot Donaldson, "The Idiom of Popular Poetry in the *Miller's Tale,*" *English Institute Essays* (1950), pp. 116–40, and Gardiner Stillwell, "The Language of Love in Chaucer's Miller's and Reeve's Tales and in the Old French Fabliaux," *Studies in Memory of John Jay Parry* (Urbana, Illinois, 1955), pp. 212–18, are concerned with the ironies resulting from the application of a courtly vocabulary to an inelegant character or situation. John J. O'Connor, "The Astrological Background of the *Miller's Tale,*" *Speculum,* XXXI (1956), 120–25; Kelsie B. Harder, "Chaucer's Use of the Mystery Plays in the *Miller's Tale,*" *MLQ,* XVII (1956), 193–98; and W. F. Bolton, "The *Miller's Tale:* An Interpretation," *MS,* XXIV (1962), 83–94, deal with sources of irony in the plot. The Rev. Paul E. Beichner, "Absolon's

This is artistic play of the highest sort, and our enjoyment of the tale arises in part from the absence of an obvious didacticism, of recourse to authority or that extravagance of exemplary materials which characterizes other tales; in short from what is for some its purity of comic intention, and for others, its ironical complexity. This complexity results from the range of theological and romantic associations which are woven securely into the comic and realistic fabric, the ornament which invests the finished product with some of its own special beauty. Obviously the comic and the romantic do not, here, add up to the conventional solutions of hero and heroine on whom we have pinned our hopes and with whom we identify ourselves. These incorrigibles remain what they are, indomitably self-willed, self-gratifying, in the world of irony, where the laws of canniness, deception, self-interest, and revenge are substituted for the conventional morality of trials and penance, reward and regeneration in the romantic world. But this latter world is ever present.

Chaucer's seriousness here is apprehensible in the range of associations with the materials of romance: ceremonial wooing and singing, the use of a vocabulary drawn from the tales of the nobility, the parody of religious materials like the Song of Solomon and the account of Noah's flood which appears like a leitmotiv throughout the major part of the story, the range of holy (and unholy) names with which the story is sprinkled. The world that is created in this masterpiece skirts the perplexities raised by the *Knight's Tale*, but at least takes account of them (as when the old husband muses about God's secrets and man's attempts to plumb them); but the emphasis is so entirely different—that is, upon the all-too-real—as to lead us to pass over them as casual or gratuitous.

Chaucer himself makes much of the description of the agents of the *Miller's Tale*, so that we cannot fail to see an intimate relationship

---

Hair," *MS*, XII (1950), 222–33, and "Chaucer's Hende Nicholas," *MS*, XIV (1952), 151–53, reminds us of the ironies implicit in the names of the agents. There are wide-ranging and insightful remarks of interest in Paul N. Siegel, "Comic Irony in the Miller's Tale," *BUSE*, IV (1960), 114–20, and in Earle Birney, "The Inhibited and the Uninhibited: Ironic Structure in the Miller's Tale," *Neophil.*, XLIV (1960), 333–38. Some of the criticism has absorbed a psychological point of view and vocabulary. For example, Charles Muscatine, in *Chaucer and the French Tradition* (University of California Press, 1957), p. 228, speaks of "the anal-retentive, squeamish spotlessness registered in Absolon's portrait and punished with terrible aptness at the end." And Birney, echoing Owen (*ES*, XXV, 52–53), speaks of his "oral-anal personality" and of the hot coulter as the "ironic symbol of his sexual inadequacy."

between their characters, talents, and inclinations and the plots in which they perform. The clever scholar or clerk Nicholas, who succeeds for a time with the wife of the old carpenter, is depicted for us as conniving and discreet, self-interested and sly, retiring in deportment and smelling as sweet as a young girl, fastidious and knowledgeable, given to the gay life but dependent upon the support of his friends, fond of music both religious and popular. The type is generalized enough to be familiar, one Chaucer anchors securely to the story to follow by appending the debased, romantic appellative "hende" to his name and thus pointing forward to his role as the prime mover of one segment of the tale and as the momentarily successful outwitter of the other male agents. He is furthermore addicted to astrology and has the ability to prognosticate either drought or rain, a talent which figures largely in the duping of the old carpenter. Part of the satisfaction we derive from the story arises out of the alternation of triumph and defeat between Nicholas and Absalom, from seeing the clever man outwitted and brought low. The reversal of fortune for Nicholas is sane and healthy as well as inevitable, a comic demand for reprisal and justice arising out of the characters as well as the form.

The old man who becomes the dupe is a jealous man, and with good cause. His wife is only eighteen, young and wild. He suspects the inevitable threat to his marriage because of the difference in their ages, and he bears the pain of this disparity as best he can.

> He knew nat Catoun, for his wit was rude,
> That bad man sholde wedde his simylitude.
> Men sholde wedden after hire estaat,
> For youthe and elde is often at debaat.
> But sith that he was fallen in the snare,
> He most endure, as oother folk, his care.   (ll. 3227–32)

And well he might; Alison's character is reinforced by affinities with the natural world: the slim weasel, the small, sour blackthorn, the pear tree which comes to be associated in the *Merchant's Tale* with adultery, the soft woolly lamb, the swallow sitting singing on the barn, the kid or calf gamboling behind its mother, the apples laid up in the hay, the skittish colt, the primrose, and the "piggesnye" fit to grace a bed—all suggesting either an irresponsible and unburdened pastoral innocence, or more specifically the barnyard world teeming with life and energy, devoid of any intellectualized sentiments, but replete with appetite, instinct, and the exuberance of nature itself.

The physical details of her dress and figure afford us further glimpses into Chaucerian ambiguity: the slim and lithe weasel provides the analogy for her body, a neat, even sinewy image later reinforced by the strength of "mast" and "bolt." The reiteration of whiteness (as of morning milk) to describe her apron, smock, and cap suggests a cleanliness and a purity to correspond with the strength and cleanliness of line just mentioned, but which are soon offset by the "likerous" eye topped by the plucked brows. If she is faintly devaluated by the terms "so gay a popelote" and "swich a wenche," she is given a specific price and value by the comparison of her visage with the newly forged and brightly shining noble. The persisting list of her physical parts, her body "gent and smal," her loins, her eyes and brows, the suggestion of a softness to the touch, her bright and shining complexion, her sweet-smelling mouth, and her legs, points insistently to the ripe and ready, impertinently vivacious and youthful creature who reaches her natural destination in the closing lines of her description. Is it any wonder that Chaucer has desisted from portraying her husband directly? She leaps to the fore, the worthy, waiting goal of the clever and conniving Nicholas.

The inescapable directness of the sexual preliminaries brings us straight to the core of the Miller's answer to the Knight. In tone and attitude, vocabulary and word choice, figure of speech and word play, in genre and philosophy, the two pilgrims stand utterly opposed.

> Now, sire, and eft, sire, so bifel the cas,
> That on a day this hende Nicholas
> Fil with this yonge wyf to rage and pleye,
> Whil that hir housbonde was at Oseneye,
> As clerkes been ful subtile and ful queynte;
> And prively he caught hire by the queynte,
> And seyde, "Ywis, but if ich have my wille,
> For deerne love of thee, lemman, I spille."
> And heeld hire harde by the haunchbones,
> And seyde, "Lemman, love me al atones,
> Or I wol dyen, also God me save!"
> And she sproong as a colt dooth in the trave,
> And with hir heed she wryed faste awey,
> And seyde, "I wol nat kisse thee, by me fey!

Why, lat be," quod she, "lat be, Nicholas,
Or I wol crie 'out, harrow' and 'allas'!
Do wey youre handes, for youre curteisye!"
   This Nicholas gan mercy for to crye,
And spak so faire, and profred him so faste,
That she hir love hym graunted atte laste,
And swoor hir ooth, by seint Thomas of Kent,
That she wol been at his commandement,
Whan that she may hir leyser wel espie.
"Myn housbonde is so ful of jalousie
That but ye wayte wel and been privee,
I woot right well I nam but deed," quod she.
"Ye moste been ful deerne, as in this cas."
   "Nay, thereof care thee noght," quod Nicholas.
"A clerk hadde litherly biset his whyle,
But if he coude a carpenter bygyle."
And thus they been accorded and ysworn
To wayte a tyme, as I have told biforn.
   Whan Nicholas had doon this everideel,
And thakked hire aboute the lendes weel,
He kiste hire sweete and taketh his sawtrie,
And pleyeth faste, and maketh melodie.   (ll. 3271–3306)

Nicholas emerges as a man of direct action; looking back to the description of him in the opening of the tale, we recognize a spareness of delineation, a compressed set of details of habitation, personal habit, and inclination, alongside of which the description of Absalom seems a dilation of bright color and attention to personal dress, verging upon self-conscious dandyism. His golden, carefully treated curly hair, his high color and grey eyes, his dainty ornamented shoes, his blue and white garments and his red hose are as colorful as those of any prissy medieval heroine. Like Nicholas he has his individualizing talents, like Nicholas he plays a musical instrument, like Nicholas he is amorous, like Nicholas he has that quality of being fastidious without which the story would lose much of its ironical point (ll. 3337–38).

That they are as subtly different in their attitudes and actions as the two knights of the previous tale, no one will deny. When Absalom sets eyes upon the cleanly scrubbed Alison in the church where she has gone "Cristes owene werkes for to wirche" (the normative world of the church suggests that standard which natural appetite carelessly violates), he is no less aroused to sexual appetite than Nicholas. But Nicholas has the faculty of solving his difficulties directly, whereas

Absalom proceeds by the prettier, more ritualistic and ceremonial way. Lacking the advantage of living in the same house as his quarry, he must woo, dress himself attractively, employ brokers, sing, offer gifts and bribes. The flamboyance of his character as well as the pressures of sexual desire make him even play the role of Herod. In short, he is all color alongside of Alison, all ceremony and prettiness alongside of Nicholas.

With the wooing of Alison by Absalom and the scheme of Nicholas to outwit the stupid carpenter, the two plots of which the tale is composed begin to coalesce. Although it is not likely that Chaucer himself combined for the first time the intrigue of the flood with the story of the misplaced kiss and the retaliatory burning, the ability to carry off the synthesis with steady control of comic detail reveals the artist at the height of his power. The humanizing details that are invested in the character of the old carpenter, solicitous for the clerk in his house, worried over the clerk's excessive learning, his humble fear of prying into God's secrets, his anxiety over Alison's safety, bring us to a limited pity. We do not pity enough, however, to resent the deception.

The action is keyed accurately and surely to domesticity and the humble actions of men: the servant boy peeping through the hole in the door intended for the cat, the analogy of the clerk stumbling through the fields and falling into a pit, the carpenter and stout Robin prying open the door so forcefully that it bursts loose from its hinges, the concrete details of the kneading tubs, the gardens, the stables are all incorporated precisely into the low style; the extravagant preparations for the deluge bring us surely into the world of comedy with its preoccupation with preposterous invention, while Nicholas' canny knowledge and connivance contrasted with the simple credulity of the old carpenter bears upon the role of the traditional impostor which he performs and which is so standard a part of comic structure. His deceitful use of astronomy and prognostication point up the age as well as the continuity of the tradition, especially when we recall Aristotle's remark that the *alazon* frequently pretends to such qualities as skill in prophesying.[4]

With the tubs tied up to the gables, and the weary carpenter asleep

---

[4] *Nicomachean Ethics* 4. 13. See the discussion of comic characters in Lane Cooper, *An Aristotelian Theory of Comedy* (New York, 1922), pp. 118 ff.

from his hasty and heavy labors, Nicholas and Alison are free to disport

> In bisynesse of myrthe and of solas,
> Til that the belle of laudes gan to rynge,
> And freres in the chauncel gonne synge. (ll. 3654-56)

Outside of their successful and secret connivance, the orderly and regulated world of moral action provides its ironical counterpoint to the successful moment.

From this point on, the two segments of the plot move unerringly towards the synapse in the cry of "Water! water!" Absalom's dainty and fastidious wooing takes on the heavier burden of acting as an instrument of poetic justice in as rare a miracle of literary contrivance as occurs in the *Canterbury Tales*. Reasoning falsely about the carpenter's absence from his customary labors and with his mouth itching for a kiss, Absalom presents himself at cock-crow to raise up his pastoral poem of prayer and pleading. The remotely Biblical tone of it, and the debased tone of Alison's reply mark once again the range and compass of irony arising out of character:

> ... softe he cougheth with a semy soun:
> "What do ye, hony-comb, sweete Alisoun,
> My faire bryd, my sweete cynamome?
> Awaketh, lemman myn, and speketh to me!
> Wel litel thynken ye upon my wo,
> That for youre love I swete ther I go.
> No wonder is thogh that I swelte and swete;
> I moorne as dooth a lamb after the tete.
> Ywis, lemman, I have swich love-longynge,
> That lik a turtel trewe is my moornynge.
> I may nat ete na moore than a mayde."
>   "Go fro the wyndow, Jakke fool," she sayde;
> "As help me God, it wol nat be 'com pa me.'
> I love another—and elles I were to blame—
> Wel bet than thee, by Jhesu, Absolon.
> Go forth thy wey, or I wol caste a ston,
> And lat me slepe, a twenty devel wey!" (ll. 3697-3713)

But so sweet a prayer and so rare an opportunity deserves the fulfillment of a comic deception. Absalom has his kiss, of sorts, and his ensuing moment of an abhorrent recognition. His cry, "Fy! allas! what have I do?" starts out of his offended fastidious soul, and is paralleled by Alison's "Tehee!" and Nicholas' remarkably apposite "A berd! a berd!" on three levels of comic experience.

What follows is an inevitable and necessary justice working out the inexorable dues: intent upon revenge, cured of romantic maundering towards "paramours" (perhaps the Miller's main point), Absalom gets his hot coulter from the smithy, replays his scene at the window, strikes his blow for justice (being nearly blinded in the act), the cry of "Help! water! water! help, for Goddes herte!" goes up—and the two parts of the plot fly together as the carpenter cuts down the tub, thinking he is about to float away on the flood. Gullible to the end, he is laughed to scorn by townsmen and clerks alike:

> They seyde, "The man is wood, my leeve brother";
> And every wight gan laughen at this stryf.
> Thus swyved was this carpenteris wyf,
> For al his kepyng and his jalousye.   (ll. 3848–51)

The question which, for many, obscures the supreme artistry of the *Miller's Tale* (and the *Reeve's Tale*) is the question of prudence, of seemliness and decorum, matters to which Chaucer himself was not insensitive. Indeed, the Retraction is itself a testament to the overwhelming sense of moral righteousness with which the instincts of the artist—to depict the whole range of human experience, even that which violates ideal patterns of thought and action and which is devoid of any purely didactic attempt to accommodate human achievement to divine commandment—are in constant conflict. Yet Chaucer chose to hold the mirror up to nature, without malice, without self-deception, without insisting that any tale represents the whole of human behavior, without intending us to believe that human nature as here depicted is intended to be a norm, or that these actions are to be emulated or imitated.

Moreover the story arises out of what is uniquely human: man is able to laugh, and what he laughs at in himself and in the actions of his neighbor emerges out of very deep layers of the mind. In the artistic depiction of a foolish human situation, in a plot of extravagant invention which looks speciously like order but amounts in the end to the triumph of disorder, the comic writer makes what is ultimately a moral statement. If such triumph of the improbable strikes the reader as more pessimistic, say, than the affirmation of order and love in the *Knight's Tale*, he may remember in this case that it is Chaucer who holds both views, and that they are both essential to the vision of the human community on pilgrimage. Man may be unique as a rational creature, but he is also perverse; the fact that he can laugh is his saving grace. For by laughing he may also learn.

It would be a grave error to fail to see that the *Miller's Tale*, like the *Reeve's Tale* to follow, has some very serious things to say about the human situation and about human character in action.[5] The tale offered is by its nature outside the pressures of philosophy, and the normative world does remain safely in the background. But it is there, and we can see that the values which it contains are based upon certain assumptions in a carefully ordered nature: the attraction of the young to each other; the peril of marriage between young and old; the temporary superiority of instinct to reason. Out of these assumptions grow the inner comic resolutions: the punishment of stupidity, the alternation of success and failure, the victory of unreason over convention. Such meanings as the fabliaux contain must take into account the values which are being vindicated.

[5] For versions of the "serious" in Chaucer's fabliaux, see R. E. Kaske, "The *Canticum Canticorum* in the *Miller's Tale*," SP, LIX (1962), 472–500; and Paul A. Olson, "The *Reeve's Tale*: Chaucer's *Measure for Measure*," SP, LIX (1962), 1–17.

THE REEVE'S TALE

*I am glad for a season to take an airing beyond
the diocese of the strict conscience.... I wear
my shackles more contentedly for having respired
the breath of an imaginary freedom.*

CHARLES LAMB,
*On the Artificial Comedy
of the Last Century*

*Deception and surprise are, strictly considered,
the* sources of laughter *par excellence, and underlie all others.*

LANE COOPER,
An Aristotelian Theory of Comedy

*Beside the pleasant Mill of Trompington
I laughed with Chaucer in the hawthorn shade;
Heard him, while birds were warbling, tell his
tales
Of amorous passion.*

WILLIAM WORDSWORTH,
The Prelude

Like the *Miller's Tale* the tale and performance of the Reeve excite
in us feelings of awe and wonder; and nothing will deepen our appreciation for Chaucer's comic gifts so much as rereading these tales
after a perusal of much else in the Canterbury pilgrimage. We are
impressed not only with the technical skill and artistry of the two
fabliaux which he has dared to place at the head of his collection, but
by the subtle differences in technique, tone, and form which distinguish them from each other.[1]

---

[1] The *Reeve's Tale* was long ago given well-nigh definitive treatment by Walter
M. Hart, "The *Reeve's Tale:* A Comparative Study of Chaucer's Narrative Art,"
PMLA, XXIII (1908), 1-44. More recently it has yielded new insights in Charles
Muscatine, *Chaucer and the French Tradition,* pp. 198-204, and in the extremely
perceptive article by M. Copland, "*The Reeve's Tale:* Harlotrie or Sermonyng?"
Medium Aevum, XXXI (1962), 14-32. Copland attempts to answer J. R. R. Tolkien,

The coarse and bawdy implications issuing from the Miller's mouth have elicited from the Reeve an angry response, not merely the response of a man who was once a carpenter taking umbrage because he has heard a tale in which an old carpenter has been duped and cruelly hurt (although Chaucer adduces this as the most available and easily stated reason for his anger), but because the very nature of the man telling the tale, private and retiring, cautious and old, crabbed and complaining, choleric and revengeful, demands a specific kind of performance. Seen alongside the hearty, garrulous, brash, and pushing personality of the burly Miller, the Reeve's antipathy for and response to the Miller does not need much explanation: their very personalities are at odds, the Miller thrusting forward with his tale of bawdiness and his bagpipes at the head of the column; the Reeve discreet and withdrawn to the very end of the column. He is sensitive to imagined slurs and is vindictive. Although he has objected strongly to the Miller's proposal of a tale dealing with a cuckolded carpenter, saying it is a sin to defame a man and to drag his wife into such harlotry, nevertheless when his turn comes, in his avid desire to be avenged upon the Miller he tells precisely the same kind of story and with much the same point.

Chaucer seems clearly to have wished the Reeve not only to corroborate certain base qualities of the Miller, to be, so to speak, at one with him in general coarseness, callousness, hypocrisy, but also to serve as a foil for him, to present to his goliardic joking nature that bitter asperity of a more humorless, tighter personality. When, for example, the Miller announces his tale of the cuckolding of an old carpenter by a clerk, the remark not merely rankles the disposition of the Reeve, it arouses his choleric nature sufficiently to overwhelm his judgment and draw him into a quarrel. He is, as we come to see, an irascible grumbler but a deadly adversary.

Having listened to the *Miller's Tale*, his anger might have been somewhat allayed: the old carpenter of the tale has some qualities of simple humanity, albeit he is stupid; he has not been recognizably patterned, save in profession and age, after the character of the Reeve, whose canny mind (we recall the portrait of the *General*

"Chaucer as a Philologist: *The Reeve's Tale*," *Transactions of the Philological Society* (London, 1934), pp. 1–70, who makes the charge that the tale is "a depressing specimen of low-class knockabout farce." "The life of *The Reeve's Tale*," writes Copland, "is, sadly, far closer to the life which most of us experience or observe around us than is the technicolour life of *The Miller's Tale*" (p. 19).

Prologue) is far removed from the credulous and simple mentality of the carpenter. But how cruel of the Miller to depict old age so easily duped! And this callous treatment of old age has revived the taste of ashes in the mouth of the Reeve as he contemplates his savorless, advancing years.

At this point Chaucer draws heavily upon a literary tradition, the topic or commonplace of old age, the continuity of which can be demonstrated with particular reference to the Latin literature to which Chaucer had ample access. It must from time to time give us pause to reflect upon the verisimilitude which Chaucer is able to invest in the words of agents like the Reeve, even when what they say is part of a long platitude. Here for example, there has been invested in the material the tone of the interior confession; the reader has the feeling of being privy to secrets which are not general comments about human nature, but specific and particular manifestations of the character and personality of a living man.

The description of the Reeve in the *General Prologue* emphasizes his intelligence, his canny wit and shrewdness. The *Prologue* to his tale goes beyond the portrait of the *General Prologue* by providing us with a dramatic monologue in which some of the mystery of this man's old age is dissipated by his statement of the ravaging passage of time. In speaking his views now the old Reeve lays bare more than he knows of his special ethos, and we witness the subjection of the conventional platitudes to the specific needs of the artistic moment.

A succession of images in the *Reeve's Prologue* all bear upon the pain of a still energetic prurience, the last vestige of passion in an old man. The grass of youth has given way to the fodder of old age (l. 3868). Not only his hair, but his heart has grown moldy (l. 3870); he is, he fears— and here we see a progression of thought—like the medlar apple that grows ripe and rotten simultaneously (ll. 3871-73); in a supporting image he is like the leek with its white head and green tail (ll. 3877-79). It is the special anguish of his old age that desire and passion should come into their maturity as the body achieves senile decay, a tormenting imbalance of the physical and emotional life now venting itself in talk.

Intermixed with persistent desire (the emotional life is now symbolized by fire) which will never die are the special defects of old age: boasting, lying, anger, greed. Now, in a note of melancholy, the Reeve speaks of the mystery of death and time, redeeming senten-

tiousness with the vivid and homely image of liquid pouring from the
tap, running steadily until the cask of life has been voided: [2]

> "And yet ik have alwey a coltes tooth,
> As many a yeer as it is passed henne
> Syn that my tappe of lif bigan to renne.
> For sikerly, whan I was bore, anon
> Deeth drough the tappe of lyf and leet it gon;
> And ever sithe hath so the tappe yronne
> Til that almoost al empty is the tonne.
> The streem of lyf now droppeth on the chymbe.
> The sely tonge may wel rynge and chymbe
> Of wrecchednesse that passed is ful yoore;
> With olde folk, save dotage, is namoore!"   (ll. 3888-98)

The Host sees the seriousness of this complaint and is impatient
with it. For him the jollity and pleasantry of the pilgrimage have
again been jeopardized. He recognizes the clerical, somewhat scholarly knack of preachment in the Reeve, which he apparently regards
as out of place anywhere but in the churches. And so the Reeve, no
longer withdrawn into his self-pitying whine, abandons his sententious, almost scriptural, tone for the preciser nuances of vengeance.

How successfully we may integrate this monologue of the Reeve
on old age [3] into his whole performance is, I suspect, a matter of
enthusiasm and zeal for seeing all that Chaucer does as a finished
performance. The Reeve's insistence (ll. 3864 ff.), for example, that
he could, if he wished to speak ribaldly, pay back the Miller for the
tale he has told of a carpenter can be taken to imply that he is not going to tell such a tale; yet in a moment he avows that he will tell just
such a tale (ll. 3909 ff.) and we must in our enthusiasm attribute this
change of intention, if it may be considered so, to the natural inconsistencies of life: We witness a man's making up his mind. But certain
questions persist. Is the elaboration of the topic of old age an outgrowth of the old age, as I have assumed, of the carpenter in the previous tale? Is it a gratuitous exploration of the character of the Reeve?
Is it a safeguard against a future larger fabric in which each person on
the pilgrimage is to tell more than one tale and in which something
more precisely related to the Reeve's opening confession will be

---

[2] See A. H. MacLaine, "Chaucer's Wine-Cask Image: Word Play in *The Reeve's Prologue*," *Medium Aevum*, XXXI (1962), 129-31.
[3] See George R. Coffman, "Old Age from Horace to Chaucer: Some Literary Affinities and Adventures of an Idea," *Speculum*, IX (1934), 249-77; and Brooks Forehand, "Old Age and Chaucer's Reeve," *PMLA*, LXIX (1954), 984-89.

created? Is it a manifestation of the emerging importance of the links asserting their own vitality and life in the framework of the pilgrimage? Was it written much earlier than the tale itself, before it could be securely oriented to the tale which was to be told? Was the interest in the convention a part of Chaucer's own sober and thoughtful process into old age? Was he somehow carried away by the complexity of the Reeve's personality but not immediately aware of how to utilize it?

Whatever we may feel about the confession of the Reeve and its function in his performance, Chaucer's interest in him is more than a mere embellishment of Maximian's treatment of old age, and a forecast of variations of the subject later in the pilgrimage, in the *Pardoner's Tale* and in that of the Merchant. The differing uses of the material enable the reader to assess for himself the quality and range of Chaucer's interest, to ponder what Virginia Woolf has called "the morality of ordinary intercourse," in which "all actions and passions are represented" and in which "instead of being solemnly exhorted, we are left to stray and stare and make out a meaning for ourselves." [4]

In the *Miller's Tale,* as we have seen, Chaucer accomplishes a near miracle of narrative art by having two incidents operate simultaneously and reach a common climax or explosion in the cry of "water! water!" We are, so to speak, coerced into laughter by watching with awe two plots going on virtually at the same time. We feel a sense of wonder at a technical prowess wedded to such remarkable richness and depth of characterization, two qualities that raise the humorous tale to the level of art. The *Reeve's Tale* also contains two incidents which form one plot, but they are arranged in a more conventional and perhaps more natural episodic way of having the two incidents follow each other in succession, the one growing more or less casually out of the other.

The two tales differ not only in plot and structure, but in the kind and amount of characterization and in the attitude of revenge which motivates the teller. The long descriptions of the *Miller's Tale* which add so richly to the texture and the interior meaning of it give way in the *Reeve's Tale* to something sparer, something more economical, something less rhetorically exuberant, less ornamental, something

⁴ *The Common Reader,* 1st Series (New York, 1925), p. 32.

tarter, less juicily flavored and savorable. The details of character in the *Reeve's Tale* which make us see the miller as proud, aggressive, suspicious, socially aspiring and his wife as haughty are precisely those necessary to our appreciation of the eventual fall from pride and the desecration of the familial hopes for social station through their daughter's marriage. The absence of description of the clerks is itself an indication that emphasis is not so much upon their characters as it is upon the function they perform in bringing about the fall from pride.

The action too is swifter than that of the previous tale, more compact. There is a shift of emphasis from the fate of young clerks in love in the *Miller's Tale* to the collapse of family fortunes in the *Reeve's Tale*. The clerks of the latter tale, now instruments of justice, are more sparely depicted than the husband and wife upon whom Chaucer centers our attention. Stress is placed upon the ethos of the family—the paraphernalia of clothes and weapons are but a counterpoint to their social aspiration—so that the effect is not so much less depth as it is a tailoring of character to suit the particular situation: thus, the miller must be depicted as sly, as thieving, as suspicious, as proud, as aspiring, as aggressive, so that in his fall we may see a comic retribution in terms that these characteristics have made inevitable. The two headstrong clerks must in some way offer as a foil their own slyness, thievery, aggression. The daughter, too, must in some way obviate the aspirations of her mother and father by going joyfully into "disparagement." The mother herself must lend herself to this disparagement, and if she is for the moment unaware of her role, so much the better for the working out of her own fall from excessive pride.

This working out of justice, this bringing low of pride, is carried out with considerably more stringency in the *Reeve's Tale* than in the Miller's, where our enjoyment is largely a matter of watching, among other excellences, the delight-and-wonder-evoking confluence of the two incidents of the plot and their bursting synapse of cry, collapse, and confusion. Indeed, whatever zest and joy suffuses the parts of the *Reeve's Tale*, the working out of justice—or the Reeve's revenge upon the Miller—may be said to constitute the point of the story taken as a whole.[5]

[5] But see Copland, in *Medium Aevum*, XXXI, 30: "...one might say that the most serious criticism the Reeve offers of the Miller is *literary* criticism."

Chaucer's embellishment and handling of his sources beautifully disguises the triteness of the originals. The strict motivation flowing from the tight personality of the teller, the clever handling of northern speech, the subtle play of the miller's anti-intellectualism against clerkish mirth and revelry, the amorous sympathy between the young, the richness of folk wisdom in the proverbial element, all point to an elevation of the banal and stock situations of old fabliaux into a story rich on its own merits, but richer by far when considered as a dramatic element in the quarrels of the pilgrimage.

Seen in perspective, the *Reeve's Tale* is composed of two incidents, one growing casually out of the other. If we divide the story into its two parts, we find a neat division almost precisely in the middle of the 404-line plot, the first incident of which alone qualifies as a lively vignette illustrating the perfidy of millers and supports the miller's own view that the greatest clerks are not the wisest men. This opening incident is, however, merely the prelude to the more hectic, more tightly organized, and more artificially contrived second part.

After a neat statement of locale, the tale opens with a sixty-line description of the miller, his wife, their daughter, and their aspirations. The descriptions are a binding element for both incidents, and what is implied or explicitly stated in the opening of the tale has a natural evolvement in the course of the whole plot. The miller we see as proud as a peacock, parading a variety of weapons that point up his suspicious, arrogant, and self-defensive nature. And we see him as thieving, and as touchily violent in the defense of his overrated family. Something of the tightness of his nature in these characteristics flows from the personality of the Reeve himself, who, in his effort to be avenged upon the Miller, describes a man in terms to which his own personality unfortunately gives validity. The pride of family which is reiterated in the character of the wife (and in the aspirations of the grandfather-priest) are a rich and pithy corroboration of her husband's personality. There is the same ingrained and arrogant contempt covering up self-defensive attitudes towards her illegitimacy and presumption. The Reeve himself is merciless in description:

> And eek, for she was somdel smoterlich,
> She was as digne as water in a dich,
> And ful of hoker and of bisemare.   (ll. 3963–65)

The daughter they have produced lacks that fleshing out of personality in the subtle details with which we were familiarized in the

Miller's Tale: the lickerish eye, the skittish barnyard winsomeness, the combination of natural wit with passion that characterize the jolly Alison of the previous tale. Chaucer's intention obviously differs in his depiction of the two women. As Brewer has commented, the subject of the *Miller's Tale* is love-making; the subject of the *Reeve's Tale* is pride and trickery.[6] In the latter tale the miller is hit where it hurts most, hence a lessening of the role played by Molly, who though cousin by instinct to Alison, presents a certain psychological —as well as physical—thickness, a certain lack of sensibility alongside the nervous and more clearly definable lineaments of Alison. Four lines in all are sufficient to describe her.

> This wenche thikke and wel ygrowen was,
> With kamus nose, and eyen greye as glas,
> With buttokes brode, and brestes rounde and hye.
> But right fair was hir heer, I wol nat lye.   (ll. 3973–76)

But it is her father's story, and she and her mother, each in her own way, figure in it mainly as instruments of justice: the one by a quick and sympathetic response, the other by unwitting cooperation both in the sexual disparagement and in the free-for-all with which the tale comes to a close.

Before the story begins to move, however, we must know of the illness of the manciple of Solar Hall, an opportunity for brazen cheating and stealing on the part of the miller.

> For therbiforn he stal but curteisly,
> But now he was a theef outrageously.   (ll. 3997–98)

The basic complication, once offered, provides the ostensible motivation for the two young scholars, John and Aleyn: they are going to prevent the miller from stealing their grain. Actually the little journey is for them a lark of the first order, an outgrowth of their being, in Chaucer's familiar words, "testif . . . and lusty for to pleye," an opportunity for "myrthe and revelrye." It is, in short, a kind of game with them, in which they will pit their wits against those of the miller; much of the irony we feel, with our foreknowledge that the miller is himself to be tricked (the Reeve has told us so), arises out of the impression of the innocence and naïveté of the two students (who are, indeed, no real match for the wily miller) which allows them so easily to be duped. Their cordial greeting to Simon is only

[6] D. S. Brewer, *Chaucer* (London, 1953), p. 146.

faintly ironical on first reading; on second reading, in the light of
what we know actually happens, it causes the helpless chuckle at
what the comic spirit has so cleverly brought into being: [7]

> ... "Al hayl, Symond, y-fayth!
> Hou fares thy faire doghter and thy wyf?"   (ll. 4022–23)

The two questions of the miller (l. 4025 and l. 4035) and the
answers offered by the two students serve to array the adversaries
against each other, and it becomes only too clear that the first victory
is to be that of the cannier and more practiced deceiver. Chaucer here
engages in artistic play of the highest order, implicating intellectual
and narrative movement with that generous sprinkling of northern
dialect and common English speech, principally in the utterances of
the two clerks, so that with their faulty grammar they manage to
suggest country lads of no station, illiterate and simple.[8] Indeed it is
virtually impossible to find another locus in Chaucer in which language is made so meaningful an adjunct to comic statement or is so
intimately welded to the larger irony of an almost mindless youthful
instinct (unforeseen by the miller in his contempt for his young adversaries) working revenge upon the miller. Through the singing
country tone we discern the childish and transparent stratagem:

> Aleyn spak first, "Al hayl, Symond, y-fayth!
> How fares thy faire doghter and thy wyf?"
>   "Aleyn, welcome," quod Symkyn, "by my lyf!
> And John also, how now, what do ye heer?"
>   "Symond," quod John, "by God, nede has na peer.
> Hym boes serve hymself that has na swayn,
> Or elles he is a fool, as clerkes sayn.
> Oure manciple, I hope he wil be deed,
> Swa werkes ay the wanges in his heed;
> And forthy is I come, and eek Alayn,
> To grynde oure corn, and carie it ham agayn;
> I praye yow spede us heythen that ye may."
>   "It shal be doone," quod Symkyn, "by my fay!
> What wol ye doon whil that it is in hande?"

---

[7] Germaine Dempster, *Dramatic Irony in Chaucer* (Stanford University Press,
1932), p. 29, writes: "...on a second reading, we find Aleyn's polite greeting
amusingly ironical because so perfectly harmless, not only in surface meaning but
in intention."

[8] Muscatine, *Chaucer and the French Tradition*, pp. 198–204, suggests an interpretation of the role of language in the *Reeve's Tale*. In brief, "the naturalistic
dialect of the two clerks is a part of the scheme" to deflate the miller "by the
crudest means possible."

"By God, right by the hopur wil I stande,"
Quod John, "and se howgates the corn gas in.
Yet saugh I nevere, by my fader kyn,
How that the hopur wagges til and fra."
    Aleyn answerde, "John, and wiltow swa?
Thanne wil I be bynethe, by my croun,
And se how that the mele falles doun
Into the trough; that sal be my disport.
For John, y-faith, I may been of youre sort;
I is as ille a millere as ar ye."   (ll. 4022–45)

It is obvious that there is more here than merely the intention to elicit laughter from language: the subtler debasement of the agents arises out of intonation as well as out of the innocent assumption of craftiness and wiles.

The miller is scornful of their attempted deceit and their obvious stratagem; in the only proverb put into his mouth he utters the sentiment that reflects a principal irony of the story, the ignorance of the college youth pitted against an older and practiced expedience: he who can read is not always the wisest or smartest man (l. 4054), says the miller to himself. His arrogant contempt for the young (later he dismisses them as playing children, l. 4098) bespeaks an anti-intellectual cast of mind that is not merely a part of the story, but a reverberation out of the description of the Reeve in the *General Prologue* in his own dealings with his younger and better lord (A 610–12).

What follows is a high point in Chaucerian comic excitement, a bit of hectic outdoor activity without real parallel elsewhere in the tales. With a "wehee!" the stallion is off after the mares, set free by the miller in his ruse to get the clerks out of the way.

This John goth out and fynt his hors away,
And gan to crie "Harrow!" and "Weylaway!
Oure hors is lorn, Alayn, for Goddes banes,
Step on thy feet! Com of, man, al atanes!
Allas, our wardeyn has his palfrey lorn!"
This Aleyn al forgat, bothe mele and corn;
Al was out of his mynde his housbondrie.
"What, whilk way is he geen?" he gan to crie.
    .   .   .   .
    "Allas," quod John, "Aleyn, for Cristes payne,
Lay doun thy swerd, and I wil myn alswa.
I is ful wight, God waat, as is a raa;
By Goddes herte, he sal nat scape us bathe!

> Why ne had thow pit the capul in the lathe?
> Ilhayl! by God, Alayn thou is a fonne!"

.   .   .   .

> This sely clerkes rennen up and doun
> With "Keep! keep! stand! stand! jossa, warderere,
> Ga whistle thou, and I shal kepe hym heere!"
> But shortly, til that it was verray nyght,
> They koude nat, though they dide al hir myght,
> Hir capul cacche, he ran alwey so faste,
> Til in a dych they caughte hym atte laste.   (ll. 4071–4106)

What emerges from the description of the stallion's "wehee!" in his instinctive search for the wild mares and the ensuing vigorous chase is an expression of natural exuberance, of lustiness and vitality in animal and humans alike without a shred of transcendental values.[9] Ironically one looks back upon this scene as a forecast of the role of appetite and instinct in the young clerks functioning as the instrumentality by which revenge is achieved. The inclination to which the miller gives release in freeing the horse he also sets free within his very house. The miller has had his opportunity to steal the grain from the clerks, whom he regards as easily duped children, but in creating his opportunity he has prepared the ground for his own defeat at their hands: the chase has taken them until nightfall and there is nowhere for them to lodge except with the miller.

It is again the miller's contempt for clerkish intelligence that links together the first and second incidents.

> "Myn hous is streit, but ye han lerned art;
> Ye konne by argumentes make a place
> A myle brood of twenty foot of space.
> Lat see now if this place may suffise,
> Or make it rowm with speche, as is youre gise."
>
>   (ll. 4122–26)

To which John with his characteristic country wisdom on the tongue answers:

> "Now, Symond," seyde John, "by seint Cutberd,
> Ay is thou myrie, and this is faire answerd.
> I have herd seyd, 'man sal taa of twa thynges
> Slyk as he fyndes, or taa slyk as he brynges.'

[9] Copland, in *Medium Aevum*, XXXI, 23, speaks of the two young clerks as "these two country loons with the merest lick of university slickness. They exhibit the countryman's directness and lack of complication. They are very like children,... and also not far from animality. Their reactions are as straight-forward as those of their horse...their lovemaking has a hard animal intensity."

But specially I pray thee, hooste deere,
Get us some mete and drynke, and make us cheere,
And we wil payen trewely atte fulle.
With empty hand men may na haukes tulle;
Loo, heere oure silver, redy for to spende."   (ll. 4127–35)

Although but a while ago they were downcast, weary, wet as beasts in the rain, that certain resilience of youth, that same head-strong quality, hand in hand with mirth and revelry, has reasserted itself. It is not mere hospitality paid for in advance that allows the miller to put the clerks up in the one chamber with his family, but a making the best of necessity and an opportunity for that same aggressive insistence upon his own wisdom and cunning as superior to that of clerkish philosophy or art.

The description (ll. 4136 ff.) that follows, of supping and drinking into the middle of the night, the miller hiccupping and slurring his speech, the wife jolly as a jay from wetting her whistle, the inevitably low and intimate detailing of the harmony that unites the miller and his wife, recalling another suggestive "burdoun" (with perhaps the same implications) comprises one of the more memorable loci in Chaucerian sketching. Such a melodious compline song is too much for Aleyn, who now reveals himself as something of a legal scholar with a quotation of a maxim:

"...gif a man in a point be agreved,
...in another he sal be releved."   (ll. 4181–82)

Clerkish wisdom has finally begun to assert and vindicate itself.

There now occurs a quick progression of events by which the clerks' revenge upon the miller's thievery is worked out. With the sexual success that is characteristic of the fabliau and entirely suitable as a mode of justice upon a family whose origins are somewhat besmirched, Aleyn has his revenge by swiving sweet Molly. Then in a rapid succession of movements John moves the baby's cradle next to his bed; the wife returning from a nightly excursion identifies the bed by the presence of the cradle as her own, gets into bed with the clerk, and progresses immediately to the same "disparagement" as her daughter. The sexual exuberance at this point (l. 4231) reaches back in tone and spirit to the "wehee!" of the stallion in the account of the "joly lyf" enjoyed by the two clerks.

Revenge is not complete, however, until the miller himself is made fully aware of what has happened to the integrity of his family. In still a further plot development, Aleyn taking tender leave of his sweetheart (she reveals her father's theft of the meal, now baked into a cake) is misled by the very cradle which had brought about John's success, and goes instead to the bed in which the miller is asleep. There he whispers a quick account of his night's prowess to the man he thinks is his fellow clerk. What ensues is an outburst of wounded family pride:

> "A, false traitour! false clerk!" quod he,
> Thow shalt be deed, by Goddes dignitee!
> Who dorste be so boold to disparage
> My doghter, that is come of swich lynage?"
>
> (ll. 4269–72)

There follows now the second major excitement of the tale to balance out the hectic chase which closed the first incident, a low-comic free-for-all in which Aleyn's nose is bloodied, the miller stumbles over a stone in the floor and falls upon his sleeping wife. In the dim light the wife beats her own husband over the head, the clerks beat him further, pick up their flour, and are off.

The Reeve cannot resist the moral tag, his own now realized revenge upon the Miller of the *Prologue*.

> Thus is the proude millere wel ybete,
> And hath ylost the gryndynge of the whete,
> And payed for the soper everideel
> Of Aleyn and of John, that bette hym weel.
> His wyf is swyved, and his doghter als.
> Lo, swich it is a millere to be fals!
> And therefore this proverbe is seyd ful sooth,
> "Hym thar nat wene wel that yvele dooth";
> A gylour shal hymself bigyled be.   (ll. 4313–21)

Somewhere Addison writes: "Man is the merriest creature in the world; whatever is above or below him is solemn." Needless to say, there is nothing solemn about this exuberantly naturalistic tale. As a work of the fantastic imagination, with its delicate mixture of failure with success; its consummate handling of irony, deception, and surprise; its use of language and proverbs to point up both character and theme; its beautifully contrived artifice of misplaced cradle and mistaken identities; its gratifying comic morality [10] in beguiling the

---

[10] Walter M. Hart, in *PMLA*, XXIII, 15, 29, 35, and elsewhere, discusses the matter of poetic justice and comic morality. In particular: "Chaucer takes special pains to emphasize poetic justice: the miller is a swaggerer who goes heavily armed,

beguiler—it emerges as a highly organized and controlled artistic form justifying the scholarly view that the fabliaux are chronologically to be dated as among Chaucer's mature pieces, that is to say, when his ironical attitudes dominated his writing so as to infuse and permeate the whole structure of a tale.

Yet, in order to appreciate the entire performance of the Reeve, we must admit that other dimension, the tale as an utterance by a pilgrim involved in a quarrel, intent upon revenge. From this point of view the laughter which the tale elicits from us all, even in the delight-and-wonder-evoking events of the conclusion, takes on a meaning deriving from the teller's private and crabbed personality, which sounds everywhere the persistent undertone of an accurate malice and spite.

---

that he may get the worst of an encounter; he and his wife are foolishly proud of her lineage and breeding, that their pride may have a fall; the parson has plans for a great marriage for Malin, only that they may be disappointed. That mother and daughter are 'difficult' heightens the effect of the clerks' conquest. The unusual thefts of the miller,—his taking advantage of the illness of the maunciple,—demand unusual punishment. His delight in the success of his own cunning directly paves the way for his downfall" (p. 29). Again, "Emphasis of a causal relation between intrigues, regarding the second as revenge for the first, results in the *Reeve's Tale,* in a kind of justification, of rough morality" (p. 35).

THE SHIPMAN'S TALE

The yarns of seamen have a direct simplicity, the whole meaning of which lies within the shell of a cracked nut.

JOSEPH CONRAD,
Heart of Darkness

Le trésor d'un homme n'est que le bijou d'un autre.

OLD FRENCH PROVERB

The *Shipman's Tale* is a species of comedy far removed from that world of happy and triumphant sexuality of the *Miller's Tale* and from that single-minded destruction of pride in the *Reeve's Tale*. By virtue of its own triumphant and immoral deception, with which it closes, it has come to be regarded as worldly, cynical, and disillusioned. Yet it is vested with a certain air of blitheness; its surface is calm and detached in its depiction of the bourgeois mentality. It is a social comedy, which tends to arouse quizzical reflection in the reader, an examination of the private and corrupt world of the family set side by side with the overly anxious and preoccupied masculine world of business and finance.

Such a story, with its emphasis upon deception centered in sexuality and money—a common topic for this type of story—seems on the face of it to be suited to the character of the Wife of Bath,[1] for whom it may first have been intended. Furthermore, the superscript of the Sercambi version, "De Avaritia et Luzuria," [2] calls readily to mind these two ingredients as the basic stuff of the Wife's character in her own long prologue. The keen enjoyment which pervades the story, the absence of any censure for the woman's role, her easy extrication from the comic catastrophe, the determined and witty verbal barrage at the conclusion, the paradoxical enjoyment of mar-

[1] W. W. Lawrence, "Chaucer's *Shipman's Tale*," *Speculum*, XXXIII (1958), 56–68, brings his years of experience to bear upon the problem of the Wife of Bath as the teller of this tale. This substantial article also strives to review within short compass the major developments in scholarship on this subject.

[2] Cf. Albert H. Silverman, "Sex and Money in Chaucer's *Shipman's Tale*," PQ, XXXII (1953), 329–36.

riage while selling its commodity—all make for a tempting ascription to the robust and somewhat lurid Wife. Contrasted with the mores of the aristocratic pageant of life in the *Knight's Tale*, or with those of the barn and granary of the *Miller's* and *Reeve's Tales*, those of this little bourgeois group afford us a glimpse into another corner of the world, viewed by the poet with the dispassionate morality of expedience. This, the jolly Wife would have approved.

At the outset of the story it seems to be her voice that we hear intruding upon the narrative:

> The sely housbonde, algate he moot paye,
> He moot us clothe, and he moot us arraye,
> Al for his owene worshipe richely,
> In which array we daunce jolily.
> And if that he noght may, par aventure,
> Or ellis list no swich dispence endure,
> But thynketh it is wasted and ylost,
> Thanne moot another payen for oure cost,
> Or lene us gold, and that is perilous.   (ll. 11–19)

This intimate exchange between narrator and audience, with its feminine tone and pronouns, hearkens back to a time in the development of the *Canterbury Tales* when Chaucer seems clearly to have had the memorable Alice in mind as the teller of the tale. Even with its uncorrected pronouns, the opening passage throws light upon Chaucer's skill in setting in motion the principal attitudes and elements of the story: its sardonic tone, its tart commentary on uxorial connivance, the forecast of adultery, and the extravagant emphasis upon material goods. Within remarkably short compass we have been introduced not only to the husband and wife, but to the "threatening third" of the tale, the trio constituting as likeable a group as we meet in any of the Chaucerian fabliaux. The ambiguity which characterizes the tale resides mainly in the sympathetic interest which Chaucer has vested in each of the agents.

The mannerly monk is a man of the world, an outrider allied in spirit and masculinity and material possessions to the Monk of the *General Prologue*, but more polished in social intercourse, more like that hypothetical person hinted at by the Host in the *Prologue of the Monk's Tale*. This monk invades the secular world, armed with its paraphernalia: jugs of wine, gifts of wild fowl, money for servants. The secular world welcomes him with glad affection:

> . . . they were as glad of his comyng
> As fowel is fayn whan that the sonne up riseth.   (ll. 49–50)

We like him, or tend to, because of his extravagance, his "heigh prudence," his gentle air; we like him because we see him in situations,
like prayer, which elicit our respect; or in actions, like blushing,
which we associate with modest bearing. Indeed, one of the fine
ironies of the tale arises from the fact that the monk's rascality is revealed only after we have been taught to like him, largely because the
other agents like and trust him; and the subsequent connivance between him and the wife causes in us a start of wonder and surprise.

There is less of this ambivalence of amiability and rascality in the
character of the wife. She is more clearly an opportunist, drawing
upon that instinctive wisdom with which the women of the fabliaux
are well endowed and with which the Wife of Bath acquaints us. Her
real needs are not always clear, but her motives are obvious. Her
relationship with the monk is that of almost instinctive rapport, and
Chaucer's narrative art brings about an alliance between them with
casual ease, a relationship of two persons exploiting each other for
personal advantage, financial and sexual.

From the first exchange of confidences (ll. 92 ff.) with the pledge
of mutual trust (ll. 124 ff.), through the monk's admission that he
comes to St. Denis only for greater acquaintance with his friend's
wife (ll. 148 ff.), with the exchange of their kiss of mutual trust, we
see the wife laying the ground for exploiting the monk. At this point
we have no indication that the monk will in his turn exploit the wife.
Her diatribe against her husband (ll. 157 ff.), although delivered in
the terms of a woman careful of her family honor, is an extravagant
falsification of the truth (her husband is the "worste" man in the
world, he is sexually inept, and furthermore a miser) which the remainder of the story rectifies.

She is too much caught up in her need for money to worry about
sex save as a bargaining point, or to worry about the morality of
seeing the integrity of family as a matter of mere finances. In order to
get the hundred francs she so badly needs she will say or do anything;
she is willing to accede to the monk's demands rather than have her
husband discover that she is in financial straits. This defect of her
anxiety about money matches that of her husband and makes them
both dupes, as we later see. Thus the monk, who is not caught up in
the business of getting and spending, is free to pit his appetite against

her need. This overanxious concern about money and financial position is a blot upon the family which the wife shares with her husband,
and provides for that dramatic irony by which the monk, exempt
from worldly concern, can act as one instrument of poetic justice.
This abstract vengeance upon immoderate care for worldly goods we
see working out as the monk first denies kinship with the merchant,
avows long-standing interest in the wife; and as with oaths on his
breviary and swearing by God, St. Martin, and by St. Denis, he
achieves his momentary success.

But it is the wife's temporary financial success which dominates the
story at this point—the monk's sexual ploy is a necessary counterpoint—and we hear the overtones of betrayal reverberate out of their
personal relationship into that which each bears ironically to the sober
merchant:

> "...God take on me vengeance
> As foul as evere hadde Genylon of France."   (ll. 193–94)

The garden in which the deception is planned, although not embellished or expanded, is familiar to the student of Chaucer. He encounters it, in amplified form, in the *Franklin's Tale* and in that of the
Merchant, as the place in which an assaulting third attempts an adulterous alliance. Here it is a casual part of the domestic scene, perhaps
a pleasure garden of the sort created by the Merchant of Prato. Chaucer avoids any kind of description of the garden (the tale is generally
devoid of descriptive ornamentation) in favor of certain more subtle
suggestions of order and propriety, like the monk reciting his office,
or the wife walking with the child who is yet under her care; details
which we associate with a regulated and secure world across which
soon fall the shadows of dalliance. The actual disorder of the household we cannot fully appreciate until we know more about the character and personality of the husband.

The character of the businessman [3] about whom the two deceivers
revolve is a curious blend of innocence and astuteness. When his wife
summons him from his counting and bookkeeping to come to mass
and dinner (the world of charity and sharing impinges upon that

---

[3] Gardiner Stillwell, "Chaucer's 'Sad' Merchant," *RES*, XX (1944), 1–18, and
Iris Origo, *The Merchant of Prato, Francesco di Marco Datini* (London, 1957),
between them cast a great deal of light upon the special ethos that characterizes
the merchant of the fourteenth century. The life of Datini, as revealed by his
letters, makes eminently clear the ground out of which so much of Chaucer's
ambiguity arises.

more corrupt, more chancy world of private enterprise), the husband speaks in those serious terms that give us with remarkable precision a sample of the merchant ethos: a careful concern for a care-ridden world that assures no man security, a world ruled by chance and fortune, a world in which a man must wear the face and appearance of success while brooding over the failures of the day and presenting a prosperous air to the world (ll. 224 ff.). These too typical utterances and his later actions make him as serious a caricature as it is possible to create of the circumscribed and limited vision of his class, inhabiting a "quaint" world from which stability is forever absent.

It is this worldly wisdom that apparently rules the household, but with sobriety and judiciousness and kindliness; for if his character is weighted down on the one side by the excessive concern for business money-making (*c'est son métier*), he is, contrary to the view expressed earlier by the wife, open-handed and open-hearted to the point of foolishness with his good friend the monk (ll. 265 ff., 281 ff.) and judicious in his attention to the provisions and finances of running a household (ll. 245 ff.). He is, furthermore, noted for his hospitality and largesse, as the opening of the story makes clear (ll. 20 ff.). The world is no doubt a constant source of dismay to the merchant, but he has been a success in business and will be again and has learned the great lesson of accommodating himself to the world of luck and change. The fruits of his success are his household and his lavishly bedecked wife. It is of course ironical that precisely at the heart of his success should develop the purely momentary breach in what is otherwise a placid marriage.

If we let ourselves be involved, we feel a touch of sadness at his plight. Although he is roughly analogous to the old carpenter in the *Miller's Tale* and to the knight in the *Merchant's Tale*, we do not feel any real satisfaction in the deception of which he is the victim. And yet, his concern with the outside world has made him curiously obtuse, self-absorbed, taking for granted the stability of the private world of the family; his innocence isolates him and makes him vulnerable. With the knight of the *Merchant's Tale* he shares the affinity of impaired vision, a peculiar blindness preventing him from seeing the connivance of his beloved wife and dearest friend; in a sense the private and neglected domestic world feeds mutely and vengefully upon his masculine world of money and finance.

Thereafter in his role as hypocrite (ll. 269 ff.) the monk easily secures the loan of a hundred francs from his "cousin," blandishing upon him affectionate care. There is that same tone of sweet amiability between the two men which we have remarked before and which adds a piquant irony to their relationship, Chaucer playing the note of genuine friendship in his noble merchant against that of careful friendliness in his scheming monk. The good merchant's concern for credit and reputation (ll. 287 ff.) provides us with some food for thought as we compare the domestic ledger with that of business. Assured of his own reputation for generous action and careful domestic economy, the merchant is thereafter off on those busy excursions that take him restlessly from St. Denis to Bruges, from Bruges to St. Denis, from St. Denis to Paris, in the quest for profit. In this contrast between the quietly conniving pair and the restlessly questing husband oblivious of the peccadillo about to take place in his own house, Chaucer wisely refrains from any comment that might disturb the dispassionate air of life studied as a specimen.

The wife and the monk reap the fruit of their bargain: the exchange of sexual pleasures and money is to take place on Sunday. The monk, like an amoral satyr, brings with him his customary attitudes and appearance of trustworthiness. "With crowne and berd al fressh and newe yshave," he comes to the house of his absent friend to claim his reward. And in all that house, says Chaucer,

> ...ther nas so litel a knave,
> Ne no wight elles, that he nas ful fayn
> For that my lord daun John was come agayn.   (ll. 310–12)

The irony of the final meeting between the merchant and the monk swells our enjoyment still further (ll. 325 ff.). The innocent merchant, "for greet chiertee and greet affeccioun," seeks out his friend the monk in Paris, and in the confidence of friendship reveals his own good fortune in business. There is nothing in their relationship of that strain that may attach to the roles of lender and borrower; nevertheless the monk cannily takes the initiative to explain that he has already repaid the loan to the merchant's wife; she, he avers, will remember the transaction. There has been up to this point (l. 365) no hint of the deception the monk will practice upon the wife.

The merchant, having completed his affairs in Paris, exults in his profit of a thousand francs, and his exultation carries him right back to the domestic scene. We are once again in the milieu of the happy marriage, with the wife waiting to greet her husband at the gate. They are the harmonious couple, with only a ripple of dissension between them, as the kindly disposed and soon sexually gratified husband is lulled back to innocence by that mother wit with which Chaucer endows the women of the fabliaux.

In a veritable burst of wit, a familiar triad of puns,[4] the story comes to its flashing conclusion:

> "Marie, I deffie the false monk, daun John!
> I kepe nat of his tokenes never a deel;
> He took me certeyn gold, that woot I weel,—
> What! yvel thedam on his monkes snowte!
> For, God it woot, I wende, withouten doute,
> That he hadde yeve it me bycause of yow,
> To doon therwith myn honour and my prow,
> For cosynage, and eek for beele cheere
> That he hath had ful ofte tymes heere.
> But sith I se I stonde in this disjoynt,
> I wol answere yow shortly to the poynt.
> Ye han mo slakkere dettours than am I!
> For I wol paye yow wel and redily
> Fro day to day, and if so be I faille,
> I am youre wyf; score it upon my taille,
> And I shal paye as soone as ever I may.
> For by my trouthe, I have on myn array,
> And nat on wast, bistowed every deel;
> And for I have bistowed it so weel
> For youre honour, for Goddes sake, I seye,
> As be nat wrooth, but lat us laughe and pleye.
> Ye shal my joly body have to wedde;
> By God, I wol nat paye yow but abedde!
> Forgyve it me, myn owene spouse deere;
> Turne hiderward, and maketh bettre cheere."   (ll. 402–26)

From "cosynage," with its double meaning of kinship (reiterated throughout the story as not really existing between the monk and the merchant) and of acting duplicitously for one's own advantage, through the associations of "dettours" with its roots both in finance and in the theology of matrimony, to "taille" with its clearly sexual as well as economic overtones, the wife speaks with that undaunted

[4] Robert A. Caldwell, "Chaucer's 'Taillynge Ynough,'" *MLN*, LV (1940), 262–65, provides a sane corrective to Claude Jones, "Chaucer's 'Taillynge Ynough,'" *MLN*, LII (1937), 570.

cleverness and presence of mind that even the jolly Wife of Bath might envy.

The merchant's serious, kindly, earnest innocence is with him even in the marriage bed, in what Germaine Dempster calls a subtly cruel form of dramatic irony.[5] As he speaks in conclusion with that same sublime ignorance—"Keep bet my good"—we see that what he was in the way of cautious, generous, tactful, but obtuse, he remains, and ever will be. It is remarkable that Chaucer, with perhaps a sympathy for the merchant class, has refrained from debasing the man so that we might see the deception as merited by stupidity, but has rather allowed that sweet innocence to flourish in the midst of deceit.

A certain urbanity of tone assures us that the marriage of the merchant and wife has not really been injured by the adulterous peccadillo in which the wife and monk have been involved. The wife's running to the gate to greet her husband as of old, the warmth of their relationship, the indifference of the monk to anything but getting off scot-free give us this assurance. The ironies may be cold, but through the tricks and guises shines something quite genial, warm and amiable, a reflection out of the mind of the author, we suspect, and an admission of an unshakable and amused wonder at and fondness for the human species.

In retrospect it is the amiability of the monk as opposed to the sober worthiness of the merchant that plagues and bemuses us. They stand paradoxically opposed: the monk belonging to the stable church, the merchant belonging to the fickle world; the monk gay, the merchant sober; the monk a minister of the sacraments, yet subtle, callous, contriving; the merchant a minister of the chancy world of business, yet simple, honest, cautious; the monk not properly in the world but tainted by it; the merchant in the world but ignorant of those closest to him; the monk calculating, the merchant philosophical; the monk financially indifferent yet astute, the merchant financially successful but obtuse; the monk without real affection for anyone, the merchant curiously trusting and affectionate.

There may be other stories or loci in Chaucer where the delicate nuances corroborate our view of Chaucer's subtle art. None of them, to my mind, maintains the ambivalence of this tale, weighing personal advantage against domestic good, innocence against craft. If our humaner feelings are called forth and mildly outraged at the decep-

[5] *Dramatic Irony in Chaucer*, p. 42.

tion of a man of dignity and enterprise, at any rate a laugh and a rueful chuckle are also elicited by the pyrotechnics of the verbal barrage
at the conclusion. With the *Merchant's Tale,* this one stands as a sample of that uncompromising comic honesty of which Chaucer is capable, in maintaining that having things work out "right" does not
always mean that they work out in accordance with our more sentimental wishes.

We can imagine the young of the *Miller's* and *Reeve's Tales* growing older and more conventional, conforming to the moral order visible in the background. The deceiving agents of the *Shipman's Tale,*
however, are not only already mature; they are supremely indifferent
to their moral obligations and have learned in their adult lives to live
successfully outside of them. What they do amounts in the fabliau
world to a mere peccadillo. Yet their triumph is achieved at the expense of honor, friendship, and the integrity of marriage, and the
reader's intuition that the success is bought at too dear a price may
produce the view that the tale, while brilliant, is either too Gallic or
wanting in humanity.[6]

Like the *Merchant's Tale* it makes a point about the power of
women to extricate themselves from difficult situations, and thus con-
firms in its rueful way a certain unpalatable truth, but it does so
without that tale's psychological richness and without its bitterness.
More philosophically, it presents a vivid picture of the businessman's
enslavement to his god, money.[7] The elaboration of this theme in
terms of transitory luck and chance provides a rationale, an affirmation of the risk in life which is as much a part of the meaning of the
tale as those other implications about friendship and marriage which
arise out of its gross ironies.

[6] Cf. Robert Kilburn Root, *The Poetry of Chaucer: A Guide to Its Study and
Appreciation* (New York, 1906), p. 189. Roy Vance Ramsay, "Tradition and
Chaucer's Unfaithful Woman" (unpublished dissertation, University of Oklahoma,
1964), pp. 339 ff., offers the view that "to require 'righteous retribution' or a moral
from the fabliau is to require of it what it lacks by definition." Yet he finds the
tale wanting in necessary comic distance because of the sympathy elicited by the
main characters.

[7] Cf. Stillwell, in *RES,* XX, 3. He writes: "While it is certainly true that as
Bedier says the *esprit gaulois* 'manque de métaphysique', and that the *Shipman's
Tale* considered as a whole is like the typical *fabliau,* devoid of any idea save that
of making us laugh, nevertheless the merchant of Chaucer's tale has a well-defined
outlook on life, if not precisely a metaphysic. It is a philosophy charged with
materialistic 'sadnesse', a philosophy of Profit and Loss, the philosophy of a middle-
class breadwinner who hopes to gain but is well aware of the dreadful possibility of
failure.... You never know when your luck may change, and so you had better
be prudent!"

The greatest ambiguity, one we may never entirely resolve, comes from the shift of the tale from the Wife of Bath to the Shipman. Coming from her mouth it would have qualified as a corroboration of one part of her admitted character: an illustration of a woman getting what she wants even at a price, and extricating herself wittily from a difficult situation. Standing as it does without sure ascription to a teller, it tends to float and so to obscure the intention of the artist in the larger design.

THE FRIAR'S TALE

> The Friar is a character ... of a mixed kind ...
> with constitutional gaiety enough to make him a
> master of all the pleasures of the world.
>
> WILLIAM BLAKE
A Descriptive Catalogue

> The devil cannot conquer or subdue any but those
> who are in league with sin; and therefore he is
> conquered in the name of Him who assumed
> humanity.
>
> ST. AUGUSTINE,
City of God

Before the Friar brings himself to speak his piece in retaliation upon the Summoner he remembers his manners and speaks with enough gentilesse (ll. 1270 ff.) for us to see his words as an overflow from the *Wife of Bath's Tale*. He is not without a satirical bent in his recognition of the didacticism of her tale: Let us leave authorities and the matters they discuss to the schoolmen and to the preachers (ll. 1276–77). He himself has the power of delivering admonishment in the style of preachers within the privacy of the confessional, the flair for citing when he must, in however conventional terms, the authority of Scripture and of Dante and Virgil. He demonstrates moreover the kind of learning suspiciously like the school matters he pretends to eschew as he makes his devil speak alarmingly like a schoolman, a true kinsman of the learned Mephistopheles of a later day.

The tale he has been nursing while glowering at the Summoner is offered with such economy and compactness of structure, with such precisely aimed point, while at the same time with sufficiently generalized conclusion, as to add another dimension to our appreciation of his character and intelligence. The story he tells does deal, as he tells us it will, with a summoner, but it is not to be a character sketch so much as the working out of the inevitable justice due an unregenerate summoner. The casual air with which he remarks to the rest of the pilgrims that no good may be said of a summoner may be taken to indicate a kind of unanimity of opinion within the limits of his definition:

> "A somonour is a rennere up and doun
> With mandementz for fornicacioun
> And is ybet at every townes ende." (ll. 1283–85)

The Host, who from time to time surprises us with his sense of decorum, reminds the Friar that a man of his estate "sholde be hende / And curteys" (ll. 1286–87). His placating words do not prevent the threat from the Summoner (ll. 1290 ff.) that he will in due course have his say; in the momentary peace that follows we are launched into a tale which affords us the satisfaction of seeing justice vanquish its violator.

Beginning with a short but inclusive list of the crimes handled by the archdeacon's court, the Friar introduces us to the sly rascal responsible for summoning violators into that court. Immediately there bursts forth from the Summoner a slurring comment (ll. 1332–33) and the Host once more restores a semblance of order, the exposition affording one more indication of the close hold Chaucer maintained upon certain sections of the whole pilgrimage and of the intimate relation between the tale and the framework which he was in the process of working out.

The interruption comes at a moment when we have just been introduced to the summoner and his spy system. Following the interruption comes the Friar's long expansion of the method by which the summoner seeks out his victims and fleeces them (ll. 1338 ff.), a minutely detailed exposure of vice, blackmail, extortion, perjury, a wholesale preying upon the weakness of human nature. The comparison to Judas (l. 1350) is a sharp thrust: he will practice his wiles for even a small "take," like food and drink, from the ignorant and fearful. This is followed by a still sharper thrust uttered with contempt:

> He was, if I shal yeven hym his laude,
> A theef, and eek a somnour, and a baude. (ll. 1353–54)

Citing all three equally as professions, the Friar plants "summoner" squarely between the two vicious extremes. As if this overt debasing of the character of the summoner were not sufficient, he now reinforces the depiction by the image of a dog sniffing out lechers and adulterers (ll. 1368–72).

In a story only 364 lines long, Chaucer has used some seventy-five lines to relate to us the whole sordid profession of summoning. These seventy-five lines he will balance subsequently with the description of the other summoning profession, that of the devil. The account is far from static; its interest lies mainly in the succinctness of expression and the lively depiction of vice perpetrated by a rascal who is safely engaged in a reputable and recognized profession that he has subverted for his own profit, and in the effect it manages to convey of a person of some power and executive ability running a successful organization. It is this same sense of power, no doubt, that enables the Summoner in the *Prologue* to the tale to affront the Friar, who is in all ways his social and intellectual superior. The story the Friar tells is a mixture of the sardonic and the bland, carrying with it the admonitory tone of the training to which our "deere maister" had been submitted; indeed it is a tone that Chaucer invests generally in the utterances of his religious, so that, while we may make the easy distinction offered to us by Chaucer himself between churls and gentles, there are other inevitable distinctions that must be made in terms of tone and interior disposition.

The devil whom we meet garbed as a yeoman has nothing sinister about him. The description of him carries with it appropriate suggestions of the pastoral life; in externals he is much like the knot-headed Yeoman of the *Prologue*. It is futile, as well as destructive to the tone of delicate contrast between external amity and interior malice, to look for obvious symbols of the sinister in the charming adversary. The summoner

> . . . saugh bifore hym ryde
> A gay yeman, under a forest syde.
> A bowe he bar, and arwes brighte and kene;
> He hadde upon a courtepy of grene,
> An hat upon his heed with frenges blake. (ll. 1379–83)

It is fetching to see in the color green the meaning of evil.[1] The garment of green here is the protective coloration ordinarily worn by a yeoman of the forest in his quest for game; obviously in this sense

[1] D. W. Robertson, Jr., "Why the Devil Wears Green," *MLN*, LXIX (1954), 470–72. See too his discussion of the moral dynamics in *A Preface to Chaucer* (Princeton University Press, 1962), pp. 266–69.

the devil is a hunter for human prey and assumes the guise of a
common hunter of game. Needless to say, as a fiend he must assume
every kind of protective coloration that will make him successful,
including the appearance of heartfelt cordiality and seductive friendship.[2] And so their meeting is couched in cordial, friendly terms; in a
moment fraught with delicate ironies the summoner utters his lie: he
is, he says, a bailiff, that is to say, an officer of justice under a sheriff,
whose duty it is to execute writs and processes, a civil function as
compared to the serving of summonses for an archdeacon's or bish-
op's court.

> He dorste nat, for verray filthe and shame
> Seye that he was a somonour, for the name. (ll. 1393-94)

Like the devil, the summoner has lied, but the exchange of the
identical lie as to profession does not prevent the demon-yeoman later
on from addressing his friend by the general term "leeve sire
somonour" (l. 1474). Chaucer manages to convey in this casual encounter with its cordial, conversational warmth the ease of pledging
friendship which is more than a casual occurrence. The gradual and
inexorable closing in of divine justice is coupled deliberately with the
speciously genial in the relationship of demon to victim; and the
supernatural air is conveyed in an atmosphere of the most vivid reality in action and speech. These two sets of ambivalent attitudes lend
the story its note of special humor, a cut above the merely sardonic.
We may recall the same blend of the genial with the corrupt in the
twinkling-eyed Hubert, and this facet of his personality seems admirably corroborated in a subtle way by his tale.

The friendship of the summoner with the demon is cemented by
something like recognition of kindred spirits but more by the promise
of gold and silver from the false yeoman's coffers, who promises such
treasures if the summoner should ever happen to come into his shire
(l. 1401). On the note of mutual profit and enticement, they swear to
be brothers until death. The advantage belongs to the demon-
yeoman, who has cleverness on his side: he has played the game of
win-a-soul before; his knowledge of psychology is keen enough for
him to entice the summoner into confessing his perversion of justice
by recounting his own indiscretions (ll. 1425 ff.). The casual air with

[2] Muriel Bowden, *A Commentary on the General Prologue to the Canterbury
Tales* (New York, 1948), p. 91.

which they tacitly assume illegal profit in the office of bailiff allows first the devil to give the impression of a shameless extortioner pressed by a difficult lord. His "confession" in turn elicits a confirmation from the summoner's experience. Deliberately graceless—"Stomak ne conscience ne knowe I noon" (l. 1441)—he is now visibly set forth as fair game for the hunter: I am a fiend; my dwelling is in hell. Like you I will do anything, go anywhere for my plunder, my prey.

Chaucer's summoner here does not take alarm. His own blindness prevents him from seeing that he may himself be the victim necessary to satisfy the false yeoman's hard and "dangerous" lord. They have so much in common that nature herself seems to have made them friends: "Looke how thou rydest..." and "Right so fare I" (ll. 1452–54).

Now follows the balance weight for the long description of summoning in the beginning of the tale. In a passage of comparable length we learn about demons, their powers, their limitations, along with incidental information about shapes and metamorphoses possible to demons. Although the devil gives a great deal of information, he leaves the impression of holding back a great deal, and his knowledge and learning contrast strongly with the blind ignorance of the summoner; he cannot understand why demons should work so laboriously at the business of garnering souls. The demon, holding back his answer, finally yields the truth: demons are sometimes instruments of God, tools for carrying out His commandments upon His creatures; if He pleases to oppose their activities, they have no power without His sufferance. Sometimes they plague men's bodies, sometimes men's souls, sometimes both soul and body, and all for one purpose: on such battlefields, by trial and ordeal of temptation and suffering, the individual Christian may be tested, taking assurance that Christ is his champion.

> "Whan he withstandeth oure temptacioun,
> It is a cause of his savacioun,
> Al be it that it was nat oure entente
> He sholde be sauf, but that we wolde hym hente."

> (ll. 1497–1500)

And yet telling as much as he does about his kind, their ability to create illusions, to raise up corpses, he does not give away the show, couching his final ironical admonition in language too rhetorically florid and too obscurely allusive for his victim to understand:

> "Thou shalt herafterward, my brother deere,
> Come there thee nedeth nat of me to leere.
> For thou shalt, by thyn owene experience,
> Konne in a chayer rede of this sentence
> Bet than Virgile, while he was on lyve,
> Or Dant also...."   (ll. 1515–20)

The summoner cannot recognize himself as victim; rather he swears closer allegiance to his companion.

The story thus far has compared two professions and prepared in us a feeling of amused irony mingled with something like awe. The wily demon, much like Marlowe's Mephistopheles, is obliged to play by the rules of testing men and proving the good. In spite of his demonic vision, he is compelled to observe the rules laid down by Another; indeed his victim may, by an act of will, escape at any time. The first limit placed upon the demon is immediately brought before us in a short scene (ll. 1539 ff.) of great vigor and fidelity to peasant life, wherein a carter curses his flagging, stumbling horses to the devil one moment and then praises them to heaven the next.

The point is simple: a curse must come from a determined heart. The short burst of anger from the lips of the carter is but a thing of the moment (ll. 1566–68). The demon has had what looked to be an opportunity, but the opportunity has dissipated. With patience and equanimity he is willing to move on in search of his true prey.

Now the summoner has *his* opportunity. He will lodge a false complaint against an innocent widow and offer her immunity for twelve pence. In the verbal altercation that ensues between the old woman and the summoner, we reach the simple but significant theological point upon which hangs the success or failure of the demon in his quest. The old woman cries out:

> "The devel ... so fecche hym er he deye,
> And panne and al, but he wol hym repente!"   (ll. 1628–29)

The summoner's hoot of derision now clinches his fate once and for all. In a flash the devil carries him off to hell, "Where as that somonours han hir heritage" (l. 1641). The old lady had meant every word of her curse within the limits of Christian charity. So simple an act as repentance by the summoner would have caused the devil to forfeit his soul. Their friendship is at once dissolved and confirmed, and the hunter has caught his prey.

This is comedy in league with melodrama, inasmuch as in the loss of the summoner's soul it meets the moral demands of the audience for an inevitable justice. Furthermore, in condemning the fictional summoner, the Friar not only holds out a warning to a vilely erring brother within the Christian community on pilgrimage, but from condemning one he passes on to the condemnation of the class: May God who made man in His image make good men of summoners (ll. 1642 ff.).

The final sermonizing words are more than conventional cadences.[3] They serve to bring into connection the two strands of the story, the lack of conscience and therefore of grace in such summoners as the one dealt with, and the role of demons in the battle for men's souls. Structurally, then, the story remains a model of delicate weight and balance: two antagonists, two professions, two tests, and a double-edged conclusion. Our "master" has the ability to make a point both specific and general for a listening audience.

One's response to the *Friar's Tale* is apt to be serious owing to its sober treatment of the function of evil, a subject in which the convictions of the age may be detected. The theological explanation of evil spoken by the demon is superimposed upon the social evil represented by the calloused summoner. The sustained balance between a surface amiability and an impersonal spiritual enmity in the devil's relation to the summoner guides our reactions over the fringes of the sardonic as we witness the consequences of a clear choice of evil.

Like the *Pardoner's Tale*, the *Friar's Tale* contains enough of the demonic—the devil and the function of repentance appear in both— to qualify as that aspect of divine comedy in which we see Dante's infernal state typified in those who subvert the good by making an idol of some personal appetite. Like it, it is a structure in which the audience concurs with the moral judgment made by the ending of the tale. Whatever one's reaction to the loss of a soul, there is a moment of melodramatic excitement in old Mabely's cursing the summoner to Hell "but he wol hym repente," and his self-damnation, "Nay, olde stot, that is nat myn entente." And the theological irony becomes

[3] See the Rev. Paul E. Beichner, "Baiting the Summoner," *MLQ*, XXII (1961), 375-76: In the closing lines "the Friar is not concerned with summoners in general, but with this Summoner, his adversary. By asking the pilgrims to pray that summoners will repent—a good work which they could hardly oppose—he implicitly assumes that they concur in his opinion of summoners, namely that they need to be prayed for, especially the pilgrim Summoner. In the context, this is a refined but devastating insult."

especially tart in the devil's parody of Christ's promise to the repentant thief: "Thou shalt with me to helle yet to-nyght."

The facile application of a moral at the conclusion illustrates the ease with which the anecdote could be converted to new uses by a preacher scourging any troublesome group. True it is different in technique and intention from the Miller-Reeve kind of comedy, and its ironies are of course vastly different from those of the *Shipman's Tale;* yet, like each of these it is a gem of its own kind, one which leaves in the mind a hard residue of thoughtfulness. Its theological implications are indeed subsumed under the comic intention, but the excess of moral statement at the end, while suited to the clerical inclinations of the teller, lifts the tale out of the class of the fabliaux momentarily and makes it the preacher's *exemplum* with an obvious moral tag. The hard core of the story is, however, its built-in flaying of the vices of summoners, its sadistic revenge upon a particular summoner. Too, the final statement by the tale is a social as well as a theological one, and it is this factor that orients the tale not only towards those making didactic or purely moral points, but also towards those in which a social meaning arises out of the action itself.

In the context of quarrel the terminal lines of the tale aiming somewhere between specific animus and general comment become fraught with psychological complexity and illustrate a delicacy of comic comment too easily lost if the tale is seen in isolation from its companion. Our enjoyment of the tale, tempered by a moral admonishment which floods out some of its comic statement and based upon our awareness of a tart blend of malice with specious charity, leads us to one conclusion: the *Friar's Tale*, seen within the context of quarrel, is one of virtually inexhaustible ironies.[4] We may laugh during the course of the tale, but our laughter becomes increasingly more thoughtful, not only because its meaning is theological as well as social, but also because the teller's malice takes on the appearance of urbanity in the destruction of an enemy.

[4] Earle Birney, "After His Image: The Central Ironies of the *Friar's Tale*," MS, XXI (1959), 17–35; Adrien Bonjour, "Aspects of Chaucer's Irony in *The Friar's Tale*," EIC, XI (1961), 121–27; and Janette Richardson, "Hunter and Prey: Functional Imagery in Chaucer's *Friar's Tale*," EM, XII (1961), 9–20.

THE SUMMONER'S TALE

> [The] Sompnour is...a Devil of the first
> magnitude, grand, terrific, rich and honoured in
> the rank of which he holds the destiny. The uses
> to society are perhaps equal of the Devil and of
> the Angel; their sublimity, who can dispute...
>
> WILLIAM BLAKE,
> *A Descriptive Catalogue*

Chaucer never approaches that tone of bitter denunciation, that *saeva indignatio* found from time to time in the *Divine Comedy*. A difference of temperament in the two major poets may explain the difference in attitude and the language that accompanies revulsion, scorn, and the determined attempt to revise and reform. Yet there is an approximation to revulsion and scorn, a something in the language and metaphor used to describe the Summoner which does not allow for the mitigating elements of pity or compassion, or the distancing elements of detachment or good-humored laughter.

For the Summoner, like the Pardoner—and there are others— affords us one more example of violation of the spiritual and social body at the hands of certain men whom, in spite of his love for the life in them, Chaucer is concerned to see as honestly as possible. The language describing the Summoner reflects in its images a deeply felt social and spiritual judgment of the age. The vicious quarreling of the Summoner with the Friar is but one means by which Chaucer is a witness to the loss of dignity in men and their offices as a symptom of disease in the century.

Chaucer clearly assumed that his listeners all knew the functions of the Summoner, functions which we must for ourselves recover before we can appreciate the depth and precision of the denouncement. Actually the office was an ancient one which was introduced into England sometime during the thirteenth century, and comprised an aggregate of subordinate duties outside the scope of spiritual ministration, constituting in the main the duties of carrying summonses from an archdiaconal or episcopal court to a person charged to appear to answer for a number of offenses. These included, in Chaucer's own words put into the mouth of the Friar, the charges

> ... of fornicacioun,
> Of wicchecraft, and eek of bawderye,
> Of diffamacioun, and avowtrye,
> Of chirche reves, and of testamentz,
> Of contractes and of lakke of sacramentz,
> Of usure, and of symonye also.   (ll. 1304-9)

The summoner was apparently paid on a percentage basis according to the levy of fines in the court; since non-payment of reparation by the charged person would bring with it the dreaded arrest by civil authority following church excommunication, any summoner guided by self-interest could, by playing upon the fear of his victims of falling into prison, practice extortion. It is easy to see how such profiteering summoners could become in literature standard illustrations of corruption and exploitation,[1] by the exacting of bribes from the ignorant and unlettered. Although these summoners may have been few, they succeeded in damaging the reputation of their brethren in what must have been a respectable profession. Chaucer is bent upon depicting a summoner of the most vulgar and depraved sort, manifesting not only the signs of professional corruption, but a personal viciousness that extends to every nook and cranny of his soul.

The account of him in the *General Prologue* opens with the ironical suggestion that the Summoner's face is an angelic visage aflame with desire for deity; he is, in fact, a negation, the opposite of all that is angelic in imagination, intelligence, and will. The fiery-red face is not the result of any impulse toward the deity, but rather of licentious living and bad diet. To his fiery-red color Chaucer adds the suggestions of psychological heat in a familiar figure: "as hoot he was and lecherous as a sparwe"; and the fiery tang of his favorite foods: garlic, leeks, onions, and strong blood-red wine. Unlike the practice of the sanguine Franklin with his sop in wine, a man of convivial hospitality, the generous action of the Summoner is reduced to allowing "a good felawe to have his concubyn" for a quart of wine, and his intelligence to the mouthing of senseless terms of Latin imitated from the consistory courts. Towards his kindred fellows he is kind in the wildest perversion of justice:

[1] Louis A. Haselmayer, "The Apparitor and Chaucer's Summoner," *Speculum*, XII (1937), 55.

> He wolde techen him to have noon awe
> In swich caas of the ercedekenes curs
> But if a mannes soule were in his purs;   (A 654–56)

reducing all guilt and innocence, not to the terms of the moral law, but to the desire for money in a corrupt clergy. Behind Chaucer's demurral ("But wel I woot he lyed right in dede") we detect something of the implied ideal of justice that should obtain under more ideal conditions. The Summoner's control over the "girles" of the diocese [2] is but another indication of the perverting of justice for his own ends.

His grotesque visage is crowned by the garland he wears upon his head, in a sense a symbol of youthful innocence crowning a cherubic face. The shield for his innocence is but the round, flat-loafed bread which reflects the material values by which he lives.

By comparison with his adversary the Friar, the Summoner comes off as considerably more vulgar, and perhaps even more depraved. Although both of them have their sensual side, the anal associations with which the Summoner's performance both begins and ends, not to mention the veiled commentary, perhaps stercoraceous,[3] with which Chaucer describes his vocal support of the Pardoner to the tune of "Com hider, love, to me!" are all of them indications of a more immediate and apparent coarseness residing side by side with a hectic and excitable ("... lyk an aspen leef he quook for ire." l. 1667) malice in the Summoner, alongside of which the "maner louryng chiere" (l. 1266) of the Friar seems coldly detached.

The tale told by the Summoner, a depiction of a progressively developing indignation and an outraged frustration, is an intimately revealing outgrowth of the character and personality we have met in the *General Prologue*. The description of the Summoner in the *General Prologue* makes eminently clear the heated and volatile character of the teller of the tale, a character intellectually limited to a few terms of Latin and hedged about by certain aspects of grosser human appetites. We may add that the purely gross appetites which glare forth from beneath his "scalled browes blake" crowned by the garland and epitomized by his bread-cake buckler assume a more terrible

---

[2] Morton W. Bloomfield, "Chaucer's Summoner and the Girls of the Diocese," *PQ,* XXVIII (1949), 503–7.

[3] "This Somonour bar to hym a stif burdoun; / Was nevere trompe of half so greet a soun." Was Chaucer here remembering that other marvelous bass trumpet in the *Inferno?*

existence from the additional lyrical horror of the alliance with the Pardoner, affirmed by the sweet vulgarity of "Com hider, love, to me!" and the frankly coarser note of the "stif burdoun." Chaucer's characteristic obliqueness offers little comment upon the grotesque two-part harmony beyond the trumpeting support provided by the Summoner.

The unmitigated coarseness of the "gentil harlot" grows out of his apparently insatiable appetites; these themselves suggest desire for the *summum bonum* faintly discernible in the background.[4] In the total performance we have the satisfaction of watching Chaucer successfully adapting for his pitiful Summoner a tale of frustration which springs from his thwarted soul. In so doing Chaucer provides us with that further revelation of character which gives the Canterbury pilgrimage its psychological complexity.

On the surface the *Summoner's Tale* seems to belie the anti-intellectual nature of its teller, being replete with French and Latin tags (Chaucer may have wished to suggest a certain continental affectation in his friar-preacher), with *exempla* drawn from rather erudite sources, and with the only mathematical joke of the *Tales*. But we may recall that the *Miller's Tale* and the *Reeve's Tale* both manifest qualities of economy, rhetorical skill, and great adeptness in characterization far beyond the powers of the tellers; the Wife of Bath too can wax eloquent in drawing material from the "wyse poete of Florence, / That highte Dant," and can recommend the words of Valerius, Seneca, Boethius, and Juvenal—truly remarkable examples of total recall from the readings of her latest husband. We have that splendid paradox of the poet's art, called to our attention by Tatlock, which does not sacrifice rhetorical art nor abandon verisimilitude for the sake of fitting the tale to an unworthy speaker. In short, even if we may cavil that the Summoner knows much that the *General Prologue* denies him, we must approve the depiction of the friar within the tale, in whom such knowledge is exquisitely apt. The foreign tags, the stock of *exempla*, all flow from the lips of an educated man who desecrates and abuses his intellectual gifts.

The *Summoner's Tale*, in fine, is an exposé of the methods employed by an unscrupulous friar, just as the previous tale is an exposé of the methods of an unscrupulous summoner. The express intention

[4] See Arthur W. Hoffman, "Chaucer's Prologue to Pilgrimage: The Two Voices," *ELH*, XXI (1954), 1–16.

of the teller is to depict a friar with such scathing contempt and adherence to general opinion as to bring discredit and personal revenge upon his hated adversary. In this way, even though it is not his express intention, the Summoner urges us to compare the selfless ideal of good clerics with love perverted into pride, anger, and envy (of possessioners) and distorted into a delicate taste in food and an overweening belief in the powers of persuasion. It is indeed this ultimate belief in his ability to get money that controls him and eventually makes him an easy victim of the person he had hoped to victimize.

Almost half the tale is devoted to the friar's self-revealing and increasingly passionate speech centering upon the vicious sin of wrath. Into it are woven the threads of personal interest and hypocritical grasping. Thomas, his intended victim, is seen mainly through the eyes of his wife, a self-pitying woman who describes her husband as disgruntled, unreasonable, unloving. In her view, he is in need of severe chiding.

> "Chideth him weel, for seinte Trinitee!
> He is as angry as a pissemyre,
> Though that he have al that he kan desire,
> Though I hym wrye a-nyght and make hym warm,
> And over hym leye my leg outher myn arm,
> He groneth lyk our boor, lith in oure sty.
> Oother desport right noon of hym have I;
> I may nat plese hym in no maner cas."   (ll. 1824–31)

Actually Thomas is a good man whose house has long been open to the friar. He is a well-to-do householder who greets the friar cordially and accepts the easy and casual familiarity with which the friar makes himself at home. He watches him sweep the cat from the comfortable bench (l. 1775), offer his chirping kiss to the wife (ll. 1804–5), hears him accept with canny grace her offer for dinner (ll. 1838 ff.). He is a man who listens with great patience to the nagging of his wife and the long preachment from the friar. He manifests for the most part an almost helpless sufferance, and is now sorely tried by the friar's insistence that he confess to the sin of anger.

> "Nay," quod the sike man, "by Seint Symoun!
> I have be shryven this day at my curat.
> I have hym toold hoolly al myn estat;
> Nedeth namoore to speken of it," seith he,
> "But if me list, of myn humylitee."   (ll. 2094–98)

In short we see him in the story as a sick and long-suffering man, perhaps crabbed and indisposed, who puts up with what he must. He acts only when he can no longer endure the shameless posturing of the begging friar, flaunting his spirituality in the face of his defenseless victim. Seeing through the dissimulation and "wel ny wood for ire" (l. 2121), and putting aside his respect for the spiritual office, he works out his contempt and anger in a humiliating trick. The friar's ability to "grope tendrely a conscience" (l. 1817) is given the exercise of another kind of groping. To his own discomfiture and bursting rage, he becomes hoist upon a petard (ll. 2144 ff.).

Onto this slim thread of a plot, a sick man avenging himself upon an overly persistent friar, with its ironical counterpoint of wrath in a man preaching against it, Chaucer weaves the subtler design of mendicant hypocritical versatility. It is worth our time and effort to examine even hastily the long preachment which reduces Thomas to calculated vengeance: The reclining figure on the couch, the windbag friar on bended knee beside him temporarily silenced—no attitudes could be more slyly pertinent to the perpetration of the deed.

The friar's speech occupies more than half the story. It takes the form of extempory preaching more or less by association, a method of preaching that characterized not only the friar of our tale but the preaching of the mendicant orders of the time. It pours from his lips in an unabated flow of rhetorical enthusiasm and abandon, announcing a theme (ll. 1834–35), departing from it to comment upon the relation of spiritual to physical nourishment, to blandish with words calculated to point up his spirituality and power the wife who recently lost a child, to speak discursively of gluttony and abstinence. He embellishes his little digression cannily with the self-flattering examples of Moses, Elias, Aaron, and Jesus, who committed the friars to

> "... poverte and continence,
> To charite, humblesse, and abstinence,
> To persecucioun for rightwisnesse,
> To wepynge, misericorde, and clennesse."   (ll. 1907–10)

And even when he has no precise text, he can gloss (glossing being to him a glorious thing) any of the Gospels to redound to the praise of friars and to the discredit of the fat, waddling, vinolent possessioners swimming in wealth and belching out their prayers.

Chaucerian rhetoric in the mouth of the hypocrite friar is a skillful thing indeed as it marks out the delicate line between connivance and the legitimate uses of his office, playing on words both advertently and inadvertently as he tells us:

> "Fro Paradys, first, if I shal nat lye,
> Was man out chaced for his glotonye;
> And chaast was man in Paradys, certeyn."   (ll. 1915–17)

Or offering bilingual play in his description of the stuffed possessioners at prayer:

> "Whan they for soules seye the psalm of Davit;
> Lo, 'buf!' they seye, '*cor meum eructavit!*'"   (ll. 1934–35) [5]

He speaks with an air of impassioned indignation and with considerable flair as he quotes a beatitude, "Blessed be the poor in spirit" (l. 1923), to the advantage of his order or resorts to the thoroughly masculine metaphor of the hawk springing upward into the air to represent the ease with which friars' prayers [6] reach the ears of God (l. 1938); he shamelessly berates a man who is his own lay brother (l. 1944) for having charities other than his order, and resorts to the cruel and vicious lie that his physical condition is the result of his mean behavior towards the friars (l. 1962). He can turn the truth to fit his need and in phrasing it inadvertently foreshadow the final problem in ars-metric:

> "What is a ferthyng worth parted in twelve?
> Lo, ech thyng that is oned in himselve
> Is moore strong than whan it is toscatered."   (ll. 1967–69)

And he subtly flatters his host by calling to mind the church-building namesake, St. Thomas of India (l. 1980).

[5] There are other possibilities in "grope," lines 1817, 2141, and 2148, and perhaps in "ferthing," line 1967, and of course in "ars-metric," line 2222. See Paull F. Baum, "Chaucer's Puns," *PMLA*, LXXI (1956), 225–46, and the "Supplementary List," *PMLA*, LXXIII (1958), 167–70; and J. E. Whitesell, "Chaucer's Lisping Friar," *MLN*, LXXI (1956), 160–61. The Latin tag has been explored, first by Marie P. Hamilton, "The Summoner's 'Psalm of Davit,'" *MLN*, LVII (1942), 655–57, and then by the Rev. Paul E. Beichner, "Non Alleluia Ructare," *MS*, XVIII (1956), 134–44.

[6] See Earle Birney, "Structural Irony within the *Summoner's Tale*," *Anglia*, LXXVIII (1960), 204–18. Birney comments, "For this 'chaste, bisy frere,' who boasts that his prayer 'up springeth into th' eir' skyward like a hawk, for this windy pedant and glosing hypocrite, a final brief gloss of air fouler and grosser than a cart-horse's." The tale itself as a masterpiece of psychological portraiture is given further examination in John F. Adams, "The Structure of Irony in the *Summoner's Tale*," *EIC*, XII (1962), 126–32, and in Thomas F. Merrill, "Wrath and Rhetoric in the *Summoner's Tale*," *TSLL*, IV (1962–63), 341–50.

Up to this point the friar has hardly done more than mention the theme he has promised to discuss in "a word or two." Indeed what he has had is a mere warm-up; in the progress of approximately one hundred and fifty lines he has projected a magnificent ideal of the mendicant's life of poverty, while subtly abusing it by his practice. More than that, he has steadily revealed himself to be guilty of those many *peccata* which add up to wrath itself, all of which the Parson calls to our attention in his long "myrie" tale, and against which the friar is now just about to speak: hatred, slander, hypocritical counsel, lying, subtle flattery, reproachful chiding, and ceaseless criticism. These all mark him as a sower of schism and scandal, violating at every turn the charity he should exemplify.

Now he moves in upon his theme, remembering his original instigation in the wife's complaint. In general his advice boils down to a bitter commentary upon marriage so familiar to us from the *Romance of the Rose* and the fabliau tradition: do not argue with a woman (l. 1986); remember all of those men who stirred up the sleeping evil in the bosom of women and consequently lost their lives (ll. 1996 ff.). Out of the antifeminist literature of the Middle Ages comes the familiar warning, the wise man does not stir up trouble in his house, advice that reaches across to the words of the Parson about the evils of a nagging wife, capable of comic expansion, but here subdued to the solemn terms of a preacher. The domestic bickering of Thomas and his wife, not found in the story but implied by the words of the wife, is seen in the fantastic connotations of wrathful murder (l. 2009), and by an easy movement of the friar's agile mind, in the connotations of wrathful murder in high places. In succession, within the space of seventy lines, we encounter the *exemplum* of the "irous potestat" who senselessly orders the slaying of three knights (ll. 2017–42), that of drunken Cambyses who shoots a child to prove to the father standing by that his hand is steady (ll. 2043–78), and that of the Persian Cyrus who, when a sacred white horse drowned in the Gyndes, delayed his march for a summer and an autumn in order to dissipate the waters (ll. 2079–84). These carry collateral didacticisms which deal with wrath and the lust for vengeance that it generates:

> "Beth war, therfore, with lordes how ye pleye.
> Syngeth *Placebo*, and 'I shal, if I kan,'
> But if it be unto a povre man.

> To a povre man men sholde his vices telle,
> But nat to a lord, thogh he sholde go to helle."   (ll. 2074–78)

and

> " 'Ne be no felawe to an irous man,
> Ne with no wood man walke by the waye
> Lest thee repente;'..."   (ll. 2086–88)

These more or less associate (if we will make the association) the wrath of wives, who are best left unprovoked, and that of lordly rulers, who will stop at nothing. Both of these classes are, it seems, equally to be feared.

This vengeful wrath is an anticipation of Thomas' desire for vengeance which springs from a thoroughly exasperated rage. He is first urged to shrive himself, although he has just been shriven by his own spiritual counsellor, and is then flagrantly importuned in the name of charity to give money to the friar's order, under the admonition that the world cannot prosper without the preaching of the mendicant order, this sun that illumines the universe.

> This sike man wax wel ny wood for ire;
> He wolde that the frere had been on-fire
> With his false dissymulacioun,   (ll. 2121–23)

writes Chaucer, and by this time the reader sympathizes with Thomas. The friar has gone too far, and the seams of friendship are unsewn; that crabbed rancor reported by the wife which the friar should have mollified he has rather kindled into flame, and the revenge which is the fruit of anger itself generates the degrading action and the humiliating gift.

The Summoner is at this juncture all too clearly the speaker, and the trumpet blast by which Chaucer characterizes him in the *General Prologue* is echoed in the language of line 2151. He is having his full revenge upon the Friar who has consigned summoners to hell.

Now we see generated a cycle or a succession of events: the friar who preached continence, the spiritual life, and the perils of wrath has fallen into the sin himself:

> He looked as it were a wilde boor;
> He grynte with his teeth, so was he wrooth.
> . . . .
> Unnethes myghte the frere speke a word.   (ll. 2160–67)

The revenge that has been wrought on him gives rise to his own desire for revenge expressed in his self-consuming anger:

> ... "by God, I shal nat lye,
> But I on oother wyse may be wreke,
> I shal disclaundre hym over al ther I speke,
> This false blasphemour, that charged me
> To parte that wol nat departed be,
> To every man yliche, with meschaunce!"   (ll. 2210–15)

—this in spite of the words of the lord of the village assuring him that he is the salt of the earth and in spite of the wife's sane appraisal of Thomas' action: a churl has done a churl's deed; God let him never prosper (ll. 2206–7). But the friar can think only that he, his order, and indeed the whole church have been blasphemed.

At this point the story is actually finished, and what follows—the musing of the lord of the village upon the devilishly difficult problem of division,[7] the straight-faced anticlericalism of the squire who suggests a solution to the problem and thereby wins a new garment as a reward—constitutes an intellectual reverberation from the main plot; a comic invention consisting of treating what has been a comic gift as a serious problem requiring the utmost scientific sobriety. It is, however, the underlying sarcasm, even the malice, of Jenkin the squire that brings us back to the dramatic motive of the Summoner as speaker. We pass back and forth between his revenge upon the Friar of the *Prologue* and the revenge of Thomas upon the hypocritical friar, enforced in the conclusion of the tale by the subtler implied revenge of Jenkin upon the whole order of friars.

Sometimes neglected because of the stercoraceous gift, the *Summoner's Tale* is *psychologically* one of Chaucer's richest stories. The depiction of the deteriorating composure of the friar ranks with the portrayal of the Canon's Yeoman, and invites favorable comparison with those of the Wife of Bath and the Pardoner.

Chaucer inflates the tale far beyond the simple model of a worthless gift bestowed upon a worthless rascal, by improvising rhetorically

---

[7] Only a word needs to be said here of the references to Ptolemy and Euclid. Chaucer's knowledge of these ancients may well have come to him from his reading of the arithmetical treatises of Boethius, in particular the *De Musica*. The problem of division posed by the tale is suggested by the precise and meticulous reasoning that went into the sectioning or dividing of the monochord, a scientific investigation to which, according to Boethius, Ptolemy and Euclid made their ample contribution.

with the techniques of spontaneous preachment. More than any other story of the pilgrimage it invites acting out so that the vividness of the character and its truth to life can be grasped. Its astonishing reality in the baring of the friar's hypocrisy, our confrontation of an appalling greed, is its meaning from the point of view of the character. From the point of view of the plot, the stercoraceous jest, in all its coarseness, is a just reprisal for the hypocrisies of the grasping friar.

The central anecdote, however, is submerged beneath the rhetorical flourishes of the bared ethos of the enraged speaker, and the contempt for vicious pretenders which the tale conveys is a large part of its comic meaning. The comment of the householder's wife at the close of the story: "a cherl hath doon a cherles dede," and the subsequent discussion of the problem in scientific and technological terms provide cooler and saner perspectives than the bursting rage of the victim.

THE MERCHANT'S TALE

Genus infirmissimae servitudinis est senex maritus.

VINCENT OF BEAUVAIS,
Speculum Majus

Morality is a duenna to be circumvented. This was the view of ... a sagacious essayist, who said that the end of comedy would often be the commencement of a tragedy, were the curtain to rise again on the performers.

GEORGE MEREDITH,
The Idea of Comedy

Both the quiet portraiture of the *General Prologue* and the more realistic bursting into life of the *Merchant's Prologue* serve their respective purposes: the one providing the terms of character, the other the situation in the Merchant's life out of which his tale naturally grows. It is the tale itself which has perplexed scholarship and which encourages speculation about the personality of the narrator. So easily does it arouse in the general reader an instinctive distaste for its central situation—the marriage of youth with age—that one's personal feelings prevent full appreciation of its themes.

The carefully savage treatment of blindness of heart and the biting commentary upon old age usurping the privileges of the young point not so much to a lapse of artistic sensibility or to a frisson of the spirit as to a level of controlled satire nowhere else achieved in the *Canterbury Tales*. The old problem of the *senex amans* is now handled in a complex way by the ironical juxtaposition of religio-romantic attitudes with realistic bourgeois ones. This setting side by side of incompatible vocabularies for the sake of oblique statement is not new. The reader has seen it in the *Troilus*, for example, and in the *Miller's Tale*. Nowhere else, however, is the tone so persistently mordant. Furthermore, the alloy of two so diverse matters or sources of vocabulary around so sacred an institution as matrimony prevents any easy definition of the literary genre. Sedgwick's suggestion that it may be called the "first psychological short story," [1] brings us inevitably back to the examination of its success or failure in producing some impression of the artist's intention, to the examination therefore of its theme and—in more practical terms—of whether we are convinced of justice in the hero's fall from fortune.

Clearly, Chaucer's intention has been to depict in specific detail a marriage which, given its carefully constructed characters, cannot possibly prosper. The young wife, herself, is depicted as thoroughly unsuited to the union; it is as though Chaucer himself has deliberately arranged a *roman à thèse* to prove a point, namely that old men should not marry young girls; for his purposes he has had to create characters of straw, intended from the outset to be destroyed. The marriage entered upon is itself shown as an antithesis to all that is implied by the religious view of marriage as a sacramental union like that of Christ with his Church, or the relation of the soul with its Creator. A union such as is here depicted is clearly as much a violation of the law of love as it is a violation of the law of common sense. The total effect is that of an upside-down world of values in which the marriage contract, instead of leading sacramentally to knowledge and moral growth, yields deception and a deserved betrayal. Blindness of heart becomes the mark of man's incorrigible will.

As a matter of fact, it is precisely the hero's insistent self-deception and a peculiar naïveté that arouse derision rather than pity in the reader. One accepts the adultery in the tree and its aftermath as the bitter but necessary compromise generated by the realistic world of

---

[1] G. G. Sedgwick, "The Structure of the *Merchant's Tale*," UTQ, XVII (1948), 337. The tale does not readily yield up any easy treatment. See J. A. Burrow, "Irony in the Merchant's Tale," *Anglia*, LXXV (1957), 199–208. Burrow points out rightly that the *Merchant's Tale*, while it has affinities with the fabliaux, has much in common with the moral fable of the Pardoner in the way of persistent irony and seriousness, and in "a perceptible drift towards allegory." He finds the tale sane and balanced, a view which is only in part agreeable to Bertrand H. Bronson, "Afterthoughts on the *Merchant's Tale*," SP, LVIII (1961), 583–96, and even less so to Robert M. Jordan, "The Non-dramatic Disunity of the Merchant's Tale," PMLA, LXXVIII (1963), 293–99. Bronson sheds light on the various levels of creation by pointing out that the tale, without its prologue, might be simply in the tradition of antifeminism; and that after the invention of domestic infelicity for the Merchant the tale took on a dimension that Chaucer himself may not have foreseen: a tale of mirth gave way to one of "mordant venom." To Jordan, the tale is "less a unified presentation than a composite of several narrative attitudes and positions, often mutually contradictory." It has, however, a "mechanic" rather than an "organic" unity, its loose composite form carrying, in spite of its inconsistent narrative viewpoint, a firm moral attitude.

social comedy. That sense of mystery or of compassion that elsewhere invests the depiction of old age—not the carpenter of the *Miller's Tale*, but the old caitiff of the *Pardoner's Tale*, even the Reeve
himself—Chaucer here carefully prevents, for the sake of a larger
condemnation of constitutional blindness of heart presenting itself to
us as the considered wisdom of age.

The narrator presents a sixty-year-old knight at the outset as suddenly desiring marriage. He has wasted his youth on a life of following "ay his bodily delyt / On wommen, ther as was his appetyt"; he
has had the world in his time, but now, at his advanced age he at-
taches new value to "that hooly boond / With which that first God
man and womman bond." This paradisical earthly state, he says,
offers him not merely the joys of "esy" and "clene" wedlock but
the possibility of multiplying mankind in the service of God. The
narrator will not say whether this conviction is the result of a sudden
access of religious sentiment or merely the foolishness of old age.

The opening debate of the story, running through line 1398, offers
us the opportunity to weigh some complexities of Chaucer's art: the
old knight sets before us the Theophrastan antifeminism for the sake
of praising the honey-sweetness that is marriage. The earlier debate
of the Wife of Bath and the Clerk gives a substantial background for
weighing these two points of view. As the old knight speaks with
bland self-interest of the necessity for taking a young wife so that he
may produce an heir, he compounds his self-deception by comparing
disordered bachelorhood to the ordered marriage state in a neat but
preposterous antithesis.

His advanced age prevents the reader from being impressed with
his words as anything but ridiculous, or even repulsive. But the voice
we hear is also ironically the voice of the Merchant narrator who just
a moment before uttered his heartfelt prayer for deliverance from the
snare of marriage. Revulsion against his own young and already disillusioned marriage invests even the sweetest praise of marriage with a
note of mordant bitterness, a kind of escape valve by means of which
his bitter self-rue pours out without let upon his surrogate, a hapless
and self-deceived man of experience. It is this voice that we hear ines-
capably. Beyond it however we hear Chaucer's own controlling
voice, recapitulating the terms of the irresoluble argument whose two
points of view human nature instinctively corroborates: the tutored

aspirations of theology and romance in which the actions of life exist for some ultimate idealized good, opposing the less rationalized instincts of the fabliau world in which appetites exist only for gratification. It is Chaucer who manipulates the character of the Merchant to utter the horror of his own marriage and then has the Merchant, a fiction himself, manipulate the character of the old knight until he stands debased and isolated upon the stage, an object of the reader's contempt and derision.[2]

The long opening soliloquy of January (to l. 1398) and his subsequent conversations with Justinus and Placebo are characterized by an almost purely intellectual movement somewhat foreign to the customary tone of the fabliau. The speeches of January and his counsellors tend to focus our attention upon the thought, the convictions of the speakers, their ethical bent. In January the recalcitrant strain of willful *luxuria* assumes the pious disguises that religious thought affords. He wishes, he says, to eschew his life of sin, but only on his own terms: his wife must be young and beautiful, no thirty-year-old taught by experience, who would drive him into adultery. Giving evidence of a thoroughly conventional knowledge of marriage and its uses, he parades before us its "leveful procreacioun" (l. 1448), the avoidance of lechery, the rendering of conjugal debt, the contract of mutual aid and solace. His conventional knowledge, seen in the light of his disregard for seemliness, becomes a prime source of irony. The notion that he can manipulate a young wife like wax (ll. 1429–30), the insistence upon knowledge beyond that of ordinary men (ll. 1443–44), the boast of sexual vigor and the comparison of his potency with that of a blossoming fruit tree and of his vitality with that of the evergreen laurel, all offer that jarring note between what is affirmed and expected and what we actually witness: namely, a sexual appetite artificially excited, a disintegrating physical vigor and an actual failure of sight, a woman whose "wax" resists his plastic stress, and a blatant deception that takes place in his very presence.

The persistent tree metaphor, with its subtle implication of an unresolved tension between fruitfulness and sterility, seems to draw upon that parable of the fig tree which, bearing leaves but no fruit, was blasted by Christ. Once having completed the tale and encountered that other fruit tree that bears such bitter fruit in the climax of the story, we see that the blossomy tree which is January is destined to bear no fruit of its own. His constitutional blindness soon cor-

[2] See Sedgwick, in *UTQ*, XVII, 345.

roborated by physical blindness is of a piece with his sterile hopes of fruitfulness and, like the blasted fig tree, represents the failure to live the life of grace and to bear the fruit of charity.

In the consultation between January and his two brothers (ll. 1478 ff.), the unctuous words of Placebo provide us with a sample of the kind of prudent behavior that blighted the courts of Europe, and which is so roundly condemned by Dante and Chaucer alike. Actually his words do little more than to encourage January in his plan. Those of Justinus (ll. 1521 ff.), suiting his name, plead for careful thought in the matter of marriage, avowing that the union of the young is difficult enough without borrowing the special and peculiar difficulties of a marriage between youth and age. To this January answers testily:

> "... Wyser men than thow,
> As thou hast herd, assenteden right now
> To my purpos...."   (ll. 1569–71)

while Placebo hastens to say, without regard to the point at issue:

> "I seye it is a cursed man," ...
> "That letteth matrimoigne, sikerly."   (ll. 1572–73)

But when January has made his choice of the young girl with whom he will lead his life "in ese and hoolynesse" (l. 1628) and expresses his sudden fatuous fear that the "so greet ese and lust in mariage" will provide him with heaven on earth and so deprive him of that other heaven which must be bought with pain and tribulation, it is Justinus who, hating the folly of his reasoning, casts aside the force of authority for the sake of hard and even bitter experience. His answer (ll. 1655 ff.), wedded securely to the theological demands of the question, yet arises out of that rueful masculine admission of the less than perfect reality in marriage which is so standard a part of domestic comedy. January, he avers, has nothing to worry about; a wife is if anything a purgatory rather than a paradise; she is an instrument of God, a whip, a scourge for bringing the soul to salvation. Less sardonic but perhaps more subtly witty is his statement that no marital joys, temperately savored, can hinder salvation, and his avowal that the truth about marriage has already been told by the Wife of Bath (ll. 1685–87). The Wife belongs to one level of fiction and the agents of this story to another, levels which do not correspond; yet for a moment they run on the same track, so to speak, for the sake of making an admonitory point about marriage and women in general.[3]

Up to this point the tale has been dominated more by talk than by action. Chaucer has not been in a hurry to put to the test the character of January which has been slowly emerging. The process of debasing the principal agent has entailed putting before us the terms of a debate about matrimony, one side of which he has given to so old a man that even with rational and persuasively religious arguments on behalf of marriage, he must perforce appear the fool by his unseemly assumption of the prerogatives of youth. A temporarily ferocious wit in Chaucer heads off any sympathy for this *senex amans*, who cannot, in the ironical context, seem anything but abhorrent.

The wedding which he now describes (ll. 1700 ff.) is a Christian sacrament, as the priestly blessing and the references to Sarah and Rebecca, the "wysdom" and the "trouthe" of marriage, make clear.[4] But he is eclectic and lavish in the embellishments, balancing the Hebrew-Christian with the more pagan and naturalistic associations of Venus and Hymen. The ironical comparison of the marriage of Mercury and Philology (l. 1734) with that of January and May is a piece of rhetorical extravagance, although some comparison may be made of the bachelors January and Mercury, both of whom are seeking wives, and of the knowledgeable (but with a difference) maidens Philology and May. More specific are the comparisons of May and Esther (ll. 1744–45) and of January and Paris (l. 1754), where the associations—beauty with feminine cunning and the instinct for survival, in the first case; youthful vigor with sexual rapacity, in the second—provide us with what the *Tractatus Coislinianus* calls the assimilation towards the better.

Obviously the wedding of January and May is not the marriage of a god with the maiden Knowledge; May is not possessed of those selfless qualities which enabled Esther to preserve the Jewish nation while maintaining the dignity of her marriage to the non-Jew Ahasuerus, and January is surely not capable of those hectic passions and that instinctive power which belong to youth, and of which he makes so lyrical and bawdy a boast:

> ... "Allas! O tendre creature,
> Now wolde God ye myghte wel endure
> Al my corage, it is so sharp and keene!"   (ll. 1757–59)

[3] See F. N. Robinson, *The Works of Geoffrey Chaucer*, 2d ed. (Boston, 1957), p. 715, for a discussion of the difficulties of this passage.
[4] J. S. P. Tatlock, "Chaucer's *Merchant's Tale*," *MP*, XXXIII (1936), 373.

January's specious attitudes dominate the tale; by comparison with them Damian's desires are as unspiritual, unhypocritical, and generally uncomplicated a sexual drive as we shall meet in Chaucer's deceivers. We will not come to know Damian, or May for that matter, as fully developed agents in the tale, nor is it important that we do. Chaucer prevents any sympathetic involvement with them; we have known their types in other contexts. May is a distinct cousin to Alison of the *Miller's Tale*, close kin to the wife of the *Shipman's Tale*, and as natural and unabashed as the daughter in the *Reeve's Tale*. Her squire-lover is a variant of Absalom and of Aurelius, with that same sudden falling in love, wooing, weeping, complaining, letter-writing, and that same determined sexual goal as Troilus. Chaucer debases them as casually as he creates them, May by her privy reading of the letter (l. 1954), Damian by his ignoble hiding behind the bush (l. 2155), and both of them by the preposterous coupling in the pear tree. But they are a necessary invention in the tale, here to provide that inevitable justice which youth metes out to usurping age.

Their impending alliance rouses in the narrator that tone of preachment which, among other elements, has led critics to see the tale as intended for a clerical speaker:

> O perilous fyr, that in the bedstraw bredeth!
> O famulier foo, that his servyce bedeth!
> O servant traytour, false hoomly hewe,
> Lyk to the naddre in bosom sly untrewe,
> God shilde us all from youre aqueyntaunce!
> O Januarie, dronken in plesaunce
> In mariage, se how thy Damyan,
> Thyn owene squier and thy borne man,
> Entendeth for to do thee vileynye.
> God graunte thee thyn hoomly fo t'espye!
> For in this world nys worse pestilence
> Than hoomly foo al day in thy presence.   (ll. 1783-94)

Out of context the passage has the ring of sincere concern, and in general it is a matter to which, like flattery in the court, Chaucer comes back time and again. In context it appears to be, like the *exclamatio* and direct address, a device for moving in theme as well as in style, towards the elevation of more serious modes. Nothing, however, prevents our remembering the uses for the domestic traitor theme in the Miller's, Reeve's, and Shipman's tales. There the generally fresh insistence upon sex as a mode of poetic justice and upon the comic ideal of youth joined to youth in lusty commerce, provides a retaliation upon old age and stupidity.

Chaucer spares us nothing: if we have had the wedding ceremony and the festivities thereafter, we must go further still into the details of the wedding night. The stimulus of Venus is enough for Damian, but not so for January (ll. 1805 ff.). He must have his aphrodisiacs before the horrid prurience of the union with May. A bride "stille as stoon" opposing the coltish "ragerye" of her aged husband, the fertility blessing of the bed by the priest, the justification of lust within marriage to an indifferent wife, the physical details of the cracked voice, the "slakke skyn," the lean neck, are all of them details written with full control of the satiric mood, exploiting the intimate horrors of a marriage in which "tendre youthe hath wedded stoupyng age."

The narrator now moves inexorably down the line of his theme, the slaying of one's self with one's own knife; within four days May is sent by her tenderhearted husband to solace the young ailing squire. And with the letter thrust upon May by Damian, the reader is launched into that extraordinary course of justice—impersonal, tart, extravagantly mordant—which brings about the permanent triumph of presence of mind over abiding and recalcitrant and invincible fatuity. In a clerical commentary the narrator makes a feeble attempt to exonerate May of responsibility; the implication is clear:

>   Were it by destynee or aventure,
> Were it by influence or by nature,
> Or constellacion, that in swich estaat
> The hevene stood, that tyme fortunaat
> Was for to putte a bille of Venus werkes—
> For alle thyng hath tyme, as seyn thise clerkes—
> To any womman, for to gete hire love,
> I kan nat seye; but grete God above,
> That knoweth that noon act is causelees,
> He deme of al, for I wole holde my pees.   (ll. 1967–76)

The sarcastic note is not completely evaporated until pity, that exonerating and divine force, that foundation stone of the courtly code, is adduced as the culprit emotion.

We are now well on the way to the culminating point of the story, and the last props are now moved into place: we are shortly within the walled pleasure garden [5] constructed by January, with its well, its evergreen laurel (which we have met before in similar symbolic context), and its own domesticated gods, Pluto and Proserpine, quarreling for all the world like any man and wife in the social scene. The fructifying deity, Priapus, could not describe the beauty of this garden which January has created so that in private he may perform such acts of love as are "nat doon abedde" (l. 2051). The mutability theme—"joye may nat alwey dure" (l. 2055)—takes on its most characteristic appearance in the rhetorical flourish:

> O sodeyn hap! o thou Fortune unstable!
> Lyk to the scorpion so deceyvable,
> That flaterest with thyn heed whan thou wolt stynge;
> Thy tayl is deeth, thurgh thyn envenymynge.   (ll. 2057–60)

January is stricken blind amidst all his prosperity, a capping detail which corroborates that inner blindness which has existed in him from the outset of the tale. In Chaucer's own pithy summary:

> For as good is blynd deceyved be
> As to be deceyved whan a man may se.   (ll. 2109–10)

The lyric (ll. 2138 ff.) whereby January invites May into the garden, like the previous allusion to the turtledove in line 2080, carries the memory back through the tradition of the *Song of Songs* with its literal emphasis on sexuality in the love relationship. It calls to mind a royal lover and a maiden of low estate, raised to glorious communion, as types of ideal conjugal love. Its allegorical suggestions recall to the mind such mysteries as the union of Jehovah with Israel, or the union of Christ with his Church. Wedded sexual love, offered as the most intimate clue in our human experience to the relationship of Christ-Solomon, the bridegroom, to the Church-Shulamite, may be called forth into the imagination for ironical comparison with the relationship of January to May as a gauge of the narrator's mordancy.

[5] Cf. D. W. Robertson, Jr., "The Doctrine of Charity in Mediaeval Literary Gardens: A Topical Approach Through Symbolism and Allegory," *Speculum*, XXVI (1951), 24–49. Although not universally accepted, this study has proved to be seminal; it is safe to say that a whole segment of Chaucerian studies has been profoundly influenced by it. For a possible source other than the Song of Songs, see the suggestion of Alfred L. Kellogg, "Susannah and the *Merchant's Tale*," *Speculum*, XXXV (1960), 275–79. The author sees Daniel 13:20 and the Song of Songs as contributing to a single point: the moral distortion of January's lust against the backdrop of "the highest love the Middle Ages could conceive." For a further statement of the moral range of this tale, see Paul A. Olson, "Chaucer's Merchant and January's 'Hevene in erthe heere,'" *ELH*, XXVIII (1961), 203–14.

The chaste fidelity of the turtledove, the expression "my white spouse" (l. 2144), the utterance "No spot of thee ne knew I al my lyf" (l. 2146) recall the view of Ambrose and Jerome that the bride of the *Song of Songs* suggests the virginity of Mary, another incongruous analogy arising out of the comparison of vastly opposite values.

January's song gives way to sententious piety and to the plea of a blind man for his wife's fidelity, with a moment of something like knowledge:

> "... whan that I considere youre beautee,
> And therwithal the unlikly elde of me,
> I may nat, certes, though I sholde dye,
> Forbere to been out of youre compaignye
> For verray love; ..."   (ll. 2179–83)

In this pathetic atmosphere of religious connotation and elderly fear we are submitted to the false-pathetic, play-acted defense by May, shocking for being brazenly couched in the terms of the soul's salvation. From here to the end, the story with its sexual and social success is hers and Proserpine's—and that of women in the fabliau tradition. Her triumph here consists of defending herself tearfully: "I am a gentlewoman and no wench," she cries while directing her lover into the fruit-laden tree. As readers, we have known from the comparison of the plight of May and Damian to that of Pyramus and Thisbe (ll. 2125 ff.) that love would find a way: their adulterous coupling in a heavily laden pear tree, aided unwittingly by January himself, however ridiculous and even preposterous, is not only richly symbolic and suggestive (as every student knows), but poetically inevitable. In the topsy-turvy world of the fabliau, casual fornication and adultery become the triumphing ideal, the instrument of poetic justice. We are forced by the ugliness of January's sensuality and by his abiding blindness to believe for the moment that the ideal of such triumphant adulterous disorder is better in the context of this story than the sanctioned lechery that passes as the sacrament of marriage.

The story has, still, a point to be made through the device of the *dei ex machina*. To Pluto's unchivalrous condemnation of women and his imperious decision to restore January's sight at a crucial moment, Proserpine counters indignantly with a vigorous defense and that unassailable, irretrievable gift to women *in perpetuo*, the power of self-exoneration:

"... alle wommen after ...
... though they be in any gilt ytake,
With face boold they shulle hemself excuse
And bere hem doun that wolden hem accuse.
For lak of answere noon of hem shal dyen.
Al hadde man seyn a thyng with bothe his yen,
Yit shul we wommen visage it hardily,
And wepe, and swere, and chyde subtilly,
So that ye men shul been as lewed as gees."   (ll. 2267–75)

As exemplars themselves of a difficult marital contract, in a distinc-
tively non-Christian (although each quotes Scripture to his own purpose), unmoral way, they are here to justify the unjustifiable, and by
so doing, to bring about what Tatlock calls "the deep-down, more
than merely worldly meaning of the whole poem ... the inexorable
chastisement for stubborn shutting of the eyes to facts." [6]

In the bitter measure for measure of the *Merchant's Tale*, the tree
of knowledge has yielded tart fruit. As for the garden in which it
grew and the better fruit which it produces, we must look to the
Franklin's Tale.

I have suggested a series of analogies between the *Merchant's Tale*
and other fabliaux: in many ways it is the richest of these, full of
overtones drawn from Chaucer's entire comic thematic range. Less
oblique in statement than, say, the *Miller's Tale*, more open in statement than the *Shipman's Tale* (to which it is most closely allied by
the heroine's successful exoneration), it goes beyond them, engulfing
the world of romance, twisting its values downward into travesty,
and bringing into existence a universal truth in the upside-down
world of bitter comedy.

Like the *Nun's Priest's Tale*—and up to a point the Wife of Bath's
performance—it is a tour de force parading before us for ironical
purposes most of Chaucer's romantic paraphernalia: destiny and fortune, pity and the gentle heart, the uses of marriage, the attainment of
knowledge through suffering, the foe in the bosom, evil in the
Garden, and here an unusual array of classical, Biblical, and historical
exempla.

Theologically, like the Wife's *Prologue*, the *Merchant's Tale* is

[6] *MP*, XXXIII, 374. For the significant role of the deities in the tale, see Mortimer
J. Donovan, "The Image of Pluto and Proserpine in the *Merchant's Tale*," *PQ*,
XXXVI (1957), 49–60.

conservative, based ultimately upon the utterances of St. Paul on marriage, a tradition which reaches back into the Old Testament and
forward into the writings of the Church Fathers. Placed side by side
with the comic tradition of antifeminism, these views take on a special
cast of irony by being placed side by side with each other. For Alice
no less than January, the recitation of the uses of marriage according
to doctrine does not assure insight into those uses. The wish-
fulfillment air of the *Wife of Bath's Tale*—perhaps many will not
agree—and the relationship of the hag in the discourse to the bliss-
with-obedience that she finally offers, point to a marriage built upon
the sacrifice of old arrogance and the acceptance of another in the
terms of an improved morality. In the light of this not quite realized
direction of the heart, the Wife's innate recalcitrance makes her an all
the more poignant figure.

The *Merchant's Tale*, by the far greater degree of its ironical vision
of marriage, indicates an impossibly self-deceived agent whose intellect enables him to argue from desire, translating personal wishes into
the theologically sanctioned acts; and whose blindness of heart and
mind amount to a constitutional blindness objectified by a loss of real
sight. The theme of sterility and barrenness—generally absent from
the Wife's performance—amidst the burgeoning of nature, the persistent analogy with pairs of lovers from ancient and modern sources,
the daring coda in which the restoration of human sight fails to
change the existing situation, after a bawdily graphic and awe-inspir-
ing feat in the pear tree, indicate a range of Chaucerian comment
upon the human scene for which nothing else in his writing has prepared us. We laugh at our debased hero who is incapable of vision,
but our laughter is rueful and our pity is grudging.

Lest we be trapped too easily by the paucity of our knowledge
about the somewhat inscrutable Merchant into the view that something in Chaucer's own life has specifically moved him to bitter disillusionment, we can Socratically aver that the man who can write
romance can also write satire. Indeed one is the inversion of the values
of the other; the story of marriage and its bitter fruit in adultery, its
assertion of a God-given superiority of women over men in the art of
self-vindication, adds up to an unpalatable truth at the furthest, most
sardonic range of comic art.

THE PARDONER'S TALE

After the Physician has told his tale, the Host cannot contain
himself. With a great oath on the crucifixion of Christ (we already
look forward to the performance of the Pardoner), he expresses in a
clerical platitude his heartfelt distress over the fate of Virginia: "...
yiftes of Fortune and of Nature / Been cause of deeth to many a
creature. / Hire beautee was hire deth, ... / Of bothe yiftes that I
speke of now / Men han ful ofte moore for harm than prow" (ll.
295–300). With considerable irony and after some fumbling with a
medical vocabulary, he opines that the Physician is much like a
churchman (l. 310). There is good reason for him to make such a
judgment: the *Physician's Tale* dealt knowledgeably with the endow-
ments showered upon a young maiden by God's vicar, Nature. It
further vigorously urged parents to guard their children from the
corruption of the world, and closed upon a moral appendage dealing
with the just deserts of sin. Platitudes all, to be sure, but learned and
highly moral sentiments such as one might expect from a prelate.

More important, however, is the heart of the story itself: evil dis-
countenanced by bold, self-sacrificing action, implying not so much

the futility of struggle against evil, but rather the poignant necessity of drastic action in the face of it.

It is, we note, a tale drawn from ancient history, and therefore without a clearly Christian orientation. The non-Christian context, the historical and pagan justification of a father's action, is not what one would expect of the clerical mind, but rather what one would expect of the mind of a tutored layman like the Physician, for whom, if we interpret his character correctly, the line between moral law and expedience is not clearly drawn.[1]

However early the *Physician's Tale* and however late the *Pardoner's Tale*,[2] the link that joins them clearly is in Chaucer's best comic vein and accomplishes its end in a more than casual way. The words of the Parson throw light upon an interesting connection between the performances of these two pilgrims:

The varieties of sin that arise out of pride, truly, when they arise from malice imagined, advised, and aforethought, or from habit, are mortal sins, and of this there is no doubt.... Now might men ask, whence pride arises and takes its being, and I say: sometimes it springs out of the good things of nature, and sometimes from the benefits of Fortune, and sometimes from the good of grace itself. Certainly the good things of nature consist of either physical well-being or riches of the soul. Certainly physical well-being consists of the weal of the body, as strength, activity, beauty, good blood, and generous candour. The benefits of nature to the soul are good wit, keen understanding, clever talent, natural virtue, and good memory. The benefits of Fortune are riches, high rank, and the people's praise. The good of grace consists of knowledge, power to suffer spiritual travail, benignity, virtuous contemplation, ability to withstand temptation, and similar things.... As for the benefits of nature, God knows that sometimes we receive them naturally as much to our detriment as to our profit.... Now truly, for a man to pride himself on the gifts of grace is also an extravagant folly; for these same gifts of grace that should have turned him to goodness and to alleviation, turn him to venom and confusion, as says Saint Gregory. Certainly, also, whoso prides himself on the benefits of Fortune, he is a full great fool.[3]

[1] Cf. Melvin Seiden, "Two Notes on Webster's *Appius and Virginia*," PQ, XXXV (1936), 408–17.

[2] This tale is psychologically and structurally one of the great performances of the Canterbury pilgrimage, with its own clear beginning, middle, and end. It represents, furthermore, a conflation of the attributes of a variety of literary types: confession, sermon, *exemplum*, moral tale. There is a strong flavor of the didactic in the tale. Yet the didacticism must be seen in the light of the speaker's intention, an intention which undermines its ostensible morality. And strict scrutiny must be given to the various devices by which rhetoric is perverted to private ends. The didactic elements may thus be seen as subordinate to a larger statement about the demonic sublime which, for Dante and Blake, is the heart of the infernal experience.

[3] The *Parson's Tale*, ll. 448 ff., trans. J. U. Nicolson, *Geoffrey Chaucer: Canterbury Tales* (New York, 1934), pp. 570–72.

The Host, reflecting a sentiment of the Parson, has provided us with the fulcrum on which the two tales are balanced: that is, the "detriment" or "profit" arising out of the possession of the gifts of nature, of fortune, and in the Pardoner, of grace. If we must limit ourselves as Chaucer does to the gifts of nature and of fortune for the *Physician's Tale* because of its non-Christian context, the entirely Christian context of the Pardoner's performance demands the inclusion of the gifts of grace. And the demonstration of evil resulting from the gifts of fortune and nature ("to deere boughte she beautee") now subtly shifts its emphasis principally to an abuse of the gifts of grace, with the consequent death of the soul. It is a long way from the recitation of the virtues of the beauteous Virginia to the material glitter of gold coins, but both of them lead to death, death received in humility and resignation, and death sought out in importunate pride.

The Pardoner's total performance, beginning with the Host's appeal to our "beel amy" for a tale and ending with their exchange of a kiss of peace, provides a structural model by which to assess the success of the other performances.[4] It provides, furthermore, the ultimate example of Chaucer's subtle handling of human psychology. In both form and function, only the roles of the Wife of Bath and the Canon's Yeoman can be confidently compared with the Pardoner's for both consummate realism and artistic control.

In the *Pardoner's Prologue* we witness Chaucer's most subtle comment upon evil emanating from the heart and mind of a man committed not only by nature but by instinct and intellectual conviction to opposing the good; or to put it another way, in Augustinian terms, to loving the goods of this world without reference to their creator. Deprived by nature, as the *General Prologue* makes fairly explicit, of parts natural to biological man, the Pardoner would seem to be, on the physical plane, a demonstration of the theory of evil as the absence or deprivation of a natural part. Chaucer is rarely satisfied, as we have seen over and over again, to depict merely the physical man

[4] Bertrand H. Bronson attributes most of the difficulties of interpretation to what he calls the "conditions of composition." Chaucer wrote the tale first, then the headlink "—not the prologue—" and the conclusion. Then, wishing to lengthen the block of narrative to the "customary hour to hour-and-a-quarter reading time" necessary for oral delivery, he wrote the Pardoner's confession, and "at a stroke created a series of problems which have strained the best abilities of several generations of critics suckled on psychological realism."—*In Search of Chaucer* (University of Toronto Press, 1960), p. 87.

without implying a relationship between the outward and the inward man. Indeed that physical evil which is so blandly insinuated both in the character of the Pardoner and in his comradeship with the sensually swollen Summoner now has its more ample assertion in the actual confession, under the influence of wine, of his interior defection of which the exterior physical flaw is but a corroboration: the loss of that vision which Dante calls the good of the intellect, a vision which sees God as the goal of man's endeavor, and the goods of this world as but fragmentary and sometimes maiming parts of a temporal order.

This perversion of the vision from the things of God to the goods of this world is amply illustrated from the Pardoner's opening remarks. In approximately a hundred and thirty lines of confession he parades before us the brazen abuses of his office. To be sure he has his letters of authority to prevent anyone from disturbing him in "Cristes hooly werk." He has his Latin tag "Radix malorum est Cupiditas" to overwhelm the ignorant; he has his false relics (ll. 347 ff.) by which to reach the credulous, the superstitious; he offers absolution (ll. 377 ff.) only to those who are without grave sin, appealing in this way to the innate vanity of human nature as well as to the proud and self-advancing arrogance of stupidity.

If the Pardoner is drunk, his tricks are yet so firmly entrenched, so practiced, that he does not fumble with them.[5] They have been sufficient to get him his hundred marks a year (ll. 389 ff.). In self-centered joy, he describes all the business he is so adept at: leaning out over the congregation, gesticulating with his hands while the words roll out over his tongue, nodding and wagging his head like the dove sitting on the barn.

It may be that some good comes out of his preaching, but the good is not his primary concern. He has been able to spit out his venom under the guise of sanctity; the malice of his nature he asserts coldly: his intention is not the salvation of souls but only personal profit. Though his own sin is avarice, his intention is to make others aware of their own greed and to bring them to a repentance profitable to himself.

As for his narrative method, he knows that the "lewed peple" love

---

[5] Of some interest here is the view of the Rev. Paul E. Beichner, "Chaucer's Pardoner as Entertainer," *MS*, XXV (1963), 160–72, that the Pardoner is a professional fund-raiser demonstrating his techniques.

stories that can be remembered and repeated. And in a burst of hunger for physical possessions that opposes the poverty of the Apostles, he reveals his inmost soul:

> "I wol noon of the apostles countrefete;
> I wol have moneie, wolle, chese, and whete,
> Al were it yeven of the povereste page,
> Or of the povereste wydwe in a village,
> Al sholde hir children sterve for famyne."   (ll. 447–51)

The deification of the self and the perverted will, as Kellogg has shown,[6] have nowhere so convincing a statement as in the seven-fold reiteration of "I wol" (ll. 439–53), the self-centered outcry of the "ful vicious man."

The Pardoner's demonic bias reveals itself from the very outset of his tale in the recitation of youth's heated vices, and more specifically in an extended metaphor: The taverns which the young dissolutes frequent are equated with "that develes temple" in which sacrifice is offered up to the demon amidst the teeming press of "verray develes officeres": shapely acrobats, singers, hawkers of fruit and cakes, panders. Through the lurid atmosphere which his preachment evokes we discern the sins he will soon describe in detail: the gambling, swearing, and "lecherye, / That is annexed unto glotonye."

The order of items in this somewhat hectic beginning is casual, from gambling to gluttony, to swearing, to lechery, and back to gluttony, and is explicable as falling from the lips of an indignantly aroused preacher who rails at the pervasiveness of evil in the world he scourges, working by general association rather than by a planned logic.

And yet, as he warms to his task he becomes logical enough, taking the great sins in turn, beginning with gluttony and drunkenness, proceeding to gambling, and finally to false oaths and swearing by the body and blood of Christ. Each sin is decked out with *exempla* and authorities and embellished with lively images. The passages on gambling and swearing, for example, are brought skillfully into confluence in a little vignette of great liveliness and realism.

> "By Goddes precious herte," and "By his nayles,"
> And "By the blood of Crist that is in Hayles,

[6] Alfred L. Kellogg, "An Augustinian Interpretation of Chaucer's Pardoner," *Speculum*, XXVI (1951), 465–81.

Sevene is my chaunce, and thyn is cynk and treye!"
"By Goddes armes, if thou falsly pleye,
This daggere shal thurghout thyn herte go!"—
This fruyt cometh of the bicched bones two,
Forsweryng, ire, falsnesse, homycide.   (ll. 651–57)

The whole process of dealing so energetically with the sins is suggestive of something deep in the Pardoner's own character. We are not so carried away by the associative vigor of his harangue as to fail to notice that the theme of avarice has been temporarily subordinated to a railing against a lust for a sinful life very like his own. Cupidity is indeed the root of *all* vices, and the sermon which describes them holds us not so much by logical argument as by the fascination with sin which the Pardoner everywhere evinces.

When he resumes the narrative of the young rioters as the principal *exemplum* in his sermon, he rectifies an oversight by making the number of the young dissolutes consonant with the three major divisions of sin. Hereafter, the rioters will embody them all as various manifestations of their proud indifference to the good. In their tale we now note that paradox of art which allows Chaucer to substitute his own story-telling skill for that of his presumably befuddled narrator. Out of the mouth of his self-centered and avaricious Pardoner now comes a tale which ironically focuses on the self-interest and avarice of others.

It is a narrative fraught with the mystery of spiritual as well as physical death, with the mystery of man's innate evil and of God's inexorable justice. In this light it is surely too narrow an interpretation to see *cupiditas* as anything less than that willful love of material goods without reference to God, which Augustine has so aptly defined. In this light, too, we may see the extent to which the distorted love of limited goods spreads its taint from the impoverished soul of the individual even to the community of which he is a sworn member.[7]

There is here a marked change of pace and tone. The random vigor of the *exempla* illustrating the various sins in the opening sections of the tale and the I-you relationship of the preacher and congregation

[7] "What lust [*cupiditas*], when unsubdued, does towards corrupting one's own soul and body, is called vice [*flagitium*]; but what it does to injure another is called crime [*facinus*].... But the vices come first, for when these have exhausted the soul, and reduced it to a kind of poverty, it easily slides into crimes, in order to remove hindrances to, or to find assistance in, its vices."—St. Augustine, *De Doctrina Christiana*, III, 10–16.

give way to the sparer, more unified lineaments of narrative art at its peak of perfection. The problem of the debased will, the mystery of divine control, the permissive view of evil, the dreadful tree of knowledge and of limited life, the terrifying but necessary triple death—all are imputed to the Pardoner as we might imagine him at his keenest edge. Our irresistible impression, however, is that Chaucer himself has temporarily taken over.

The gay day-and-night abandon of the devil's temple has disappeared. Death itself encroaches upon the lives of the young rakes as they learn of the burial of a crony much like themselves. The tone of admonition with which the Pardoner threatened spiritual death is now muted to the simple yet mysterious warning put in the mouth of a serving boy:

> "Me thynketh that it were necessarie
> For to be war of swich an adversarie.
> Beth redy for to meete hym everemoore;
> Thus taughte me my dame; I sey namoore."   (ll. 681–84)

The rioters' response is one of profane and arrogant pride: pledged to a community of evil action they set out to slay Death himself. The allegorical temper enables us to see Chaucer's ironical purpose. Physical death cannot be avoided; spiritual death can, but manifestly not by the perverse commitment to evil. The degree of their commitment Chaucer spells out more subtly in the encounter with the Old Man.

By contrast with their surly rudeness the Old Man is all courtesy and resignation. From his lips fall persistently prayerful greetings and salutations as well as a quotation from Holy Writ; these reflect conventional aspects of Christian patience with which Chaucer's audience could empathize by contrast with the proud recalcitrance of the young men. Such a comparison between Age waiting painfully yet meekly upon the will of God and Youth waiting impatiently upon the accident of Fortune has a purely psychological validity for us. We understand the two ages of life. Theologically, however, a Boethian commonplace throws light upon the moral conditions of all: The more a man participates in material goods, the less he partakes of God. In Chaucer's tale material goods become a divisive force; and the gold soon disrupts the brotherhood to which the three rioters had pledged themselves. The gold, which was to them "so fair a grace" (l. 783), becomes the inspiration for secret and private devices. God's

law governs to the end, even to allowing the demon himself to work
upon the youngest of the rioters:

> For-why the feend foond hym in swich lyvynge
> That he hadde leve him to sorwe brynge.
> For this was outrely his fulle entente,
> To sleen hem bothe, and nevere to repente.   (ll. 847–50)

Shortly the poison is procured, for use upon rats, polecats, vermin
—a sardonic suggestion. And with the swift conclusion of the
murders ("What nedeth it to sermone of it moore?" l. 879), we are
back in the more flamboyant style and tone of the original sermon, of
which the tale has been but the chief embellishment. What we recognize again is the false piety, the calculated sincerity, the deliberate
histrionic passion, recapitulating all the sins:

> O cursed synne of all cursednesse!
> O traytours homycide, O wikkednesse!
> O glotonye, luxurie, and hasardrye!
> Thou blasphemour of Crist with vileynye
> And othes grete, of usage and of pride!
> Allas! mankynde, how may it bitide
> That to thy creatour, which that the wroghte,
> And with his precious herte-blood thee boghte,
> Thou art so fals and so unkynde, allas?   (ll. 895–903)

It is a summing up, now wedded to his formerly iterated and reiterated purpose, that of getting money: "I will absolve all who make
offerings. Heaven is yours; I will take anything you have to offer:
nobles, silver, brooches, spoons, rings, wool."

He has exhausted his confession, but he has still to make us see the
full extent of his villainy. This he does by making clear, once and for
all, the ultimate truth:

> And Jhesu Crist, that is oure soules leche,
> So graunte yow his pardoun to receyve,
> For that is best; I wol yow nat deceyve.   (ll. 916–18)

It does not seem to come from him as a paroxysmal burst of sincerity, not does it seem agonized, as a very great scholar, Kittredge,
has interpreted the scene. We recognize it as a necessary part of the
experience and performance: no one can doubt that the Pardoner has
always known the truth. He has not unawares given us a glimpse into
a spot of decency in an otherwise blemished nature. He is, furthermore, speaking to a group that includes clerics whose rights he has

usurped; they too know the truth. But the Pardoner, in his supreme contempt for the good, to make his confession complete must state clearly the truth against which he is embattled so that we may see the extent of his commitment to personal profit. The point of his own story unfortunately is lost on him.[8]

The *Pardoner's Tale* invites comparison with the *Friar's Tale* as another example of a preacher's anecdote successfully employed; like the *Friar's Tale* it deals with the unwitting encounter with spiritual death through the pursuit of material gain, a theme which grows beautifully out of the Pardoner's own commitment to subverting the good. Although its irony is more somber than that of the *Friar's Tale*, it affords us the pleasure of witnessing a punishment gratifyingly commensurate with the wickedness of the agents.

The story of the three rioters is praiseworthy for its economy, its atmosphere of a mingled excitement and quiet foreboding, its swift characterization. The Old Man, representative of old age as a time of somewhat bitter resignation, is used as an instrument which tests the young impartially. Since the young men are clearly devil's disciples from the very outset, they are destined for a sinister end. The community of evil in which they are united by pledge dissolves in an instant under the pressure of self-interest.

A mystery pervades the tale: Does an implacable Providence bring about a wrathful catastrophe, or is the fate of the rioters the inevitable result of their characters? The movement towards death is so steadily maintained that one wonders how much is divinely ordained, how much humanly determined. The lurking mystery leaves a residue in the mind; perhaps it is this power to perplex the highest imagination which is the tale's special virtue. As spoken by a vicious man, the sublime awe which it inspires is its supreme irony.

It is to Chaucer's everlasting credit that he has given us by one device or another the whole range of the moral experience from unswerving dedication to divine law to the shifting material values of a recalcitrant humanity. But because for Chaucer the experience of men is in its theological aspect comic, the last act even of the Pardoner's performance is to have its happy ending.

[8] For the allegorical bearings of the tale, see Robert P. Miller, "Chaucer's Pardoner, the Scriptural Eunuch and *The Pardoner's Tale*," *Speculum*, XXX (1955), 180–99.

The Host, as we have seen over and over again, is a barometer of sensibilities and a reflector of the general opinion. That this heartiest, most robustly masculine man should be singled out by this "beel amy," and that he should be named by a confessedly wicked man as one most enveloped in sin brings forth an appropriately low-comic outburst: a gross, cruel, and intimately revealing comment.

> "Lat be," quod he, "it shal nat be, so theech!
> Thou woldest make me kisse thyn olde breech,
> And swere it were a relyk of a seint,
> Though it were with thy fundement depeint!
> But, by the croys which that Seint Eleyne fond,
> I wolde I hadde thy coillons in myn hond
> In stide of relikes or of seintuarie.
> Lat kutte hem of, I wol thee helpe hem carie;
> They shul be shryned in an hogges toord!"   (ll. 947–55)

Its aptness defies comment. Very shortly the Knight interrupts the general laughter; the warrior becomes a man of peace, the Host and Pardoner dissolve their quarrel with the kiss of peace, and order is restored.

This little epilogue to a play asks for explanation, and it does not seem like straining the point to expand a little upon the Host's function here of destroying the finishing touches of the Pardoner's plan. In essence, by calling attention to a physical defect, he has made all too clear the Pardoner's psychological and spiritual sterility. But the pilgrimage is life in small, the human community in the process of movement and becoming. To have come to know the Pardoner for what he is is salutary, as it is salutary to recognize a vile disease. The cure lies at the end of the pilgrimage. But in the meantime the kiss restores him to the community from which his villainy and anger have isolated him; and its bespeaks a special kind of charity in Chaucer that the social harmony implied by the kiss of peace should admit an occasional discordant note.

THE CANON'S YEOMAN'S TALE

Mare tingerem si mercurius esset.

ATTRIBUTED TO RAYMUND LULL

Ora, lege, labora et invenies.

THE ALCHEMIST'S MOTTO

*I believe that those err who expend their energies
on this art, standing with long and continuous
vigil always ardent in their desire and in the conduct of their operations, more inflamed than the
very coals in their furnaces in the effort to see
whether they can bring the adamantine hardness
of such fruit to ripeness. God's aid would be
needed to do this and those who knew how to
do such things would be called not men but gods,
for they would extinguish the insatiable thirst of
avarice in this world and in the extraordinary
excellence of their knowledge would by far out-
strip the power of Nature.*

VANNUCCIO BIRINGUCCIO,
The Pirotechnia [1]

While the terms of alchemy have an interest for us from our
vantage point of a developed science of chemistry, for Chaucer the
alchemical data are employed for other ends than to test their intrinsic
value. What he knows of the intellectual adventures of his time he
converts to the uses of poetry, in this case a lengthy comment upon
the fondest delusion of the human heart, the hope of converting base
metals into gold. The instrument of commentary is the character of
the Canon's Yeoman; the method employed is that of the confession,
with its inadvertent revelation of the ethos of the speaker.[2]

[1] Trans. Cyril Stanley Smith and Martha Teach Gnudi (American Institute of
Mining and Metallurgical Engineers, 1942), p. 37.

[2] There are general discussions of the tale in Raymond Preston, *Chaucer* (London
and New York, 1952), pp. 282–85; D. S. Brewer, *Chaucer* (London, 1953), pp.

Leaden-hued, disheveled, impoverished, the Yeoman is knowledge-able about the ability of alchemy to separate the greedy from their money. Yet he is himself unable to withstand the fever for gain and the will-o'-the-wisp promise of power. His bitterness against the master he has served, his excited recitation of dismal failures, and the tale he eventually tells of the charlatan duping the stupid priest become the means by which Chaucer depicts the very epitome of disillusion-ment. The Yeoman, after seven years of addiction to the lust for gold, now vents his ire upon the whole science which has enslaved him. By comparison with his pessimism, his master the Canon, however doomed to failure in his own fanatical commitment, provides a very type of optimistic scientific zeal.

We must be wary of attributing to Chaucer himself the attitudes towards alchemy expressed by the disillusioned Yeoman. The unfail-ing optimism of the Canon in the chancy world of experiment tends, within the tale, to arouse in us a moderated yet sympathetic interest and as such provides a balance to the intellectual jaundice of the Yeoman. Both the optimism of the Canon and the pessimism of the Yeoman, we remember, are Chaucerian. We may, with Lounsbury,[3] share the impression that Chaucer had a "far sounder perception than [his contemporaries] of the nature of what was true and false in the evidence upon which scientific conclusions are based," and even that "his knowledge, so far as it went, stood on surer and firmer ground than theirs," but we are closer to Chaucer's intention in the *Canon's Yeoman's Tale* in seeing the relation of the scientific matter to the mind and heart of the Yeoman in much the same way that we see the relation of theological and social views of marriage to the heart and mind of the Wife of Bath. The confession of the servant who, now permanently disillusioned, looks with his sickly eye upon all experi-

173–76; John Speirs, *Chaucer the Maker* (London, 1951), pp. 194–99; and a more extensive and highly provocative interpretation in Muscatine, *Chaucer and the French Tradition*, pp. 213–21. Paull Baum has some acute observations to make in "The Canon's Yeoman's Tale," *MLN*, XL (1925), 152–54. More recently there has been a renewed interest in the major problems of interpretation: Judith Scherer Herz, "The Canon's Yeoman's Prologue and Tale," *MP*, LVIII (1961), 231–37; R. G. Baldwin, "The Yeoman's Canons: A Conjecture," *JEGP*, LXI (1962), 232–43; Joseph E. Gren-nen, "The Canon's Yeoman and the Cosmic Furnace: Language and Meaning in the Canon's Yeoman's Tale," *Criticism*, IV (1962), 225–40, and Bruce A. Rosenberg, "Swindling Alchemist, Antichrist," *CRAS*, VI (1962), 566–80.

[3] T. R. Lounsbury, *Studies in Chaucer: His Life and Writings* (New York, 1892), II, 389.

menters, quite naturally becomes the prelude to the confidence game; the attitude towards alchemy attributed to the Yeoman is to be seen as a necessary ingredient of his debased character, which quite naturally takes its own kind of joy in the account of the swindling of a greedy priest.

This is not to deny that a judgment, perhaps even a condemnation, is in the process of coming into existence before our eyes. But it is a judgment made within the purview of comedy and irony, one that comes into existence by the individual stages of the Yeoman's performance.

First we witness the interruption of the pilgrims by the Canon and his servant, in which the animosity of servant to master grows before our eyes to the point where, in order to preserve some sense of respect, the Canon flees from the pilgrimage "for verray sorwe and shame" (l. 702). Here in small is prognosticated much that the subsequent confession amplifies: the hint of madness, the misuse of the clerical intellect ((ll. 648–49), the relation between secretly practiced science and physical disease (ll. 663–72), the alternation of hope and inevitable failure (ll. 678–79), the suggestion of guilt (ll. 684–89), and the first hint of an affinity with the community of Hell (l. 705). This preliminary engagement makes way for the confession proper, in which the Yeoman reveals his intelligence and ethos (*Prima Pars*). This in turn, gives place to the extension of his disillusioned cynicism into the tale of *Secunda Pars*, to which Chaucer adds a final word, forcing us to look at the subject both practically and morally. The structure, it may be noted, bears comparison with that of the performances by the Pardoner and the Wife.

The judgment that is coming into existence becomes clearer if we admit the pressure from the metaphor of a pilgrimage into which people willingly enter, and from which others wilfully depart. The interruption of the already established pilgrimage by the Canon and his Yeoman is a piece of excitement for which we have not been prepared, but which, once witnessed and accepted, provides both appreciation for Chaucerian invention and joy at the impression of a steadily more inclusive community growing before our eyes. The failure of the Canon to remain in pilgrimage, for whatever reason, implies a truly terrible judgment. Couched in no moral terms, Chaucer lets it happen before our eyes without express concern for its significance. Apostasy from his order is terrible enough; to extend by comic action his apostasy to self-ostracism from the community on pilgrimage is a judgment of a more fearful order.[4]

The terms of such a judgment can be more fully spelled out by reference to Dante, prior to Chaucer, and to Erasmus[5] and Ben Jonson,[6] after his time. Comparison with Dante's inclusion of alchemists as one instance of fraud within the social body is especially instructive. Dante's economic attitudes toward property, toward money, metals, toward natural resources in general are a significant part of his total moral view; in them proper respect for the right uses of the substance of life arises out of respect for the community of men involved in its use. Any selfish exploitation of the means by which the social group acts and prospers, as well as any misuse of the institutions by which it carries out its affairs are versions of "adultery" or violations upon the ways of life which God himself has sanctioned. Nature, too, being a bridge between God's intellect and man's mind and the source of much of man's economic well-being, has of course its legitimate uses for the common good. For Dante the itching alchemists tamper selfishly with the "things" by which society prospers; their loathsome disease is the external sign of the illness at the heart of the society they corrupt.

Dante's allegorical purposes encompass over and over again the Scriptural view: we are members of one another; and the depiction of a corrupt, demonic community at variance with itself in quarrels, recriminations, betrayals, and fruitless competitions steadily implies the city as the fulfillment of God's plan for his creatures. Within these purposes, and within the steady availability of a moral structure which is minutely defined by stages, the sinners of the *Inferno* function as exemplars of particular defections from reason and law. Overt moral statement of this sort is not to be found in Chaucer's comic fictions; yet, even with the very real differences of intention, Chaucer, as well as Dante, by means of a dramatically revealing confession, implies a judgment: the suggestions of a diseased passion manifesting itself in physical form, the diversion of the intelligence from true

---

[4] Cf. Muscatine, *Chaucer and the French Tradition*, p. 221; and Marie P. Hamilton, "The Clerical Status of Chaucer's Alchemist," *Speculum*, XVI (1941), 103–8.

[5] *Ten Colloquies*, trans. Craig R. Thompson (New York, 1957).

[6] *The Alchemist*, ed. Charles M. Hathaway, Jr., Yale Studies in English, No. 17 (New York, 1903); the introduction draws together much of the tradition of alchemy.

vocations to alchemical arts, the frustration of any final goals, the analogies with demonic life—all indicate a convergence of comic and satiric energies upon meaning revealed obliquely through dramatic utterance.

In the *Canon's Yeoman's Tale* character in the grip of a destroying passion is created directly before our eyes. Our interest is cleverly aroused first by the excitement of an unexpected intrusion into the pilgrimage, then sustained by the Yeoman's protestations of his master's special abilities. And as in other tales in the realistic vein, Chaucer's skill in the placement of meaningful detail, in the planting, so to speak, of ideas that cast their shadow forward over the whole work, is readily apparent: the comment, for example, upon the uses of the intellect and an implied distinction between two kinds of clerkish intelligence. That of the Canon has gone astray; to it stands opposed that of the lowly Clerk of Oxford, who, satisfied to be without gold in coffer, is devoted to knowledge, to study *and* to moral virtue. The one is indifferent to money except as a means of purchasing books; the other is ever anxious for coin to pour into endless experiment. They present to us two aspects of poverty, the one placidly accepted, the other anxiously borne.

The Yeoman says of his master,

> "He is to wys, in feith, as I bileeve.
> That that is overdoon, it wol nat preeve
> Aright, as clerkes seyn; it is a vice.
> Wherfore in that I holde hym lewed and nyce.
> For whan a man hath over-greet a wit,
> Ful oft hym happeth to mysusen it.
> So dooth my lord, and that me greveth soore." (ll. 644-50)

As he tells of their wretched dwellings among robbers and thieves (ll. 657 ff.) and explains his discolored face as the result of his fruitless and money-exhausting labors (ll. 673 ff.), there is in the pejorative associations a shift of attitude from praise to vilification, implied even, perhaps, in the juxtaposition of "hope" and "grope" (ll. 678–79), which have debased associations elsewhere in the *Canterbury Tales*.

Fearful of exposure, the fanatically self-protective Canon ("... he that gilty is / Demeth alle thyng be spoke of hym, ywis") flees from the Host's goading interest and the Yeoman's new independence (ll. 697–99).

We may, with justification, see the Canon in a sympathetic light which history affords. In him we see the plight of all the early students of alchemy, to be driven by constantly frustrated hopes to the exhausting sacrifices of money, friends, social status, prestige, and even, as with this religious, the integrity of his order. Constantly experimenting, limited in their technical knowledge and tools, they were unable from day to day to repeat or reproduce their previous experiments.

This is, however, not the sympathetic interest of the disaffected servant. For him, all has been for naught. Tainted by lust for gain, and now devoid of money, clothes, and health, he can only damn this "slydynge" and "elvysshe" science, replete with special vocabulary, which has bleared his eye and impoverished him (ll. 720 ff.). He bears witness to the contagion of the gambling fever which unites its devotees into a community of destitute wretches (ll. 740 ff.). All labor is lost no matter what the experiment or what the materials, he tells us amidst those long interpolations (ll. 754 ff., 784 ff., 852 ff.) of scientific jargon in which Chaucer's rather extensive knowledge of the alchemist's tools and equipment are poured out in a dramatically revealing and controlled disorder, a strange literary paradox in which the yeoman's ignorance reveals Chaucer's grasp upon the objective data of alchemical experience.

For the Yeoman, no amount of learning will yield the ultimate secret of the craft, and ignorant as well as learned come to the same ultimate failure (ll. 830–51). Apprentice and master alike, each is goaded by hope (ll. 862 ff.) and "supposynge" (l. 871) to give up even his last garment for the money to continue the quest for the Elixir. Alas, their equipment is so bad that even with the control of the master alchemist himself, "the pot tobreketh, and farewel, al is go!" (l. 907).

Out of the failure of their experiment grow the quarrelsome recriminations of all involved in it (ll. 920 ff.), a comic disunity amidst the community of workers supported by the familiar demonic analogy:

> . . . Withouten doute,
> Though that the feend noght in oure sighte hym shewe,
> I trowe he with us be, that ilke shrewe!
> In helle, where that he lord is and sire,
> Nis ther moore wo, ne moore rancour ne ire.

Whan that oure pot is broke, as I have sayd,
Every man chit, and halt hym yvele apayd. (ll. 915-21)

Yet over the failure is raised up the perennial optimism of the master
—"Plukke up youre hertes, and beeth glad and blithe,"—and his
hopes that the mistakes of the moment will provide success for the
next experiment in the chancy world of science:

"Pees!" quod my lord, "the nexte tyme I wol fonde
To bryngen oure craft al in another plite." (ll. 951-52)

But all is raving madness (l. 959), according to the Yeoman, and in
his disaffection he can go on to assert that their apparent wisdom is
really ignorance; that even the wise man, when put to the test, is a
fool, and the most honest man a thief. The utterance is useful not
only as a transition to the three-part trick of the gulled priest and the
charlatan-canon alchemist of the tale that follows but as an indication
of the extent to which the disillusionment of the Yeoman has so
permeated his character as to poison heart and mind.

Pars secunda is a continuation of the voice which we have heard in
the first section. We hear in it first an aggressively sardonic and admonitory tone, the Yeoman's personal grievance against his former
master now disguised as a righteous warning to canons about the
Judas in their midst, a surprising return to the theme of the foe in the
bosom which we have encountered before in Chaucerian comedy. In
it the theme of the passionate lust for the philosopher's stone is extended to demonstrate the abuses to which the craft lent itself in the
hands of deliberate charlatans, not merely in the hands of the self-
deceived. It contains much that we associate with the mature Chaucer:
the comment upon human blindness (ll. 1074 ff.), the easy manipulation of a comic situation, the lively dialogue, a casual ease in versifica-
tion, a reportorial detachment and clarity in describing complicated
tricks. Our interest is sustained, says one writer, by "the convolutions
of the confidence trick itself, which is of course related to the characters of the subtle alchemist and his stupid victim." [7]

A final section of the poem (ll. 1388 ff. of *Pars secunda*), delivered
by a faintly ironical voice of unusual sobriety and balanced judgment,
is a capstone comment upon the misguided passions of all who see in
alchemy a means of getting rich quickly. The secrets of alchemy are
for the experts, not for ordinary men; if we are burned by its fever

[7] Brewer, *Chaucer*, p. 175.

and are drawn into it, we blindly venture forth into perils we can hardly assess. This is practical advice from a plain-speaker, a warning both against the allurements of the misty vocabulary of the philosophers and against the enslavement to an insatiable appetite; the ironist's voice rings out its seasoned admonition: "Save your money!" The ultimate secrets of the art, if we read Arnold of New Town and Plato aright, the voice continues, are for those rare souls whom Christ himself chooses, a cryptic warning against tampering and meddling with nature. In the final lines, the admonition becomes more overt:

> I rede, as for the beste, lete it goon.
> For whoso maketh God his adversarie,
> As for to werken any thyng in contrarie
> Of his wyl, certes, never shal he thryve,
> Thogh that he multiplie terme of his lyve.   (ll. 1475-79)

The appearance of the devil in oaths and metaphors, the associations of brimstone and hellish stench, the references to madness, to Judas, the continued isolation of the Canon from the society on pilgrimage, the quarrel amidst the community of scientists, the general contagion of greed-motivated commitment to the art, with all the implications about the exhausting of substance—these add up to a vision of a community living by sinister values. The enslavement to an appetite as real, as sharp, as consuming as lust produces an irresponsible exploitation of the natural world for the sake of power, an arrogant and presumptuous quest for a secret which is not man's to have.

There is good ground for reading Chaucer's intention so explicitly; indeed, one can if he wishes spell out with Dante's aid, or even that of Chaucer's Parson, much that Chaucer's comic irony implies but does not state: for example, that the pursuit of knowledge for the sake of money or power is socially irresponsible; that the use of power acquired through the exploitation of the natural world without regard to transcendent Law, is, in the long stretches of time, ethically and morally a form of destructive folly; that the uses of knowledge and the power it tends to generate are not, nor can ever be, divorced from rational and moral responsibility. The Canon's apostasy, his power to persuade others to this art, the sacrifice of the wealth of others to his passion, and the surrender of his proper vocation amount to a comment upon the perversion of the intellect from better uses.

In all of this, we can, if we wish, see Chaucer as a backward-looking medieval man, derisive of the spirit of scientific curiosity. But whatever Chaucer thought about psychology, or medicine, or astronomy, or alchemy he has kept to himself, for the most part. He refrains from passing overt judgment upon matters which others of his time were accepting with credulity, and takes a certain satisfaction in presenting the beliefs and attitudes of the various sciences with amazing clarity (proof enough that he understood them insofar as they could be understood), using them when they suit his purely artistic purposes. Whether he "believes" in the various scientific endeavors of his time is not nearly so important to us as whether in his fiction he has misrepresented their aims, and in misrepresenting them committed the graver error of falsifying the vision of men laughing or suffering in the pilgrimage of this life.

No one can deny that Chaucer saw all around him, both in England and on the Continent, tremendous strides in technology.[8] Given the coolness and dispassionate sanity of his mind, we cannot pretend to believe that he would not have known the value of processes and machines which would make his life easier or more comfortable. He seems to have preferred the practical usefulness of the astrolabe to the abstract speculations of astrology; in the *Canon's Yeoman's Tale*, he renders at the close an eminently practical ironist's demurral rather than a purely intellectual or religious one. Further, Chaucer is not favorably inclined to novelty, nor anxious for the hitherto untried, although he bears witness to the passion for novelty in the characters he creates. His own pose at the close of the *Canon's Yeoman's Tale* is that of the plain-speaker offering common-sense advice to the uninitiated; but the whole comic structure carries much the same common-sense warning against any ambition that isolates and divides, that destroys trust and confidence, that destroys health, that wastes money, that violates natural talents or obligations, that injures the society of men. These attitudes are not merely medieval; they have a permanent validity for the community of men.

We may not wish to go so far as to see in Chaucer's treatment of alchemy anything *more* than the means by which character is revealed.[9] Yet, in the literary tradition in which alchemy has figured, Chaucer's attitudes are thoroughly consistent with those of Erasmus

[8] Cf. Lynn White, Jr., "Technology and Invention in the Middle Ages," *Speculum*, XV (1940), 141–59.
[9] S. Foster Damon, "Chaucer and Alchemy," *PMLA*, XXXIX (1924), 782–88, offers the view that Chaucer "intended to attack false alchemists because he saw that they were becoming a public menace (and that they were such a menace is obvious from the laws so soon passed against them), but that under cover of this attack, he

and Jonson, and with Dante before him, in reflecting through their subject, not the truth or untruth of the science, but the tremendous temptations it offered to the spirits of man. Whether we can successfully impute to Chaucer a distrust of technology and an especially acute prescience with regard to the subsequent development of applied science, I am extremely doubtful. His judgments are those which the comic structure will support; in this case, through a depiction of an irrational passion, a comment upon excessive zeal as a type of *hubris*. The poet *qua* poet need go no further.

To conclude, the *Canon's Yeoman's Tale* looks on the surface to be a drastic change in form and subject matter from what we have come to expect in the *Canterbury Tales*. We recall, however, that disjointed structure and an emphasis upon the extravagant are signs of comic art; we recall too that Chaucer's interests embrace the science of his time. Actually, the tale is not formally different from the performances of Pardoner, Wife of Bath, and Reeve: ideally an invitation to the game of story-telling, a preliminary confession, then the tale itself as an extension of character, with some terminal moral statement.

Psychologically like the *Summoner's Tale*, Part I of the *Canon's Yeoman's Tale* is the depiction of a mind dominated by a passion. In general it is comedy of disillusionment, commenting practically and spiritually upon the perils of alchemy to the average man. In it the jargon of a special vocabulary from the mouth of a jaundiced apprentice serves the needs of satirical statement, in essence a mockery of the hopes of deluded and misguided alike. As a form of confession revealing heart and mind, its meaning makes very clear the speaker's melancholy deviation from the higher law. A substantial part of its worldly meaning, however, in the trickery of the second section, has to do with the duping of the stupid or pretentious. This

---

deliberately introduced material calculated to stimulate those rare experimenters who knew something of the real secret" (p. 782). Cf. also G. L. Kittredge, "The Canon's Yeoman's Prologue and Tale," *Transactions of the Royal Society of Literature*, 2d Series (1910), No. 30, pp. 87–95. He writes (p. 92): "How far is the Yeoman's denunciation of alchemy and its practitioners indicative of Chaucer's own views and of the character of his mind? Some critics (like Tyrwhitt) have fancied that the poet was expressing his individual resentment, that he was labouring under a sense of injury. But this is certainly a misconception. Chaucer's attitude is that of complete detachment. He may agree with the Yeoman's opinions, but he does not share the Yeoman's disappointment and indignation. We may, perhaps, infer *what Chaucer thought of alchemy*, but we cannot infer *how Chaucer felt towards the alchemists*. The distinction is vital."

double stance of moral comment in one episode of the tale and of a suggestive social meaning in another is brought into one focus at the close when the narrator himself, in a personal voice, utters his own ironical judgments.

CODA TO THE COMIC AND
IRONIC TALES

Earlier in this book I tried to describe the structure of the Canterbury pilgrimage as a literary form. To recapitulate briefly, it is romantic in the sense that it deals with a quest moving from alehouse to temple: an original plan entailing a round-trip—departure, arrival, return—was changed from the rather grandiose promise of more than a hundred and twenty tales to one of vastly fewer stories (an accommodation of theoretical to practical considerations) strung along between a departure and an arrival at a goal. In the changes from one scheme to another, in the shifting of tale from one teller to another, in the readjustment, cancellation, and expansion of links, appears something of the architectonic principle by which Chaucer was guided, which yet left room for creativity and inner movement. In short there comes into existence before our eyes an artistic concern, at once obvious and undeniable, with a new form *and* meaning.

When we consider Chaucer's subtle grasp upon the variety of literary types, his experimentation with them in order to sharpen their focus or widen their range of meaning, we are forced to a truism: he is uncommonly knowledgeable about the subject matter the type can carry, about the appropriate level of style; he knows furthermore how meaning can be rendered more complex by the mixture of subject matters and their proper styles. The distinctions Chaucer makes between churlish, ribald tales and those dealing with morality, nobility, or holiness, between tales of profane content and those of spiritual interests are conventional distinctions between the two great divisions of literary materials. But they are not distinctions to which Chaucer slavishly clings.

Chaucer rarely, if ever, writes tales which belong securely in one or the other of these two divisions. Even dominantly comic tales contain ingredients drawn from the conventional, romantic, or spiritual sphere—elements which undermine their surface meaning. It is necessary to recognize, too, the degree to which the tales function thematically as parts of a pilgrimage frame. In short, we are in the process, constantly, of assessing the tales individually, and then as part of the larger poem.

When we look at the tales individually, we are forced to modulate the terms "seriousness" and "irony." It is theoretically possible to write ironical tales which are not in any sense moral, are in fact immoral because of a deliberate attempt by the author to subvert the beliefs of his audience or to cater to their fondness for the sensational; or because the writer is yielding to some personal morbid emotion, or is indifferent to the power of literature to persuade and to arouse the passions. As a matter of fact, when we look at the realistic tales, we discover that they are indeed, all of them, built upon the triad of trickery, deception, and surprise, but that they deal with recalcitrance and folly, that they go to the lengths of bringing into existence, in their more forceful statements, an infernal community bent upon subverting the good. Nevertheless a normative world is a part of the texture, the background against which they act; and the higher values of the community of men moving towards salvation are never far to seek, either by ironical implication, by underlying assumption, or by overt statement.

The *Miller's Tale*, for example, has its wide range of Biblical associations; the *Reeve's Tale* has its gnomic wisdom, its theme of pride brought low; the *Friar's Tale* has its disquisition on the problem of evil and the functions of devils; the *Shipman's Tale* has its hint of a garden, of innocence in the child under the tutelage of the merchant's wife, its monk with breviary; the *Merchant's Tale* has its Christian theory of marriage; the *Canon's Yeoman's Tale* sets up vivid pictures of an infernal community at work; the *Summoner's Tale* makes its chief agent a friar and a hypocrite simultaneously. These are of course only the most obvious matters. They point up the conclusion here that moral seriousness in the comic and ironical tales is a matter of weight and tone, a matter of the amount and kind of moral statement conveyed by the tales individually. Taken as parts of the total pilgrimage which is being carried on, they are seen as functioning within a larger moral vision in which the follies and vices depicted— whether innocent or injurious—must be put off, before the reader, as participant in the pilgrimage himself, may present himself before the shrine of St. Thomas.

The moral standards which Chaucer is using to measure his characters are in essence not different from those of Dante. But Chaucer's humane common sense counters the moral vision and is bolstered by a Plautine spirit. In the tales most obviously in the fabliau vein, Chaucer's Roman comedies, the subject matter is the outwitting of convention and propriety by instinct and craft. Ironically the plots advance the triumph of youthful folly, for the most part, over the normative forces in the world. In all of them, over and above the wrangling between deceivers and the deceived, there is a sympathy with the young, a willingness to entertain the notion rather innocently that the natural sympathy of the young for each other makes them right in their opposition to the rigidities and possessiveness of somewhat ugly old age. The laughter that arises from their comic justice is for the most part laughter of approval, although older readers may have a feeling that there is something faintly subversive in the thematic statement that comes through to them.

There is, of course, less innocence, a colder irony in the *Shipman's Tale* with its succession of deceptions, its coolly cynical statement about the integrity of friendship and of marriage. But this irony still lacks a larger infusion of philosophical and romantic matter to deepen its tone of mordancy, as in the *Merchant's Tale*. The latter presents something of a special case in that, among the ironical tales, although it is not the most skillful, it has a richness and denseness of texture, of style, a crustiness of allusion and association not found to the same degree in other fabliaux. Here the subject matters of farce and romance are made to serve each other. Theological disquisition, Biblical and classical allusion, the questions of destiny and expedience, all lend a special "bite" to the tale. Here more explicitly than anywhere else in the comic and ironic tales, the thoroughly conventional uses of marriage are tested impossibly by the special relationship of youth and age. Youthful drives and passions in the decaying body of the old, the selfishness and blindness of age are displayed as utterly ridiculous. Fate, destiny, the stars do not dictate the final meaning of the action for the audience: a certain recognition of the decora of age and the natural sympathy of the young. These are worldly truths which are allowed to overwhelm the notion that marriage, sanctioned even in these difficult terms, is possible in the given circumstances and which hence preclude the view of marriage as a paradise on earth.

Marriage may be a sacrament, but for living men it cannot be divorced from the dictates of, if not reason, at least good sense.

Obviously none of the sensual tales deals with a world of complete innocence; none deals with happy marriage. Although the values of the stable world are discernible in the background, convention and propriety are not allowed to defeat triumphant instinct and craft. A husband exists to be found a fool, and there is an uneasy feeling that the situations just witnessed are capable of repetition; as for example, at the end of the *Shipman's Tale*, where the forces of order and disorder are reconciled—perhaps merely held in abeyance of each other—by means of verbal puns and double entendres. Blindness of heart or stupidity invite deception. In Chaucer's comic irony, deceivers triumph.

The other performances in the ironical vein invite an Aristophanic rather than a purely Plautine comparison. All of them are studies in vice deliberate, rampant, self-conscious. All of them entail a consideration of the honest, moral community which is here opposed by another vicious and demonic group. All of them deal with impostures of one sort or another, containing characters who assume that they are wiser, more in control than in fact they are. Their arrogance and pretenses earn for them a compensatory defeat, death, disillusion.

Chaucer, like many another in his time, saw a special relationship between the common good and the spiritual reform of individuals. In these tales the meanings projected go beyond the subject of folly to a deeper, more trenchant comment upon the relation between the corrupt and corrupted person and the society of which he is a part. Thus the *Canon's Yeoman's Tale*, while it has in common with even the sexually oriented tales a realistic background, a principal episode which is an involved piece of trickery, and an effect of laughter through deception and surprise, shares with the *Friar's Tale* and that of the Pardoner the attempt to bring into life before our eyes the overtly demonic community. The imagery makes this clear: hell, devils, Judas, disease, secrecy, madness, and the like. With the friar of the *Summoner's Tale*, the protagonists have in common their overwhelming dedication to private goals opposing the good.

In the sensual tales, there was no attempt to accommodate the conclusions of the tales to the sentimental wishes of the audience. What happened in them happened because the comic spirit demanded it. But in the *exempla* of the Friar and the Pardoner, the demon's disquisition on permissive evil and the Old Man's impartiality and resignation point up and gratify certain needs in the audience: a belief in an ordered universe in which evil has a part, a corroboration of their convictions about human freedom. Similarly in the psychological sketch of the Summoner's friar and in the Introduction and Part I of the *Canon's Yeoman's Tale*, the reprisals of disintegrated composure, of disease, of spiritual death, are felt as moral necessities of the plot.

Thus in the tales of Friar, Summoner, and Pardoner we have the satisfaction of seeing the deceivers deceived. Spiritual death, discomfiture become the desired revenge as the values of a morally oriented audience are vindicated. Avarice of one sort or another has been their common vice, and membership in an infernal community has been their mark. Repentance and recalcitrance are interwoven into somewhat grimmer ironies in these tales; where recalcitrance persists, disillusion and death take over. Character becomes fate, and destiny takes on the mysterious chill of watching from on high the passion for choosing damnation. In the end, if society is not able to reassert its values and work out its revenge in its own way (as in the *Summoner's Tale*), the slaying of vice is somehow accomplished from afar. It is God who watches.

The ironical tales then range from playful to serious, from an ostensible indifference to conventional values to a conscious concern with them. The more serious thematic interests are discernible in a variety of ways other than the obvious evolution of the plot: in the background details through which a stable world affords the counterpart to disorder, in the loading-on of theological disquisition, in the depiction of ethos through imagery and rhetoric.

By one means or another the views of a stable community are set over against the folly or willfulness of the individual. In the farces the will is not as important a consideration as the exalted instinct; the subject is for the most part man at play. In the others we see various aspects of the diverted will. The plans of the agents of the *Shipman's Tale* are the plans of the adult world working a cool deception upon husband and friend. The hypocrisy of the friar in the *Summoner's Tale* is active and deliberate vice. The tormented will of the Canon's Yeoman supplies a further example of a mind struggling with choice after years of service to greed; he is now demonstrated as hovering in a kind of vacuum between disillusion and a new attitude toward life.

Whether he is bright enough to take advantage of the new vision which is about to be born we cannot say, owing to the confusion of voices and tone at the conclusion of his tale; nevertheless he is now on pilgrimage, in a sense restored to his proper, penitent community.

The emphasis, in the *Friar's Tale* and the *Pardoner's Tale,* upon a choice of conscious repentance illustrates more than the other comic and ironic tales the role of the will in a securely and overtly theological kind of irony, in which the outcome can be an escape from spiritual death if the right choice is made. The Canon's Yeoman has achieved some vision about his craft. And having made his grave choice, he must now face the consequences of that choice. The others in this category are lost.

III
FUNCTION:
ROMANCE

THE KNIGHT'S TALE

Armi, amore, e virtu ...

BOCCACCIO, Teseida

What is this world? What asketh men to have?

Thanne is it wysdom, as it thynketh me,
To maken vertu of necessitee,
And take it weel that we may nat eschue,
And namely that to us alle is due.
And whoso gruccheth ought, he dooth folye,
And rebel is to hym that al may gye.

If there is a grand manner in Chaucer's *Canterbury Tales*, one comes closest to it in the leisurely, pictorial, philosophical account of the two knights who momentarily sacrifice friendship and their knightly pledge of mutual fidelity for the love of a lady. As a literary type, the story falls generally into the class of romance, although it leans on the one side toward a kind of tragedy leavened by detachment and sober stoicism in the face of certain imponderables, and on the other toward a kind of high comedy made possible not merely by Chaucer's penchant for the ironical, but by the Boethian definition of love and its operations, within which the agents function. The problem of the human will and its responsibility, merely hinted at, is supplanted by the gradual depiction of destinal forces controlling the lives of men within the plan of Providence and creating that delicate philosophical topic "necessity" which seems at once both to tantalize and to fatigue the mind of the poet.[1]

[1] Paull F. Baum, *Chaucer: A Critical Appreciation* (Duke University Press, 1958), pp. 84–104, offers an unusually stringent treatment of the tale, an appraisal of the trend in literary estimates of the *Knight's Tale*. It is somewhat at variance with the essay by Charles Muscatine, "Form, Texture, and Meaning in Chaucer's Knight's Tale," *PMLA*, LXV (1950), 911–29, and with the earlier essays of William Frost, "An Interpretation of Chaucer's *Knight's Tale*," *RES*, XXV (1949), 289–304, and of H. S. Wilson, "*The Knight's Tale* and the *Teseida* Again," *UTQ*, XVIII (1949), 131–46; also with my own earlier version of this chapter, "Some Philosophical Aspects of *The Knight's Tale*," *CE*, XIX (1959), 296–302; and more recently with the esays of Dale Underwood, "The First of *The Canterbury Tales*," *ELH*, XXVI (1959), 455–

In spite of the readily apparent parallelism and symmetry, the *Knight's Tale* presents a number of stumbling blocks to the new reader, principally in the free admixture of styles, the presence of comic stringencies within passages of considerable solemnity, the adducing of personal attitudes, not found in Boccaccio, which from time to time ruffle the surface tone. The reader unaccustomed to the manner of romance may feel that the two heroes are not distinguishable from each other, that sympathy is not enlisted in favor of one to the exclusion of the other, or that the imposition of philosophical statement upon the pagan and astrological machinery of the tale seems at the outset to oppose mutually exclusive world views. Yet, in spite of all such objections, and taking into account that occasional note of levity which invests and hence defines Chaucer's attitudes towards experience, the reader who peruses the *Knight's Tale* even as moderately serious poetry is apt to see in the conflicting loves of the two knights, in the exploration of the question "What asketh men to have?" and in the accommodation of the destinal order to Providence, that Chaucer has employed the vocabulary and exploited the themes of the didactic romance.[2] Indeed these larger concerns so pervade the story that, taken with the pictorial and descriptive element of the tale, they tend to mask whatever defects it may contain.

The sober elevation of this romance, with its encompassing of the weighty subject of man's destiny and the necessity of death within the chain of being, manages, by virtue of the union of Palamon and Emily with which it closes, to fall within a range of Christian comedy opposing that more carefree vision of the all-too-human and sometimes irrational creatures in the fabliaux. Because of the affinity of Chaucer's vision to that of Boethius as well as to that of Boccaccio, his writing reflects the whole range of comedy from the most serious and elevating to the most realistic and merely amusing sort. Although we cannot accuse Chaucer of being a philosopher, he is so sympathetic with the Boethian view that he adduces with considerable frequency

---

69; John Halverson, "Aspects of Order in the *Knight's Tale*," *SP*, LVII (1960), 606–21; and Richard Neuse, "The Knight: The First Mover in Chaucer's Human Comedy," *UTQ*, XXXI (1962), 299–315.

[2] I am remembering here Dante's division of the best subjects for the vernacular into safety, love, and virtue. He writes: "I mean the things which are most important (in terms of what is useful, pleasurable, and right), as prowess in arms, the fire of love, and the direction of the will."—*De Vulgari Eloquentia*, II, ii, 63–78, trans. A. G. F. Howells, in *Latin Works of Dante*, The Temple Classics (London, 1904), p. 71.

attitudes and commentary of the more moral kind from the *Consolatio*. Not only were these views compatible with the religious views he held; artistically they were useful and provocative. They may even have been the means, as Nevill Coghill suggests, by which Chaucer's native genius was released from the mechanical world picture of the dream allegory.[3]

If he is philosophic at all, it is in the broadest sense of confronting the truths of experience in as many ways as possible through literary type and character. If the variety of moods, tones, styles, or attitudes within a single complex tale like that of the Knight resists any unifying pressure, it is because Chaucer's own ironical mind resists a rigidly encompassing moral system within which to secure all the facets of experience. Reality is for him the infinite data of man acting, thinking, suffering, laughing, making choices, deceiving and being deceived. This does not mean that Chaucer did not appreciate what he found in Dante, nor that he does not reflect in his poems the relationship of the natural order to the supernatural and the capacity of the individual to cooperate with grace. It means only that Chaucer's proclivity is for the particular and immediate in personality and experience, for the comic and ironic which tend to override the serious and solemn.

But we need not go so far as to maintain that Chaucer is not interested in the human heart or the ways of the soul;[4] whether they are matters of poignant personal belief or merely attitudes which were inescapable in his time, Chaucer has an intellectual interest in the matter of evil, in reconciling God's goodness with the existence of evil, in God's foreknowledge and the moral freedom of human beings. They are so clearly a part of the artistic process, and so clearly a part of the rationale within which many of Chaucer's agents have their existence that they must be taken to be a meaningful part of Chaucer's whole reaction to his time, and a necessary part of the equipment of an educated man, even one whom posterity persists in

[3] *The Poet Chaucer* (Oxford University Press, 1949), p. 165. A statement such as this cannot be read as an absolute formula, nor can we make rigid divisions of Chaucer's work into periods. Yet as he grew older and continued to labor at his art he succeeded to more substantial views and allowed these views more and more to supply the backdrop against which his agents act. What we generally think of as Chaucer's large humanity becomes "large" in the judgment of posterity precisely because of the presence of the deep moral tone of his major poetry.

[4] John Edwin Wells, *A Manual of the Writings in Middle English, 1050–1400* (New Haven, Conn., 1916), p. 602.

regarding as non-speculative. If anything may be deduced from Chaucer's chariness about repeating performances precisely like the *Knight's Tale* in the Canterbury collection, it is surely not that he is incapable of vision or of serious thought, or even that it is antipathetic to his genius; but rather that his métier is the more realistic, ironic modes into which he has grown and developed as an artist.

One problem of the critic in handling the *Knight's Tale*, then, is that of deciding how good, how persuasive, how gratifying Chaucer's handling of his theme is—in short, of deciding whether as a dominantly serious work, it is successful. That there are defects in the tale, in the manner and the style, scholars have reminded us.[5] But beyond the clumsiness, or the inconsistencies, even the occasional silliness which some have noted, lies its strong interest in the quest for meaning beyond merely human experience, the sobering resignation to life as well as to Law, the search for a way to reconcile man's experience to the certitude of God's providence. With all its defects, it marks one phase of Chaucer's attempts to conflate romance with realism and to accommodate philosophical commentary to human suffering, such as we see accomplished with greater success in *Troilus*. The fact that Chaucer in the *Knight's Tale* so freely intermixes elements that are tragic and romantic, comic and ironic, elements better combined in the *Troilus*, seems to indicate an experiment of sorts, an artistic endeavor that perhaps does not bear excessive repetition.

On most of the matters on which there is contention, the student who rereads the tale will form his own judgments, and will have to content himself with the tendency of his own attitudes to fluctuate and change as he perceives new facets of Chaucer's genius and achieves new insights in the light of his own growth in literary experience. Some matters, however, demand explanation over and over again, among them the relation of the philosophical additions to the existing pagan, astrological system, or in short, the accommodation of the Prime Mover of the Boethian system to the variety of pagan deities who figure so largely up until the conclusion of the story. It is here, in the role performed by the gods and goddesses in frustrating, or molding, or advancing their favorites that we see a threat to the interior coherence of the tale, newly conceived, which holds in bal-

---

[5] Ralph Baldwin, *The Unity of the Canterbury Tales*, Anglistica, Vol. V (Copenhagen, 1955), pp. 68–69, and Baum, *Chaucer: A Critical Appreciation*, pp. 84–104.

ance a God-centered universe, orderly and reasonable, and a polytheistic system which seems to deny it.

A steady and persistent passing back and forth between the One God and the many gods may be charted in the tale, in effect a passing back and forth between the older Boccaccian structure and the newer Boethian form which makes its impress first in the long speeches attributed to the young knights in prison. Arcite, by way of example, may attribute his woes to the working of some ill disposition of Saturn (A 1086–90), and at the same time, in his speech dealing with the vanity of human wishes, hold views about the providence of God, and more surprisingly even mention purgatory and hell. Palamon may himself in his speech dealing with innocence and suffering vacillate between his "God woot" (l. 1282) or "For Goddes sake" (l. 1317) and his "O cruel goddes" (l. 1303) . It is obvious that in attributing their suffering to cruel Saturn both Arcite and Palamon (l. 1328) are referring principally to the planet and to astrological influences upon their lives, but it seems equally clear that Palamon, in attributing their suffering as well to the influence of Juno refers specifically to a deity and that throughout the body of the action, what is not attributed to the stars or to the deities is attributed to fortune or destiny as a facet of God's providence.

The lives of the agents, within this system, are acted out in a world through which, even in the end, the way is not entirely clear. Such a view of a destinal order over which men apparently have little influence can be seen as bearing upon a kind of pessimism or at best a kind of noble resignation, a view which results from Chaucer's chariness in using those parts of Boethius' treatise in which the will is vindicated as the means by which man transcends the destinal order. Chaucer has stayed out of his story, has indeed allowed Theseus to interpret the higher law to which he himself is subject and for which he supplies a severely delimited Boethian explanation. One feels, almost irresistibly, the tug of that completer view supplied by Books IV and V of the *Consolatio*, but at the same time recognizes the propriety of keeping within the purview of the Boccaccian system of Fate. Indeed, that completer view, lurking, it seems to me, in the long Boethian speeches of Palamon and Arcite, is at the same time denied as an issue in the tale, and so does not enter into the explanation of God's law by which the resolution is brought about.

Like Boccaccio, Chaucer is interested more in the pattern of destiny than in character in action. Hence the emphasis upon the providential scheme; hence the correspondences between agents and highly individualized deities whose personalities and influences are described in the temples; hence the collusion between Venus and Saturn as part of the determinism of the tale. The indifference of the *Knight's Tale* to the troublesome matter of providing moral freedom within the prescience of God, more than any other factor, gives the impression that the heroes are not acting but being acted upon.

Although it seems to belabor the obvious, it is necessary to state that the Middle Ages managed to salvage the ancient gods by accommodating them to their own customs and beliefs.[6] By a series of sometimes ethical, sometimes theological, sometimes psychological accommodations, the gods could be seen as providing correspondences with and influences upon man's existence.[7] The gods become means of presenting on a pagan plane the *vera* that underlie the pilgrimage of this life. In a variety of contexts mainly allegorical they define the power of God to work out what his Providence encompasses. In the *Knight's Tale*, for example, Venus epitomizes the irresistible and overriding passion in the lives of men, a passion with which no one may vie successfully. The collusion of Venus with Saturn indicates still further the greatness of this power before which even that of Mars, however fierce and destructive, is ineffectual. Mars too represents an apparent element in the heart of man, something aggressive, something warlike, something destructive, while Diana is presented both in terms of her virginity and in her role as patroness of those in the pangs of childbirth. (Chaucer here, in his passion for symmetry has created out of his own sources and resources the depiction of Diana.)

Chaucer himself brings about the conflation of the pagan machinery and the Boethian providential scheme of things by equating, in his final section, the role of Jupiter with that of the Prime Mover. The influence of the gods has been but the working out of a Master Plan; the fate against which the agents have struggled bitterly is but the

---

[6] Jean Seznec, *The Survival of the Pagan Gods*, trans. Barbara Sessions, Bollingen Series, XXXVIII (New York, 1953), does much to illuminate this fascinating episode in the mythological tradition and its influence.

[7] Boccaccio calls them ministers of opportunities and vicissitudes. Cf. Charles G. Osgood, *Boccaccio on Poetry* (Princeton University Press, 1930), pp. xx-xxi, and 65 ff.

ordering of Destiny, given objective and concrete form in the personalities of the gods and goddesses who order the individual actions of life. Taken together they yet constitute but a fragmentary view of the whole plan of the universe as it exists in the regulative mind of God in the design called Providence. All the deities used in the tale, even the fury that starts up out of the ground, are but manifestations of the power of the Prime Mover. It is a view to which Boethius was led by means of the ancient Greek philosophers, one which bears ultimately upon a Hebraic tradition which is able to encompass and absorb it. Boethius, by virtue of detachment from revelation, by virtue of his emphasis upon human reason as sufficient for man to know himself in relation to God, serves as a kind of bridge between a rather meaningless pagan cosmos in which men suffer at the hands of the apparently capricious astrologized gods and a universe in which change is but an illusion in the highly regulated and orderly progression of time, and in which chaos in the lives of the heroes is seen no longer as chaos but as a dimly describable formal plan. In the development of Chaucer as a thoughtful poet, with an eye to insoluble problems, the *Knight's Tale* may be the first serious application of the philosophical attitudes of the Roman writer to the subjects of poetry. The fact that it continues to perplex the mind may itself result from that persistent strain of irony, corroborated by Boethius, which prevents in him any facile affirmation.

Weakness in the characterization of the two heroes and Emily has been often noted.[8] It must be stated that Chaucer intended the deflation of Emily's character and performance since she is merely the instigator of the conflict, while the equalization of the knights was already a fact of Boccaccio's version. There are no significant changes from the Boccaccian treatment of the characters of the knights, although there are some rearrangements of materials that may be construed as subtly preparing additional sympathy for Palamon. Nonetheless, to say that Chaucer has equalized the performance of the knights is not to say that he fails to distinguish between them. By excluding Arcite's prayers to Apollo, Fortune, and Venus (in the fourth book of the *Teseida*) and restricting his pleas entirely to Mars and those of Palamon to Venus, Chaucer has managed to dissipate

[8] E.g., J. R. Hulbert, "What was Chaucer's Aim in the *Knight's Tale?*" *SP*, XXVI (1929), 375–85.

certain unnecessary complexities and oppose the two knights more simply by the alignments expressed in their prayers.[9]

Indeed, we do not come to know the knights by any of the conventional means of characterization; in what they say, a normal source of insight into character, the distinctions that we may make are limited.[10] Psychological analysis tends to be fruitless inasmuch as the agents merely exemplify or express certain attitudes which are, in the resolution, to be corrected and amended; the vision towards which the poet moves demands formalized and conventional views by which the destinal pattern may be demonstrated. In attempting analysis, however, we may discern why the philosophical attitudes of the *Knight's Tale* prevent either the full range of the tragedy of fate or the full range of serious comedy and produce a kind of quizzical and thought-provoking literary type somewhere between them.

Chaucer's changes from the Boccaccian text are not those bearing upon the depiction of character and any special distinctions between the two heroes. We may note that the prayer which Arcite utters to Venus (Book IV) is omitted, probably in the interest of simplifying the alignments between Arcite and Mars; the rearrangement of the order in which Arcite, Palamon, and Emily (Boccaccio's order) offer up their prayers to their respective deities, placing Palamon in the position of priority and Arcite last, with Emily between them, serves to suspend the fate of Emily between the fortunes being evolved within the temples of Venus and Mars. Like the other changes or modifications, the creation of the role of Saturn, relieving Venus of the function of directly producing the fury, is in keeping with increasing the sense of a destinal pattern within which men seem to be powerless victims of fate. Chaucer seems not to have wished to complicate the already existent irony of the central situation: two admirable men in love with the same girl, two powerful deities pitted against each other, two prayers which are to be answered. The very symmetry of the structure bearing ultimately upon diverging fates

[9] Robert Pratt, "Chaucer's Use of the *Teseida*," *PMLA*, LXII (1947), 615, makes the judicious comment: "...their personalities are somewhat heightened and differentiated, as befits the slightly dissimilar roles they are called upon to play. Yet, like Boccaccio, Chaucer does not do much to encourage the heroine or the audience to favor either rival until the *deux ex machina* has removed the loser. Palamon's complete submission to love and Venus perhaps makes him a little more attractive than the more practical and aggressive Arcite; but Chaucer wisely does not overdo the differentiation between these two, thus avoiding Dryden's eventual error."

[10] But see the discussion of the two knights in Percy Van Dyke Shelly, *The Living Chaucer* (University of Pennsylvania Press, 1940), pp. 135 ff.

for the two knights, both of which, on the basis of attitudes produced within the tale, may be seen as good, does not depend upon or evolve out of the characterization of the knights. The issue into death and marriage preserves to the very end a deliberate ambivalence of intention and necessitates as resolution, not the transfiguration of the spirit (Chaucer omits the flight of Arcite's soul to paradise), not the "excellence achieved through suffering," but rather the explanation of the law which, once defined, must be accepted.

In the translation of pagan gods into forces familiar to a Christian audience, the relationship of Venus to Mars is of considerable interest. It throws light upon the means Chaucer uses to prepare us for Palamon's ultimate victory. The rationale of the School of Chartres which made Venus the executrix of Nature and gave her the task of perpetuating species in "unwearied continuation" went so far as to explain love as an imitation of and participation in the eternity of God. As employed by Chaucer in various of his poems, Venus-love takes on the protective coloration of Christianity, is even equated with the ultimate law of the universe and defended as the path to virtue. These views, which are either implicit or explicit in the depiction of Venus in the *Knight's Tale*, all contribute to increasing our vaguely felt impression that Palamon prays knowledgeably indeed. "Venus tames Mars, but Mars never subdues Venus," writes Plato, and Ficino long after him.[11] The recounting in the temple of Venus of those who succumbed to love, the prayer to her in terms of both licit and illicit associations, the promise of victory, the use of Saturn to bring about Venus' wish, although not overtly equated with a liberating, humanizing, virtue-producing emotion, yet lead over and over again to the same conclusion:

> "Love is a gretter lawe, by my pan,
> Than may be yeve to any erthely man;
> And therfore positif lawe and swich decree
> Is broken al day for love in ech degree." (ll. 1165–68)

> O Cupide, out of alle charitee!
> O regne, that wolt no felawe have with thee!
> Ful sooth is seyd that love ne lordshipe
> Wol noght, his thankes, have no felaweshipe. (ll. 1623–26)

[handwritten margin note: But Mars is not a law! Both M. & V. are urges toward a goal, which the story shows is ultimately insufficient!]

[11] See S. R. Jayne, "Marsilio Ficino's Commentary on Plato's *Symposium*," *University of Missouri Studies*, XIX (1944), 176–77. See the discussion on the two Venus-loves in D. W. Robertson, Jr., *A Preface to Chaucer* (Princeton University Press, 1962), pp. 105–6, 126–27, and 372–73.

"The god of love, a, *benedicite!*
How myghty and how greet a lord is he!
Ayeyns his myght ther gayneth none obstacles.
He may be cleped a god for his myracles;
For he kan maken, at his owene gyse,
Of everich herte as that hym list divyse."   (ll. 1785–90)

Thus may ye seen that wysdom ne richesse,
Beautee ne sleighte, strengthe ne hardynesse,
Ne may with Venus holde champartie,
For as hir list the world than may she gye.   (ll. 1947–50)

"Youre vertu is so greet in hevene above
That if yow list, I shal wel have my love."   (ll. 2249–50)

"The Firste Moevere of the cause above,
Whan he first made the faire cheyne of love,
Greet was th'effect, and heigh was his entente.
Wel wiste he why, and what thereof he mente;
For with that faire cheyne of love he bond
The fyr, the eyr, the water, and the lond
In certeyn boundes, ..."   (ll. 2987–93)

It may be that Chaucer intended our sympathies to be subtly swayed toward Palamon who prays to the source of life rather than to the source of death and who evinces a wisdom greater than he knows:

I think
not!

"I recche nat but it may bettre be
To have victorie of hem, or they of me,
So that I have my lady in myne armes.
For though so be that Mars is god of armes,
Youre vertu is so greet in hevene above
That if yow list, I shal wel have my love."   (ll. 2245–50)

Alongside of his prayer that of Arcite seems unsubtle and direct, the warrior's rather than the lover's prayer, touching in its admission of passionate commitment to the prized Emily, but uncomplicated, without confusion about the right thing to do: "Yif me the victorie, I aske thee namoore" (l. 2420).

Again we must remember that Chaucer's source had laid down a quasi-philosophical pattern of the resignation of the agents to the fate provided for them by the gods, and their noble acceptance of, or even transcendence over, the destinal forces which frustrate their hopes. It is upon this foundation that Chaucer builds the more overtly philosophical scaffolding and framework by which to extract meaning from the suffering of the agents. In any final search for character we cannot attribute to Arcite anything like an error of judgment in praying to Mars; what he is doing is a glorious part of the knightly life. Nor can we attribute to Palamon any special rationalized wisdom in doing what turns out, for him, to be the right thing. Indeed, there is curiously absent from the context any note of that excellence which human dignity may extract from suffering, outside of Arcite's sense of the mystery of life upon his deathbed and his reconciliation with Palamon (ll. 2765 ff.). Chaucer's heroes complain and suffer, they express doubt and confusion, but answers to their plights are not explicitly given in the final discussion of the chain of being with which the tale is brought to a close. Yet this is all the answer that Chaucer has deemed it necessary to give. It is sufficient to bring knowledge of God's law to the dimly comprehending Palamon and Emily, but we note that the knowledge which is offered does not grow out of the moral responsibility of the agents for their actions. It qualifies rather as a freely adduced reassurance that the actions of life are not divorced from a larger, all embracing plan for the universe within which the events of life have meaning. Whether man is free, responsible, significant does not become an issue of the story. The issue is, rather, the accommodation of man to the working of the Law which he cannot always interpret, but which in certain moments he may affirm.

The character of Theseus emerges from Chaucer's pages as the most interesting, the most subtle, the most satisfactorily depicted agent of the tale. He alone among the human agents embraces the whole range of experience delineated in the tale, as the slave of Venus in his youth and the husband of Hippolyte in maturity, as the close friend of Perotheus, as a conqueror and devotee of Mars, and on the philosophical plane, as a defender of the natural law against the assertions of Creon's positive law at the outset of the story (the Theban dead deserve burial), and as the explicator of the natural law at its close. When it is necessary to speak his explanation of God's law, he becomes a kind of divine instrument by which the errors of mankind are rectified and amended; one has the faint impression of a voice speaking through a mask the wisdom of a god out of a machine.

He is a man capable of detachment and irony, pity and sober judgment, anger and sternness. The attitude of wise, faintly bemused common sense with which he evaluates the "trespas" of Arcite and Palamon ("Fy upon a lord that wol have no mercy . . .") demonstrates his normative function of providing a sane vantage point from which to view the confused actions of the heroes. From beginning to end we see him, too, not only as the defender and interpreter of the law, but as himself a part of the destinal order and an instrument in it, able to stand apart from it and to comment upon it without destroying the mystery, within both the pagan and the Boethian rationale. His intimately human involvement and explanation in the one (ll. 1623 ff.) and his faintly godlike detachment and pronouncement in the other (ll. 2987 ff.), as expressions of the same personality, serve artistically and structurally as a device by which to bridge the gap between the two systems.[12]

When, after the passage of "certeyn yeres," we finally arrive at a parliament convened to decide certain matters of "alliaunce" and "obeisaunce," the stage is subtly prepared for his apologia on behalf of universal order. Theseus now speaks a stern philosophical view, in essence an embellishment of his own remarks on mutability in the *Teseida*. (These Chaucer assigns to Theseus' old father Egeus.)

> "This world nys but a thurghfare ful of wo,
> And we been pilgrymes, passynge to and fro.
> Deeth is an ende of every worldly soore."   (ll. 2847–49)

What the all too human Arcite and Palamon have been unable to settle, what Theseus himself has been unable to prevent in Arcite's death, the wisdom which he speaks embraces and resolves. The means by which the grand resolution can be brought about are indeed built into the original structure of the *Teseida* (the marriage of Theseus to Hippolyte, the superiority of natural law to positive law in the slaying of Creon, the contrast between a shifting Fortuna and a stable destinal order), and Chaucer has obviously made a virtue out of the necessity of retaining the essence of Boccaccio's first two books in his opening 174 lines. Taken together they provide the bases upon which

---

[12] Cf. the opinion of J. A. W. Bennett, *Chaucer: The Knight's Tale* (London, 1954), pp. 23–25, that Theseus may possibly be considered the "hero of the Knight's story," that he is more human than his Italian original, more godlike: ". . . in his wisdom and equity . . . and in his function as an arbiter of Fate he comes much nearer than Teseo to the divine ruler, to the Jupiter who arbitrates among the Gods, the First Mover whose 'greet effect' and 'heigh entente' he himself extols." See, too, Robertson, *Preface*, pp. 260–66, for a discussion of Theseus as a type of wisdom and virtue in the traditions of classical iconography.

to erect the Boethian meaning of the tale: the definition of the natural law within which fortune is but a reflection of Providence and to which the marriage of Palamon and Emily is a sanctioned, even a necessary accommodation.

Whether, in adopting Boethian attitudes, Chaucer admits the possibility of implications not directly stated, we can only conjecture. It is true that Theseus' speech in praise of the Great Chain of Love may be read simply to mean that Emily and Palamon must cease mourning for Arcite and reconcile themselves to his death as a necessary penalty of imperfection. Yet the Neo-Platonic burden of those very loci which Chaucer has borrowed from Boethius deal not so much with the necessity or even the fact of death, but rather with the attempt by living creatures to imitate the eternity, the unity, the singleness, the permanence of God by means of the continuous existence assured to species by progressions and successions. This perpetuity allowed to creatures by the law of love is the counterpart of God's eternity; indeed participation in the divine *is* participation in the law of love. On more than one occasion Chaucer calls our attention to the popular meter of the *Consolatio*, which now becomes the ground note of Theseus' speech: "This love halt togidres peples joyned with an holy boond, and knytteth sacrement of mariages of chaste loves; and love enditeth lawes to trewe felawes. O weleful were mankynde, yif thilke love that governeth hevene governede yowr corages" (*Boece*, II, m. 8). It would seem strange if, in a tale of such persistent symmetry and balance, the law of love should encompass the death of Arcite but not provide for the living.

The degree to which the definition of natural law both reconciles Palamon and Emily to their future and provides a palatable attitude toward the death of Arcite—in short the degree to which this speech accomplishes a reconciliation of the past with the present—marks in a sense the success or failure of its symmetrical structure, and the success or failure of the shift of emphasis from fortune and fate and astrological determinism to a clearly defined Boethian Providence. A cursory glance at the principal Boethian additions will make clear the statement of the philosophical problem which has been translated into human terms, along with the attempted solution. Arcite, it will be remembered, as well as Palamon, posits the hand of God in the rule of the universe, admitting that men produce their own destruction in pursuit of the fragmentary goods of the world.

> "Allas, why pleynen folk so in commune
> On purveiaunce of God, or of Fortune,
> That yeveth hem ful ofte in many a gyse
> Wel bettre than they kan hemself devyse?"   (ll. 1251–54)

Palamon voices a confusion arising out of the suffering of the guiltless and gives vent to the larger consideration of man forced to restrain his passions for fear of divine reprisal:

> "And yet encresseth this al my penaunce,
> That man is bounden to his observaunce,
> For Goddes sake, to letten of his wille,
> Ther as a beest may al his lust fulfille.
> And whan a beest is deed he hath no peyne;
> But man after his deeth moot wepe and pleyne,
> Though in this world he have care and wo."   (ll. 1315–21) [13]

Taken together their views are reflections of that total intellectual and emotional disaffection of Boethius before his long re-education by philosophy, which gives way to the larger view of the *summum bonum* as the sum of all the goods desired by man, a view which denies the existence of evil and allows for participation in the divine through acceptance of the larger law. With the entrance of Theseus upon the scene of the battle between the two knights, we are assured that the providence of God is effected in the changing bond of the world through the agency of destiny, and that

> ... oure appetites heer,
> Be it of werre, or pees, or hate, or love,
> Al is this reuled by the sighte above.   (ll. 1670–72)

Thus the way is made for the resolution of the problem as stated by Arcite; his protest that life consists of a blind pursuit of false felicities and that man is the victim of impersonal fortune is countered by a description of a universe held in bounds by love, a universe in which nothing is left to chance, and evil has no absolute existence. His life has come to an end because

> "That same Prince and that Moevere ...
> Hath stablissed in this wrecched world adoun
> Certeyne dayes and duracioun
> To al that is engendred in this place,
> Over the whiche day they may nat pace."   (ll. 2994–98)

---

[13] This distinction between all animals' natural instinct and man's capacity to restrain "what nature desires" is made by Boethius, Book III, Prose xi, ll. 185 ff.

It is this universal principle of love operating in the reconciliation of Palamon and Arcite in the last moments of the latter's life which allows to him the purchase of a glorious name to outlast his body.

The flight of Arcite's soul to the eighth sphere of the heavens and his laughter from beyond, the student will note, is absent from Chaucer's version. This scene, we recall, is put to good use in the conclusion of *Troilus and Criseyde,* and expanded there to provide the necessary religious distance from the pagan ethos which motivates the agents of that poem. One might ask why the flight of Arcite's soul is not retained in its proper place instead of in the other work; indeed the answer might be more easily reached if we knew more about the chronological relations of *Troilus* and the *Knight's Tale.* If Chaucer had already used it in the *Troilus,* he would naturally omit it in the later work. On the other hand, on purely artistic grounds, it is possible that cosmic laughter might have been construed by Chaucer's audience to mean that Arcite had indeed made off with the prize by escaping from the foul prison of this life, that with his purified vision, he tends through laughter to make a mockery of the anguished attempts of the living, involved in the law of progressions and successions, to accommodate themselves to the will of God. In short, would not such a law, which necessarily involves the living, preclude an incident which forces us to see the marriage of Emily and Palamon as less meaningful than the death of Arcite at the height of fame?

But what of the living? Is their chief duty simply to accept the fact of death? Are we not to accept their marriage too as a foreseen and foreordained part of that wise plan

> "That speces of thynges and progressiouns
> Shullen enduren by successiouns,"   (ll. 3013-14)

as the means by which, in the Boethian scheme, the unity of God is imitated. If we accept the view, we may then assume that out of the necessity of death man may yet snatch the assurance of a gracious cooperation with the forces of nature. The freedom which is granted to Palamon and Emily, then, is freedom to cooperate with what God has ordained, to attain virtue through cooperation.

Such seems to be the double pattern of consolation *and* reconciliation [14] invested in the tale by its philosophical statement. It would be

[14] Opinion as to meaning ranges from that of Robert Kilburn Root, *The Poetry of Chaucer* (New York, 1906), p. 172, who sees in it, "the terrible reality of the mystery of life, its tragedy and its pathos," to that of George Kane, *Middle English Literature:*

curious indeed if the law of love should reconcile Palamon to the inevitability of dying as the end of man without offering him the necessity and grace, however Platonized, of living. And we faintly discern why the marriage of Palamon and Emily should, within the purview of elevated romance, prevent Arcite's laughter from beyond.

A Critical Study of the Romances, the Religious Lyrics, Piers Plowman (London, 1951), p. 88: "...the *Knight's Tale* is almost all show; it awakens little emotion, and the bright pictures which it leaves in the memory are cold." John Speirs, *Chaucer the Maker* (London, 1951), p. 123, comes close to an essential truth about the tale: "The *Knight's Tale* is continually on the point of moving beyond itself (as par excellence a courtly romance) into a substantiality that would be that of comedy or tragedy; yet it never completely does move beyond courtly romance, as does *Troilus and Criseyde:* it continues to be a courtly romance but with an inner tendency towards a completer reality."

THE MAN OF LAW'S TALE

As ... riding ryme serveth most aptly to write a merry tale, so rhythm royal is fittest for a grave discourse.

GEORGE GASCOIGNE,
*Certain Notes of Instruction
Concerning the Making of Verse
or Ryme in English*

The first link of the *Canterbury Tales* to provide us with insoluble problems is the *Introduction to the Man of Law's Tale*. We detected something of a difficulty in linking the Reeve's discourse on old age to his tale; although it was psychologically revealing, it was not dramatically and inevitably connected with the tale he tells. It was however in keeping with the notion of a loose-structured comedy in which the pilgrims could push forward with their opinions and maxims, their oaths and arguments, as protagonists of the dramatic action. The revelation of the Reeve's disquisition is but one instance of the gradually emerging importance of the links as an examinable meaningful entity, and it serves to reveal both the intellectual and the ethical bias of the speaker as an agent within the frame.

So dynamic is the frame and so manifold the problems of articulating the links and the tales that it becomes clear that Chaucer did not find any set pattern which would answer all his needs. All the changes in intention which we detect—tales which do not materialize (B² 3160, A 4360), tales cut off, links cancelled or reincorporated into others, shifting of tales to new speakers, the introduction even of a new person into pilgrimage—could have arisen only in the process of breathing life into what might easily have been a rigid frame.

It is clear that Chaucer is attempting what he has not essayed before. The *Legend of Good Women* is a collection of tales appended to a prologue, but without psychologically valid, comically realized agents, without a great variety of views of experience, without the compass of comic vision from the highest to the lowest attitudes. The

very vastness of the conception of the *Canterbury Tales* may have
been the factor that prevented Chaucer from bringing into a final
harmonious unit the variety of stories which he was in the process of
fitting into a frame.

The more burdensome tasks of art, we presume, were those of
assuring that the tone of the tale, its narrative technique, its themes
and thought, its emotional and ethical bearings be all in keeping with
the personality of the teller. This is indeed a most complicated matter
implying that the personalities of the pilgrims were firmly grasped,
brought into literary existence, and immediately assigned a tale. Common sense counsels otherwise: in some instances certain tales seem to
have been accomplished as literary exercises before the idea of the
Canterbury Tales; others seem to have come into existence on their
own merit while the *Tales* were being evolved, to be later attached
to the frame by whatever adjustments seemed necessary; in some
cases, regardless of when the tales were composed, posterity remains
puzzled as to the suitability of the agent to the tale, for example the
Physician's Tale, or that of the Shipman and that of the Manciple, to
cite only the more obvious examples.

Something of the unresolved nature of the details appears in the
Introduction to the Man of Law's Tale:[1] Is April 18 the first or the
second day of the pilgrimage? What do we make of the citation of
"Seintes" legends of "Cupide" which do not exist in the *Legend of
Good Women;* and what of those in the *Legend* which are not cited
here? What of the promise of a tale in prose? Does the promise of a
prose tale, which does not appear, indicate a shift in purpose from
some original or as yet unformed intention?

And what of putting into the mouth of the Lawyer the commenda-
tion of himself (Chaucer) with regard to stories dealing with incest?

> And . . . he, of ful avysement,
> Nolde nevere write in none of his sermons
> Of swiche unkynde abhomynacions,   (ll. 86–88)

to which the lawyer adds , "Ne I wol noon reherce." In spite of what
some object to in the fabliaux, Chaucer has not felt a need to justify
himself there in anything but conventional assertions that the word
must be cousin to the deed; here, whether or not a jibe at Gower is

---

[1] The problems are fully discussed by F. N. Robinson, *The Works of Geoffrey
Chaucer,* 2d ed. (Boston, 1957), pp. 689–92, and by Robert A. Pratt, "The Order of
the *Canterbury Tales,*" *PMLA,* LXVI (1951), 1149–56.

intended, he draws a moral line, manifesting even pride in the avoidance of such plots, perhaps defining some as yet obscurely felt principle for the range and limits of the kinds of tales he would tell. If he were determined to illustrate in any rigid scheme all the ramifications of love, he could easily have justified the subject of incest on artistic grounds and embellished it with florid rhetorical patterns and injected it with pathos, drawing upon such familiar sources as the *Wretched Engendering of Mankind* (which he translated at one stage of his development), the *Complaint of Nature* (which is clearly an influence in his poetry), or his own version of the *Parson's Tale*. But we can see from even a cursory glance that the *Canterbury Tales* resists such schematism; and Chaucer's mind, while not squeamish, yet turns away from the subject with deliberation.[2]

The facts urge us in another direction. The *Knight's Tale* has been a tale of love in which an irresistible law of human love is brought into conformity with God's providence. The Miller and the Reeve thereafter offer us reactions to the elevated views of the *Knight's Tale* in a healthy response on a lower plane of comic action. With the tale of Constance, a tale built upon the notion of an implicit and perfect love existing between creature and Creator, Chaucer seems to be defining the upper limit of love stories; the love between the sexes in the world of comedy may be fundamentally immoral, but it is normal human love, normal human passion which forms the lower limit of the range.

The tale of Constance has been grouped by Lounsbury[3] with the *Second Nun's Tale* and the *Prioress's Tale* as exhibiting "the development of Chaucer's poetical method in the treatment of themes essentially similar." It is a useful collocation to which we must surely add the *Clerk's Tale*, their common properties being their seriousness and the use of rhyme royal. They evince, however, different manners of treatment and different tones which may be demonstrated by a comparison of the tales of the Man of Law and the Clerk.

In mood and in degree and kind of rhetorical embellishment, the *Man of Law's Tale* and that of the Clerk are markedly opposed; but in that core of religious statement which both make, and in the movement either toward or away from an allegorical focus, they have a

---

[2] This matter is discussed at some length by T. R. Lounsbury, *Studies in Chaucer: His Life and Writings* (New York, 1892), III, 353 ff.
[3] *Ibid.*, II, 485.

demonstrable relationship. They cannot, to be sure, be equated with each other in manner: one is obvious, the other subtle; one makes its point by overt statement, the other by implication. The tale of Constance makes much—perhaps overmuch—of a didactic burden interpretable on an easily available *quid credas* level of statement. The tale of Griselda is virtually bare of flat didactic utterance, indeed makes an effort to withhold statement in favor of a more restrained, a more rarefied, and ultimately a more spiritual vision, the limits of which can be approached on the highest level of medieval literary interpretation, the level designated as *quo tendas*.

Both tales deal with the marriage of the heroine. For Constance the marriage is but one of many vicissitudes, albeit the central one, by which whatever Constance represents is tested and proved; for Griselda the marriage is the whole expression of reality, the whole experience by which to define something of the unutterable mystery of man's relationship to God, or of the soul's willingness to live by any law its Creator deems valid. Both of them are touched by that note of tenderness and pity towards oppressed innocence, innocence which itself elicits from the off-center world that it inhabits, undeserved calumny, chastisement, expulsion.

The Griselda story eschews extravagant ornamentation. Whatever Biblical elements exist in it are subtly interwoven into the texture of the plot; and the overtones of Biblical sentiments, while pervasive and diffuse, emanate from few loci. Its simplicity of presentation gradually accrues its own grave burden of intellectually apprehensible truths in a statement of so great a spiritual profundity that any attempt to "explain" its meaning, even within the poem itself (ll. 1142 ff.), tends to vitiate a part of its poetical strength.

The tale of Constance makes its statement by repeating over and over again rhetorical questions that can be answered only in one clearly perceived way, offering its screen of obvious riddles and exacting its answers from a bemused audience in what amounts to a charming preachment. It has a certain easily definable beauty, along with what appears to be a weighty burden of doctrinal meaning; this meaning, even through the touches of sophisticated wit and momentary lapse of taste, does not obviate the impression of a curiously childlike naïveté. Its ornamentation draws overwhelmingly upon religious beliefs in apostrophes, allusions, and exclamations. These are adduced throughout the story in so many crises that one must reckon with a flamboyant rhetoric with which to point up even simplest pieties. The bravura virtuosity goes well with the extravagant invention of the plot; indeed one has the feeling that the outrageous and fantastic episodes have necessitated the overblown and dilated insistence upon the presence of a Higher Power whose influence molds the life of this Christian woman, and provides, from the point of view of the plot, its informing spirit.

Fundamentally the tale of Constance deals with the character and faith of the Christian who puts himself with complete confidence within the control of his Maker. In its purely didactic religious aspect, it deals with the power of God to transcend all the influences of nature. A recitation of the religious additions made by Chaucer to support the didactic purpose of the tale would include the following: the power of the stars to dictate the occurrence of either good or bad events in the lives of men, but the power of God to nullify this influence; the death of Christ for the salvation of men; the ancient power of Satan to subvert mankind through Eve; the control of fortune and destinal patterns by God; the power of the sign of the cross; the power of faith; God's willingness to perform miracles for those who trust in him; a permissive view of evil; God's control of the elements; the victory of Christ over Satan; the sending of a teacher to those whom God wishes to convert; the exoneration of the faithful by divine intervention; the power of Mary as intercessor; the forgiveness of repented sin. One could go on multiplying instances by means of which Chaucer makes his story the vehicle for the more credulous kind of religious element, and insists by implication upon the wisdom of the Christian surpassing learning and experience. This wisdom is arrived at through the sublime resignation of the totally loving creature to the will of the totally loving Creator.

This is not to say that the tale is without humor and an occasional descent into a sardonic or witty comment, but only that the overwhelming effect is that of religious enthusiasm and insistence alongside the quieter and rarer atmosphere of the *Clerk's Tale*. If the affirmations seem too easily adduced, too facile, too self-conscious, they serve nevertheless to gloss over the difficult nature of the materials, so full of improbabilities as chronicle, with long stretches of historical time so difficult to translate convincingly into poetry. Not only do they afford the poet a device by which to elevate his historically oriented sources; they succeed in providing the justification by faith, which gives meaning to Constance's suffering. For the reader they provide one means by which we may make some estimate of the new form towards which Chaucer was moving in accommodating Trivet's account to poetry: we may consider, for example, the relationship between the purely narrative biographical account of Constance's life and the lyrical and occasionally rhapsodic passages which embellish it.

As with Trivet, so with Chaucer the dominant effect of the tale of Constance is pathos arising out of the continuing plight of a heroine who has no human defenders. Everywhere in Chaucer's careful manipulation of his sources is that quality of religious affirmation which we have noted above. Everywhere is that sharp distinction between the forces of good and those of evil, evil appearing somewhat symmetrically in an essentially duple structure (owing to the source) as the two women, the Sultaness and Donegild, and as the two men, the knight and the steward, who are both slain for their attempts upon the virtue of Constance. With the heroine's goodness placed so determinedly in the foreground of our sympathies, we cannot help feeling that Constance is not so much acting as acted upon, a feature which is up to a point demonstrable in Trivet. Actually, in order to make clear some statement about the perfected religious experience, Chaucer goes farther than his source by making Constance still more than ever the victim of a variety of adversaries, a victim who never raises her hand in self-defense because God Himself is her champion.

By the addition of religious elements [4] Chaucer encourages us to see the impingement of the supernatural upon the life of creatures. By the heightening of the purely human element (the realistic tears and lamentation, the pathetic concern of mother for child, the raising of anxious prayer), he makes his heroine more believable on the literal plane, and enhances the theme of his tale on any other by allowing

---

[4] The fullest account is that of Edward A. Block, "Originality, Controlling Purpose, and Draftsmanship in Chaucer's *Man of Law's Tale*," *PMLA*, LXVIII (1953), 572–616. Two papers of interest to students who wish to assess the intention of the poet are those of Bernard I. Duffey, "The Intention and the Art of the *Man of Law's Tale*," *ELH*, XIV (1947), 181–93, and Paull F. Baum, "The *Man of Law's Tale*," *MLN*, LXIV (1949), 62–63. For a brief list of the religious teachings of the tale, see Paul Ruggiers, "The Form of *The Canterbury Tales: Respice Fines*," *CE*, XVII (1956), 442–43. See also John A. Yunck, "Religious Elements in Chaucer's *Man of Law's Tale*," *ELH*, XXVII (1960), 249–61, for a discussion of the transformation of Trivet's account into "a romantic homily on the virtues of complete submission to divine providence."

her faith in God to flourish as a stable source of strength amidst very real human weaknesses.

Any attempt to extract the allegorical implications of the *Man of Law's Tale* leads into more rarefied religious and literary experience, and necessitates a recovery of a vocabulary. Yet, even when we fail to assess what seems from Chaucer's additions to be so obvious, we can look back to the *Knight's Tale* as a method of comparing the differing intention of the poet: the *Knight's Tale*, with its infusion of philosophical thought, carries a Neo-Platonic implication that the trials of this world are the corrective means by which man's will accommodates itself to Divine Necessity; indeed that tale goes far towards providing a rational order within which man's suffering has meaning and justification. This noble burden of ideas is superseded now, within the contexts and meaning of the pilgrimage pattern, by a thoroughly Christian point of view in which the will has not had to be corrected or shaped or molded, but is correctly oriented toward the Deity from the outset in a wholly salutary trust in the Lord. It is here, precisely, that the tale of Constance bears an interior and intimate relationship with the tale of Griselda. Both offer thought-provoking statements on the means by which worldly experience may be converted into love and service; both suggest an ideal relationship of the Church to Christ, perhaps, or more surely, of the soul to the Deity. Perseverance, fortitude, patience, loyalty, obedience, unswerving love as exemplified in Chaucer's two heroines suggest irresistibly the way of the soul in the process of salvation.

These are matters which, according to Dante, "chiefly attract the longing of mankind." [5] For the Christian audience Constance's homecoming and reconciliation with her father confirm poetically even the most wistful hope of an all-too-rare rapport between creature and Creator and an anagogical destination *in patriam*.

The *Man of Law's Tale*, a free adaptation of its source with amplifications, invites comparison with the *Clerk's Tale*, a translation with

[5] *Letter to Can Grande*, 19. It seems clear that Chaucer is constraining the recalcitrant materials of Trivet's pseudo-history towards poetry. Whether he has done this by expansion or constriction, by additions or omissions, by humanizing or dehumanizing the chief agent, the proof of the success of his version is its ability to render its audience well-disposed, attentive, and as Cicero would have it, tractable. The triumphant affirmation of Law in the life of the faithful commands attention by the steady application of the marvelous, while the reproach implicit in Constance's near-perfection renders the listener humble. So the Christian audience might have received it.

small additions. For the most part the *Clerk's Tale* implies its moral meaning; the *Man of Law's Tale* overwhelms us with its overt statement. Both deal with the improbable and romantically idealized, the *Man of Law's Tale* in the relation of God to one of his creatures, the *Clerk's Tale* in the relation of a creature to Lord and Master. Both of the accounts impose more than a suspicion of a strain upon Chaucer's credulity, and the reader's. Chaucer's main effort seems to have been directed in the *Man of Law's Tale* at making moving and appealing the character of Constance, and of presenting the frankly incredible with sufficient rhetorical persistence and didactic force to overshadow the unbelievable. Chaucer calls upon us to respond to rhetorical outbursts, to imprecations, to rhetorical questions about the source of Constance's strength. He makes free use of religious materials drawn from the life of Christ or Mary, and thus he makes lyrical and pathetic the plight of mother and child set adrift on the sea.

The general pattern of reconciliation worked out in the whole tale indicates on one level or another an artistic experiment with literary genre. The emotional extravagance from time to time seems hollow. The borrowing from far and wide in moral readings leads to matters not perfectly integrated, as for example when upon the death of Alla observations about human psychology are tied in with the theme of mutability.

Nevertheless the *Man of Law's Tale* is a thing of considerable beauty in its parts, particularly in those passages in which Constance is given the chance to display emotional responses to her incredible predicaments. When she acts at all she acts as the saints who act by suffering the fate doled out to them. In this sense, whether fate is seen in terms of a human injustice or oppression, or as an accident, or as a matter of astrological destiny, her life is that of a dedicated and providentially protected virtue, a vessel of purity amidst the wickedness and oppressions of the world.

THE PRIORESS'S TALE

And al was conscience and tendre herte.

The fierce bigotry of the Prioress forms a fine background for her tender-hearted sympathies with the Mother and Child; and the mode in which the story is told amply atones for the extravagance of the miracle.

WILLIAM WORDSWORTH,
Selections from Chaucer Modernized

Between them, Eileen Power and Sister Madeleva, more than twenty-five years ago, put to rest among the welter of scholarship many of the fanciful notions about Chaucer's Prioress, Madame Eglantine.[1] The fact that the work of these two fine scholars is not totally in agreement may be accounted for partly by the very ambiguity of character depiction in the *General Prologue* and by its customary ironical manner, partly by the different vocations of the two ladies writing about the Prioress. The emphasis of Sister Madeleva is upon the quite natural interaction of the religious vocation with the actions, life, and disposition of the Prioress, and arises out of her own experience as a nun. That of Miss Power is upon a certain worldliness to be found in the fourteenth-century convent, a worldliness which her studies as an historian corroborate. Both writers show charity no less than intelligence. And if Miss Power calls our attention to what the lady Prioress was before she entered upon the religious life and what the external affairs of her life as a prioress subsequently entailed, Sister Madeleva has shown us in the light of the Benedictine Rule what her daily interior life, a life of prayer and its effects upon action, must have been.

The fact, however, that two points of view so different may have

[1] Eileen E. Power, "Madame Eglentyne, Chaucer's Prioress in Real Life," *Medieval People* (Boston, 1924), pp. 59–84. See too her account of life in the nunnery in *Mediaeval English Nunneries* (Cambridge, England, 1922). See also Sister Madeleva, "Chaucer's Nuns," *A Lost Language and Other Essays on Chaucer* (New York, 1951), pp. 27–60. This essay was originally published in 1925.

validity demonstrates the characteristic ambiguity of Chaucer's descriptive portraiture. The Prioress's good manners, her storybook eyes and nose and smile "simple and coy," topped by the visible high forehead, her attention to careful dress, her pleated wimple, her romantic name, her fancy "beads" with the mysterious brooch and motto *Amor vincit omnia*, not to mention the ownership of well-fed puppies, and the sentimental attitude toward animals in general—all of these may be seen on the one hand as the irresistible lure of the world or, as Lowes has suggested,[2] as the eternal woman peeping through the restricting bonds of the religious vow; although we must exert our common sense to recall that entering upon the religious life does not automatically divest one of nature, or warmth, or essential humanity. Chaucer knew his good clerics from his bad and has managed to make the gradations between them psychologically provocative not only by his descriptions of them in the *General Prologue*, but by the stories he attributes to them. We come to know the Monk and the Friar, the Clerk and the Parson, the Pardoner, and the Prioress herself by the tale he gives each to utter as well as by the kind of relationship that Chaucer builds up between the particular agent and others on the pilgrimage.

Thus if there is an ambivalence of character in the depiction of the Prioress in the *General Prologue*, we can with some confidence look for confirming dichotomies of thought and action in her tale.

After the *Shipman's Tale* is over, the Host reveals a comic antipathy for the villain of the piece:

> "Wel seyd, by *corpus dominus*," quod oure Hoost,
> "Now longe moote thou saille by the cost,
> Sire gentil maister, gentil maryneer!
> God yeve the monk a thousand last quade yeer!
> A ha! felawes! beth ware of swich a jape!
> The monk putte in the mannes hood an ape,
> And in his wyves eek, by Seint Austyn!"   (ll. 435–41)

---

[2] John Livingston Lowes, "Simple and Coy: A Note on Fourteenth Century Diction," *Anglia*, XXXIII (1910), 440–51. He writes (p. 442): "In a word, not only in his account of the amiable foibles of the Prioress herself, but in his own choice of words and phrases, Chaucer suggests the delightfully imperfect submergence of the woman in the nun." Cf. F. N. Robinson, *The Works of Geoffrey Chaucer*, p. 653: "Chaucer's characterization of the Prioress is extremely subtle, and his satire—if it can be called satire at all—is of the gentlest and most sympathetic sort." For a new reading of the Prioress as a "grotesque" see D. W. Robertson, Jr., *A Preface to Chaucer*, pp. 244–48.

and draws his robustly comic moral:

> "Draweth no monkes moore unto youre in," (l. 442)

before offering us a marked change in his own manner and attitude as he speaks with heightened and self-conscious politeness to the Nun:

> "My lady Prioresse, by youre leve,
> So that I wiste I sholde yow nat greve,
> I wolde demen that ye tellen sholde
> A tale next, if so were that ye wolde.
> Now wol ye vouche sauf, my lady deere?" (ll. 447–51)

Since she and the whole company have just heard a monk debased and have had the monk's wily character brought to their attention more forcefully by the opening remarks of the Host to the Shipman, however triumphantly the monk has carried the day, we may suppose some faint embarrassment which prompts the politeness of the Host as he asks the Prioress for a tale. And we may look for a certainty and exultant holiness in the prologue to the tale of the Prioress, if we remember that she is vindicating not only an impulse of her own nature, but the religious life that has just been scandalized in the actions of the monk. So that when she begins to speak, it is with the gladness of her heart and considerable artistic craft that she utters the heartfelt cry of the Eighth Psalm:

> "O Lord, oure Lord, thy name how merveillous
> Is in this large world ysprad," quod she;
> "For noght oonly thy laude precious
> Parfourned is by men of dignitee,
> But by the mouth of children thy bountee
> Parfourned is, for on the brest soukynge
> Somtyme shewen they thyn heriynge." (ll. 453–59)

Then drawing more or less freely from the Divine Office, she makes direct application of her prayer to the need of the moment, passing from praise of God to praise of Mary as next worthy of honor. In the third stanza, progressing by degrees, she makes a direct plea to the Virgin Mother, addressing her in terms made available though the Little Office of the Blessed Virgin Mary as "bussh un-brent, brennynge in Moyses sighte" (l. 468), a detail which was in Chaucer's memory not only from the Office, but from his own early translation of Deguilleville's *Le Pèlerinage de la Vie Humaine*, in which he writes:

> Moises, that saugh the bush with flawmes rede
> Brenninge, of which ther never a stikke brende,
> Was signe of thin unwemmed maidenhede.
> Thou art the bush on which ther gan descende
> The Holi Gost, the which that Moyses wende
> Had ben a-fyr; and this was in figure.

Chaucer's version of the Prioress's now direct prayer to Mary is especially interesting for its violent figure of Mary's humility ravishing

> ... doun fro the Deitee,
> Thurgh thyn humblesse, the Goost that in th'alighte,"
>
> (ll. 469–70)

and for its metaphorical and doctrinal treatment of the conception of Christ, in the lines immediately succeeding these:

> "Of whos vertu, whan he thyn herte lighte,
> Conceyved was the Fadres sapience."   (ll. 471–72)

It is a conceit which we have seen in the opening lines of the *General Prologue* ("Of which vertu engendred is the flour."), now more securely oriented to the great mystery of Christ's origin. Then following a Dantean reminiscence (repeated in the *Second Nun's Prologue*) which vows that Mary, in her goodness, sometimes anticipates the prayers of men, the Prioress returns to her opening figure of the child lauding Deity, but with a difference: the child that the Prioress feels herself to be needs the help of Mary in order to sing the song in her praise.

What the Prioress has just uttered is a prayer of an elevated sort, its elevation resulting from that curious mixture of an almost rhapsodic impulse natural to the heart of the speaker with that doctrinal core inherent in the antiphons of the Divine Office. It stands as a kind of pause between the performance of the Shipman and that of a dedicated religious, and serves to preserve and sustain a deliberate distance between the profane and the holy, the impious and the sacred. Coming after the account of an errant and worldly monk (her own worldliness is not of the offensive sort which characterizes the monk of the tale and that other Monk of the *General Prologue*), it serves, with her own interpolated remark,

> This abbot, which that was an hooly man,
> As monkes been—or elles oghte be—   (ll. 642–43)

to restore a sense of religious balance to the situation. In this way Chaucer strips her for the moment of any worldly tone and by so doing preserves that element of dignity which is dominant in her character, and gives us witness to the devotion and conscience which are the better parts of her personality.

The tale that follows is linked to its prologue by its internal sentiment, that of children lauding God and Mary and of innocence becoming the instrument of the supernatural; and it belongs to that category of art which we may call the pathetic. The matters of belief that we encountered in the invocation of the Prioress have given way to the credulous and wondrously naive, and in the tenderness of the theme of a child suffering death at the hands of perfidious Jews because of his love for Mary, yet serving as a means by which God's justice through Mary will out, played against that plangent note of motherhood pitiful in bereavement, we see that the tale extends the sentiment expressed in the *General Prologue:* the Prioress is all heart. This Mary legend has a special inner pertinence too in that a mother who has lost a son appeals to Mary, who also has lost a son.[3]

The story is familiar enough: a seven-year-old school boy, the son of a widow, must pass through a ghetto on his way to school. He has been taught to say his *Ave Maria*, but not his *Alma Redemptoris*. Hearing this latter sung, he memorizes part of the Latin by rote and finally gets an older friend to tell him what the words mean. Pleased to have a song to sing in praise of Jesus' mother, he memorizes the whole prayer and thereafter sings it to and from school. Satan, who is ever the villain in Chaucer's more moral tales, inspires the hearts of Jews with hatred, they hire a murderer, the boy is slain and cast into a privy. The heartsick mother searches for her child, ever calling upon Mary for help. Finally as she approaches the place in the ghetto where his body has been thrown, the boy's voice is heard singing the *Alma Redemptoris;* the body is recovered and taken to a nearby abbey. The culprits are cruelly punished. But before the child can be buried, the abbot clarifies the mystery of the child who can sing although his throat is cut: Christ who wishes his glory to be remembered allows his mother's praises thus to be sung. Mary herself has

[3] Margaret H. Statler, "The Analogues of Chaucer's *Prioress' Tale:* the Relation of Group C to Group A," *PMLA*, LXV (1950), 896–910. She writes: "The very nature of the Cult of the Virgin in the Middle Ages with its worship of the Mother of Christ indicates the reason for the popularity of the theme of a son's death, the grieving mother, and his restoration to her by the Virgin."

placed the "greyn" upon the child's tongue, promising that when the object has been removed, she will fetch him away. The abbot removes the grain, the child expires, and the monks, after praising Christ's mother, bury the child in a tomb of marble.

There can be no doubt, to answer those who find much of the tale objectionable, that the treatment of the murderers is callous and cruel:

> "Yvele shal have that yvele wol deserve";
> Therfore with wilde hors he dide hem drawe,
> And after that he heng hem by the lawe.   (ll. 632–34)

As in the first *exemplum* of Chauntecleer, the punishment of homicide is in the context "murder will out":

> And right anon, ministres of that toun
> Han hent the carter and so soore hym pyned,
> And eek the hostiler so soore engyned,
> That they biknewe hire wikkednesse anon,
> And were anhanged by the nekke-bon.   (ll. 3058–62)

The close reader of Chaucer may further recall the more horrendous and useless cruelties of the *exempla* in the *Summoner's Tale* illustrating the sin of wrath. But the tale is a good enough example of medieval anti-Semitism, if one is looking for this trait in Chaucer; a much better example of it is to be found in Gower's *Confessio Amantis*,[4] and there are others. Chaucer does not shirk the facts of his sources, but his primary concern is for the truth and validity of the mind and heart of the Prioress. It is her own divided nature that encompasses compassion for animals and tolerates the drawing and quartering of villains; her nature which encompasses purity in a privy, a human nature which strives for earthly graces of deportment while holding rarefied spiritual values.

[4] VII, 3207–3360. Gower uses the tale to prove that pity and charity go hand in hand. See the discussion in Ruth M. Ames, "The Source and Significance of 'The Jew and the Pagan,'" *MS*, XIX (1957), pp. 37–47. T. R. Lounsbury (*Studies in Chaucer*, II, 491) found it regrettable that broadminded Chaucer "should have allowed his genius to pander, for the sake of literary effect, to a cruel slander which, begotten of superstition, was kept alive by ignorance." More recently R. J. Schoeck, "Chaucer's Prioress: Mercy and Tender Heart," *The Bridge: A Yearbook of Judaeo-Christian Studies*, II (1956), has suggested (p. 255) that there is in Chaucer's treatment of the Prioress "a clear-eyed recognition of the inhumanity of her Tale, its violation of the deepest sense of charity which fourteen centuries of Christianity had been laboring to develop, and its failure to carry the burden of charity which is enjoined on all Christians, but especially on religious."

It is this other side of her nature, the ecstatic note which Speirs calls to our attention,[5] that we hear counterpointing its opposite when the tale is done. The "O mooder Mayde! o mayde Mooder free!" of the invocation reiterated in the emotional and rhetorical attitude of "O martir, sowded to virginitee," through "O grete God, that parfournest thy laude / By mouth of innocentz, lo, heere thy myght!" together with the rich ornamentation and religious suggestion of "the white lylye flour," "The white Lamb celestial," "This gemme of chastite, this emeraude, / And eek of martirdom the ruby bright," as well as the "greyn" placed upon the child's tongue by the Virgin—all point to a controlled elevation and a controlled artistic goal, right through the triple cry for mercy in the last stanza:

> Preye eek for us, we synful folk unstable,
> That of his mercy, God so merciable,
> On us his grete mercy multiplie. (ll. 687–89)

There is, beyond the unity of effect impressed upon us by the rhapsodic tone, another kind of unifying embellishment which contributes to its religious meaning and heightens it. I refer to the investment in the tale of certain parts of the Mass and liturgy for the Feast of the Holy Innocents, which falls on December 28. The theme of the Mass for that day, developed through the proper prayers, is, like that of the *Prioress's Tale*, the perfecting of God's praise, and the bringing of confusion to God's enemies, through the utterances and acts of children. The commemoration of the death of Bethlehem's male infants within the octave of Christmas is a token of the Church's belief, given expression by St. Augustine, that these children slain by Herod's command, not only died for Christ, they actually died in His stead; martyrs in fact, if not in will, for whom the Church assumes the garments of mourning and suppresses any expression of joy. Interwoven into the Ordinary of the Mass, the Introit for the day, reversing the opening stanzas of the Eighth Psalm, strikes the keynote, that the praise of God even in the mouth of babes confounds His enemies: "Out of the mouth of infants and of sucklings, God, Thou hast perfected praise, because of thy enemies. O Lord, our God, how marvelous is thy name in the whole earth." By their death, not their word, the Collect goes on, innocents praise and confess God. The Epistle for the day (Apoc. 14:1–5) points to their triumph by calling to mind the "hundred and forty and four thousand" virgins,

[5] *Chaucer the Maker*, p. 179.

"not defiled with women," standing with the Lamb upon Mount Sion, while the Gospel (Matt. 2:13–18) recounts Herod's attempt to slay the infant Jesus through the broad command to murder all the male children of Bethlehem under two years of age, forcing the flight of the Holy Family into Egypt and fulfilling both the prophecy "Out of Egypt have I called my Son," and that of the mothers of Bethlehem who would weep, like Rachel for her children, for their own. The beautiful theme of the Mass, as I have said, is the perfecting of God's praise even in the youngest of His creatures, who, on this occasion, have died for Him; their triumph, as the Epistle implies, is to be with Him in Paradise. The thematic similarity in internal movement may further be seen in the view expressed in the liturgy (third nocturn of matins) that the suffering of the young and innocent for God is "the exaltation of Christ," and in the words of the Prioress:

> But Jesu Crist, as ye in bookes fynde,
> Wil that his glorie laste and be in mynde.   (ll. 652–53)

All of these elements appear in the *Prioress's Tale;* and it is entirely possible, as one scholar has speculated, that the tale may actually have been suggested to Chaucer by a sermon for the feast day,[6] or as another has advanced, that the tale was suggested by the liturgy for that day.[7] Indeed, we may go so far as to say that the seven-year-old "clergeon," with a prayer upon his lips, as a martyr not merely in fact but also in will, is an improved, speaking type of the Holy Innocents; that the villains who slew him offer some figural analogy with Herod's soldiers, as his widowed mother, like the mothers of Bethlehem, suggests the archetypal Rachel who cannot be comforted.

In this way the popular Mary legend is wedded inextricably to the more substantial authority of the Church and offers one more perplexing dichotomy to add to the appreciation of the subtly depicted narrator, whose character and personality are deepened as well as amplified by her performance.

Like her companion the Second Nun, the Prioress assumes the stance of a humble adult striving to be as a child before the divine and pleading for the assistance of Mary in the labor at hand. The story which each nun tells belongs to the miraculous and so demands the

[6] Marie Padgett Hamilton, "Echoes of Childermas in the Tale of the Prioress," *MLR*, XXXIV (1939), 1–8; revised for inclusion in *Chaucer: Modern Essays in Criticism*, ed. Edward Wagenknecht (Oxford University Press, 1959), pp. 88–97.
[7] J. C. Wenk, "On the Sources of the *Prioress' Tale*," *MS*, XVII (1955), 214–19.

suspension of disbelief by which the miraculous may make its special appeal to the contemplative mind. We do not have to strain for their meaning: what they have to say is obviously stated in terms of the demonstrated rapport between the transfigured soul and providential power.[8]

Some scholars, with Wordsworth, have noted the Prioress's fierce bigotry.[9] What we tend to remember, however, is a tale of transcendent innocence uttered in Chaucer's sweetest verse. The theme that comes through even the dreadful details of drawn and quartered villains is that of the special relationship of innocence to wisdom. The tale carries its meaning by a series of correspondences with the account of the Holy Innocents. It is not necessary to know about the liturgical substructure of the tale, however; by entrusting simple pieties to a child, by eliciting the utmost pathos from the spectacle of a bereaved mother, Chaucer corroborates at one and the same time our dimly felt convictions about spiritual and domestic relations.

[8] Germaine Dempster, *Dramatic Irony in Chaucer* (Stanford University Press, 1932), pp. 91–92, writes: "That power is more than an object of firm faith; it is a reality, a close and immediate reality not only for the author but for the reader, whatever his personal beliefs may be."

[9] It is difficult, in handling the problems of interpretation, to resist falling into the trap opened up many years ago by G. L. Kittredge, *Chaucer and His Poetry* (Harvard University Press, 1915), p. 155, of viewing the Prioress as a psychological case of "thwarted motherhood," and of allowing such a view to awaken in us the more sentimental responses. It is more difficult to resist the other view, equally "psychological," of "the overt streak of cruelty masked as pious hatred which is the visible obverse of the rather shallow sensibility that marks this nun's temperament."—Bertrand H. Bronson, *In Search of Chaucer* (University of Toronto Press, 1960), p. 78. One has to be satisfied with an irresoluble residue of ambiguity; to succumb to either of the temptations is, to my mind, to yield to the self-persuasion that verbalization often brings, or to read one's own sensibilities into the fictional character. It has been suggested that if we examine the details of the tale we will find perhaps that Chaucer has produced an "exemplar of the grotesque—a contrast between extreme polish and beauty of *surface finish* on the one hand, and a sentimentality and cruelty that jar sharply with the surface beauty." The suggestion offers a tempting possibility, though it runs the risk of becoming more subtle than the poet.

THE NUN'S PRIEST'S TALE

Toute est pour enseignement.
Roman de la Rose

From many points of view the *Nun's Priest's Tale* may be considered a high-water mark of complex thematic statement in the *Canterbury Tales*. Even with its proliferation of exemplary materials (such as we note in the tales of the Pardoner and Franklin), it constitutes a complex of most that is happy in Chaucer's artistic and intellectual equipment: a grasp of form, a subtle ironical tone, cleverness without slavery in the literary allusions, the subjection of high seriousness to the needs of the form, a casual finesse with rhetorical conventions, a sharpening of the theme of marital dissension, a suiting of moral utterance to the narrator, and a delicate balance between the romantic and comic modes. It is, in short, *sui generis*.

Its meaning has to do, in one sense, with the way in which reason and instinct are embattled (a sentiment common to the fabliaux), but it places these firmly against the larger questions of love, the destinal order, and human responsibility, and casts a final vote in favor of self-control. If this shift of balance to the side of reason suggests survival through canniness, we have, I feel, a merely ironical tale. By adducing the more serious questions of a rational universe, Chaucer widens the theological ambience in which his agents live, and tests the familiar triad of love, crucial adventure, and virtue acquired which are the heart of romance.

Coming as it does after the limited range of the Monk, the tale evinces an intellectual complexity which is its characteristic tone; just how far removed we are from the mechanical world of Venus, or Fame, or Fortuna, or from a vague retributive Justice meting out good and ill through apparent caprice is demonstrated by the tale of a cock, hen, and villain fox, all of whom have responsibility in a world they not only must interpret, but create for themselves. It is a world seen not from the point of view of tragedy, but of thought and laugh-provoking comedy. It is comedy that comes as a response to the plea of the serious-minded Knight, a man of moderate disposition, albeit a slayer of his foes and a mighty warrior in fifteen battles. The complexity Chaucer attributes to him is not merely a matter of having such a man cry out for gladsome tales. If we compare his character in detail with that of the lugubrious and doleful tale-teller the Monk, we discover new ironies inherent in their actions.[1] The purely physical details of the Monk's hulking figure, his fine horses, his taste for fine food and clothes, his overbearing assertion of service to God outside the monastic world afford a sharp contrast to the figure of the Knight with his meek and maidenly deportment, his restraint of tongue, his avoidance of the signs of wealth, his fruitful activity in defense of the faith. To attribute to the one a limited vision of the meaning of suffering and to the other a preference for tales with a happy ending is to point up in yet another way an expanding complexity of character in the pilgrimage community. Chaucer is, as it were, focusing his own attitudes upon the perplexities of tragedy and comedy in preparation for a new kind of tragi-comic vision far beyond the Monk's limited range.

In the *Monk's Tale*, the concept of tragedy, although it does not entirely omit the role of the will, is more mechanical than human, the effect of character upon action being restricted mostly to the defect of "mysgovernaunce" and to the "unwar strook" dealt out by Fortune. We note in it an absence of character development and the tendency to see human suffering only as the result of a fall. The form itself prevents a thoughtful interest in the development of ethos in the agents, in their ability to argue themselves into or out of situations and in the important consideration of the degree of human responsibility which the agents may assume in this life. In all justice to the tales related by the Monk, we must consider that any long treatment of these tragedies would conceivably entail a great deal of thought upon precisely such matters; indeed their defect is their brevity as much as it is the incompleteness of the whole view regarding Fortune and man's lot which they imply.[2]

The interruption by the Knight calls for something more in literature; if not a correction of the view of Fortune in its relations to the

---

[1] See R. E. Kaske, "The Knight's Interruption of the *Monk's Tale*," ELH, XXIV (1957), 249–68.

[2] Still useful is Theodore Spencer, "The Story of Ugolino in Dante and Chaucer," *Speculum*, IX (1934), 295–301.

law of the Prime Mover such as he himself has already presented in his tale of Palamon and Arcite, at least an amplification of a view of life which allows for quite another way of fictive presentation:

> "... whan a man hath been in povre estaat,
> And clymbeth up and wexeth fortunat,
> And there abideth in prosperitee:
> Swich thyng is gladsom, as it thynketh me,
> And of swich thyng were goodly for to telle."   (ll. 2775-79)

To this the Host gives scolding assent. His point of view may not be that of the Knight, a representative of quite another class of society, but he does know that what he has heard has become a heavy burden to the mind, if not an outright bore:

> "For sikerly, nere clynkyng of youre belles,
> That on youre bridel hange on every syde,
> By hevene kyng, that for us alle dyde,
> I sholde er this han fallen doun for sleep,
> Althogh the slough had never been so deep."   (ll. 2794-98)

And so the Knight and Host are united in common intention if not in comprehension of the issue at hand. Both have objected to the performance of the Monk, the Knight we presume because he objects to the statement of a not entirely sound view of life (if we may judge him from the story he has told) and because "litel hevynesse / Is right ynough to muche folk, I gesse." The Host objects because there is "no desport ne game" in these tales, and furthermore the reiterated theme has become monotonous. Both views have their healthy side.

The Monk, however, had had his say and declines to relate a tale of hunting; his natural discretion, which has held him back from engaging in badinage with the Host, again urges upon him the better course of keeping his private life to himself. We turn instead to another religious, the "sweete preest, this goodly man, sir John," who is urged to tell us a happy, cheerful tale. His horse, a jade "bothe foul and lene," offers a contrast to the sleek berry-brown palfrey of the Monk, whom the Nun's Priest now supersedes. But as we read we see that the paucity and poverty of material goods in the Nun's Priest do not preclude a richness of natural gifts and a depth of cheerful goodness absent from the performance of the materially endowed, self-limiting Monk.

For reasons which we can only surmise, Chaucer has not given explicit details about the person and character of the Nun's Priest. In the *Prologue of the Nun's Priest's Tale* the Host describes his horse, and in the famous epilogue, regarded by some as a cancelled link, substantially repeats a line and a sentiment which we have already heard him apply to the Monk: "Thou woldest han been a tredefowel aright" (B^2 3135). We can only conjecture that Chaucer has, by the shift of the line to the previous performance, exhausted one view of the ecclesiastical male and temporarily, at least, abandoned the matter of expanding upon the character of the Nun's Priest. On artistic grounds it seems suitable too to explore the matter of celibacy and marriage (the lives of Monk and Host) immediately following upon the *Melibee*, a natural enough movement from the admonitions of Dame Prudence in that tale to the bodily threats of Goodelief in the Monk's *Prologue*, and thence to the plight of matrimony in a world from which the best men have escaped. It would seem that Chaucer is by degrees opening the door on the many-faceted subject of marriage, so that when he has finished the *Nun's Priest's Tale*, there is little reason for him to revert to the matter of priestly celibacy inasmuch as it diverts attention from the subject of the tale itself and repeats elements now applied to the character of the Monk.

Since Chaucer himself has told us little about the character of the Nun's Priest (some deductions may be made from the tone and attitudes of the tale assigned him), critical opinion has perforce to be conjectural. One commentator describes him as "a handsome, strong, rosy-cheeked youngster, with a sense of humor unequalled in the company," who can "deftly satirize the personal characteristics and the literary style of his predecessor without for a moment arousing the suspicion of his dignified superior." [3] Another later writer suggests that he is "Scrawny, humble, and timid, while at the same time highly intelligent, well-educated, shrewd and witty," and further that he is "weak in body and fawning in manner." [4] These are tantalizing surmises; in the end, each reader will feel that the personality of the Nun's Priest is best derived from an examination of the story Chaucer chose to assign him.

As we have said, the tale masterfully integrates many elements which we have seen or noted singly or in combinations in other tales. More important perhaps than these elements taken one by one or in

[3] Samuel B. Hemingway, "Chaucer's Monk and Nun's Priest," *MLN*, XXXI (1916), 479–83.
[4] Robert M. Lumiansky, "The Nun's Priest in the *Canterbury Tales*," *PMLA*, LXVIII (1953), 896–906.

combination is the creation of a frame or envelope in which to contain the moral and quasi-mythic structure. This outer frame presents to us those human agents necessary to provide for the reader some ideal of human behavior, some rule of continence and contentment. The old widow, with her little cottage and her careful economy by which she provides for herself and her two daughters, offers by such details as temperance of diet and exercise and a contented heart an image of temperate law, of self-restraint and self-control, of sobriety and reasonable discretion. It is the widow's yard that is the world, apparently safe and secure, for Chauntecleer and his wives; it is into this world that evil intrudes in the shape of the sly fox; it is to this world that the widow wishes to restore Chauntecleer at the conclusion of his adventure, setting in motion the final boisterous attempt at rescue.[5]

But it is Chauntecleer's plight which holds our interest and for which the outer human frame exists. It is Chauntecleer's character and his virtues or absence of virtues, his self-assurance and braggadocio, his pride, his sensuality, his susceptibility to flattery, and his sly intelligence that engage our minds. The opening description of Chauntecleer, replete with instinctive passion and joy, follows immediately upon the associations of poverty and patient, passionless temperance. Style itself echoes the contrast as Chaucer begins to employ the language of the romantic mode, and what is austere or even pedestrian in the opening of the tale gives way to something courtly, perhaps, and descriptively elevated, with even a momentary flight into lyric: "My lief is faren in londe!"

This may be considered the high style, in keeping with the poet's intention to parody the purely tragic view of the Monk and to supply a corrective through the device of comedy. Hence the necessity for enhancing the character of the cock so that he may appear to be regal, hence the fall from good fortune, hence the philosophical rumination about the relation of will to necessity, the elevated speeches, apostrophes and exclamations, the comparisons with figures of classical antiquity, and hence the errors in judgment and the final moral tag. The subjects and mannerisms of tragedy must be present,

---

[5] Needless to say this interpretation is somewhat willful, an insistence that the opening section has pertinence to the whole tale. Paull F. Baum, *Chaucer: A Critical Appreciation*, p. 134, sees it as a false start. See Mortimer J. Donovan, "The *Moralite* of the Nun's Priest's Sermon," *JEGP*, LII (1953), 505, for the identification of the widow with the Church.

even in ironical contexts, seen in contrast to the subjects and mannerisms of comedy: the world of love and marriage, of domestic quarreling, of deception and jokes, of personal arrogance and instinctive
passions, of personal vanity and wishing to be right at all costs, of wit
and hairbreadth escape, of chases and rueful laughter. The result is, in
its way, like the relation of the *Franklin's Tale* to the *Merchant's
Tale*, a saner, more humane attitude than the one stated in the previous tale.

A large section of the tale is composed of the debate between
Chauntecleer and his beauteous paramour Pertelote on the subject of
dreams. Their speeches reveal a great deal of their character; Pertelote's lines beginning "Avoy! Fy on yow, hertelees!" with their
repeated exclamations and questions are full of feminine excitability
and concern. Her admonitions are purely domestic: "For Goddes
love, as taak som laxatyf." Her wisdom is for the most part the wisdom of the home dispenser. Chaucer is clearly enjoying the game.
Chauntecleer's long-winded answer, beginning with an elaborate politeness ("Madame, graunt mercy of youre loore.") is a rejoinder of
some haughtiness of tone. More than a refutation answering the al-
leged authority of Cato, the long recital of superior authorities allows
us to see Chauntecleer as one of Chaucer's more self-conscious
orators, more thoughtful, more playful and sly, more pompous and
self-assured. The cock is a narrator of no little skill, constructing his
two initial *exempla* with great care as to form and tone and attention
to detail. Indeed he is so careful a constructer of plot, with its inevitable conclusions, that the moral statement with which the first one
closes tends to overshadow the principal concern with the credibility
of dreams:

> "O blisful God, that art so just and trewe,
> Lo, how that thow bewreyest mordre alway!
> Mordre wol out, that se we day by day.
> Mordre is so wlatsom and abhomynable
> To God, that is so just and resonable,
> That he ne wol nat suffre it heled be,
> Though it abyde a yeer, or two, or thre.
> Mordre wol out, this my conclusioun."   (ll. 3050–57)

But the point is made, first through a reluctant believer in dreams, and
then through an actual non-believer who is proved to be wrong.
Thereafter Chauntecleer warms to his task, and in a rapid mélange of

instances drawn from Biblical, literary, and historical sources, within a space of some 40 lines as compared with the 126 of the first two *exempla*, he rattles off six additional stories to refute his wife's authority. His conclusion is inevitable, a mixture of the tragic assertion with the most bathetic comic statement:

> "Shortly I seye, as for conclusioun,
> That I shal han of this avisioun
> Adversitee; and I seye forthermoor,
> That I ne telle of laxatyves no stoor,
> For they been venymous, I woot it weel;
> I hem diffye, I love hem never a deel!"   (ll. 3151–56)

And the action that follows upon this long debate, in which each agent has but one major speech, bears out this prediction. But before the action there intervenes his love speech to Pertelote containing its bold and unself-conscious *ludum*, a joke at the expense of his less tutored wife:

> "...*In principio,*
> *Mulier est hominis confusio,*—
> Madame, the sentence of this Latyn is,
> 'Womman is mannes joye and al his blis.'"   (ll. 3163–66)

Whether we cheer or blame him in this joke upon his wife-paramour, the speech is that of the passionate lover, embellished with sincere regard, expressing gratitude for God's grace, joy and comfort in her companionship, as well as that up-surging confidence that enables him to defy dreams and visions. They have had their quarrel or debate, but their relationship is a happy and a natural one elevated by the poet through the language of love. The jest that Chaucer puts in his beak hints at that double-edged truth to which the Middle Ages were dedicated by tradition on the one hand and by human nature on the other: in the beginning Eve was the source of Adam's fall. And yet, Chaucer's humane and comic realism forbids the dour anti-feminist implications [6] and provides a counterpoise in that other truth, that other affirmation, *Amor vincit omnia.*

> "For whan I feele a-nyght your softe syde,
> Al be it that I may nat on yow ryde,
> For that oure perche is maad so narwe, allas!

---

[6] But see Arthur T. Broes, "Chaucer's Disgruntled Cleric," *PMLA*, LXXVIII (1963), 156–62; Charles A. Owen, Jr., "The Crucial Passages in Five of the *Canterbury Tales*: A Study in Irony and Symbol," *JEGP*, LII (1953), 309; and J. Burke Severs, "Chaucer's Originality in the *Nun's Priest's Tale*," *SP*, XLIII (1946), 37.

> I am so ful of joye and of solas,
> That I diffye bothe sweven and dreem."   (ll. 3167–71)

We see Chauntecleer here in all his pride, hardly deigning to set his foot to the ground, royal as a prince in his hall, says Chaucer, summoning all his wives with a mere cluck.

Up to this point (l. 3186) the narrative has supplied us with a situation which is to be fulfilled in the remaining part of the tale, and with some intellectual attitudes that are to be tested. Chauntecleer's pride has been placed before us not only in the details of his dainty high stepping and his grim lion's look, but in the whole context of his long answer to Pertelote. Chaucer hereafter plays against each other instinct and rational control in much the same way that he assays willfulness and human responsibility in *Troilus and Criseyde.*

With the return to a purely narrative tone in lines 3187 ff., Chaucer seems to take a deep breath before providing the catastrophe foreseen by Chauntecleer in his dream. In the midst of the beauties of May, when Chauntecleer's heart is full of "revel and solas," he is to discover that the latter end of joy is woe. The Nun's Priest now raises the whole question of destiny and man's freedom as the catastrophe impends, and the fox waits to fall upon the cock. It is a burst of rhetoric in a variety of tones: the extravagant comic sublime ("O false mordrour . . . / O newe Scariot, newe Genylon, . . . o Greek Synon, / That broghtest Troye al outrely to sorwe! / O Chauntecleer . . .") merges into a more arid statement of simple and conditional necessity familiar to readers of the *Consolatio,* and finally into the traditional indictment:

> Wommennes conseils been ful ofte colde;
> Wommannes conseil broghte us first to wo,
> And made Adam fro Paradys to go,
> Ther as he was ful myrie and wel at ese.   (ll. 3256–59)

In the mouth of the Nun's Priest, such a statement is a kind of bold impertinence; in Chaucer's mouth it is not less so if we bear in mind the tradition of oral presentation at court. And yet it has a kind of arch humor about it. It can be carried off by welding it fast to the narrative context:

> My tale is of a cok, as ye may heere,
> That tok his conseil of his wyf, with sorwe,
> To walken in the yerd upon that morwe
> That he hadde met that dreem that I yow tolde.   (ll. 3252–55)

And so the narrator escapes responsibility both for philosophical explanation and for the indictment of women. Just how much involvement we can impute to Chaucer himself, or how much the poet has made the indictment of women a statement assessable only in terms of the priest's character—these are questions that we solve only with a kind of presumption.

And yet there may be a level of artifice here, a trick of narrative in which the artist-writer stands behind his creations and allows some of his own personal attitudes to be expressed through one of his agents, a form of play in which we sometimes discern the remoter *ludum* beyond the situation in which the agents are involved: Chauntecleer has had his intellectual fun in deceiving his wife with a Latin tag; Chaucer has had the Nun's Priest offer us, in Chauntecleer's translation of the Latin, two definitions of love which threaten to cancel each other out: Adam fell through Eve's counsel and bequeathed to their children similar falls without number; yet in the relationship of Chauntecleer and his wife-paramour there is a certain careless and lovely sensuality, a springtime "revel and solas," an overtone of one strong tradition that sees the love of woman as the means by which man perfects himself. It constitutes a perennially perplexing ambiguity which man's mind declines to resolve, even if it could.

We pass out of the romantic and sensual into the mutability theme, into a commentary upon the turn of fortune's wheel, with which we have been bludgeoned in the previous performance. The joke becomes more serious; the sarcasm, faintly antifeminist in the priestly attitude towards women's taste in literature, is kindly enough if it is Chaucer's own view; if it is the Priest's, there is a want of decorum in his speaking even in so veiled a fashion before the Prioress, the Nun, and even the Wife of Bath, who can make a moral point herself, with considerably less ambiguity. But in the familiar lines dealing with the opinions of worthy clerks on the problem of evil and the relation of God's foreknowledge to man's free will, the universal problem of the freedom of all men arises, and one feels that it is not the Priest's reluctance to provide a solution, but Chaucer's own disinclination that is expressed in the line, "I wol nat han to do of swich mateere." It seems strange that this priest should not know what he believes, when all the other clerical tales stand squarely upon the strong base of assertion. It seems less strange that Chaucer should do what writers have always done in the spirit of play: allowed their creations to toy with notions they themselves would decline.

But the context is comic and philosophical. The elevation of Chauntecleer's fortunes to a level we expect of the epic and tragic has the obvious effect of comic incongruity and disproportion. The narrator's special task is to accommodate the mysteries of the destinal order, dreams, Venus, nature, and the rest to a Divine Foreknowing which yet allows to man significant action and a saving self-knowledge. As the subsequent appearance of the fox makes clear, Chauntecleer's original assertion was correct, and Pertelote was wrong: he will indeed have adversity as a result of his dream. Seduced by the confidence which may be the fruit of love, and following his wife's advice so far as to "fly down from the beams," Chauntecleer makes obvious the difference between believing with conviction and acting upon that conviction. No matter how bad the advice of Pertelote, Chauntecleer cannot be exempt from the trials and temptations of his temporal existence. Indeed, the trials and temptations are themselves the means by which the Christian comedy achieves its happy goal, the battlefield upon which the soldier's mettle is put to the test.

The test offered by the appearance of the fox is compounded of flattery and deceit which in some measure balances out Chauntecleer's own towards his wife. In both deceptions there is that curious inter-mingling of instinctive self-preservation with soothing, blandishing flattery. Both deceptions are successful, the fox's more obviously so inasmuch as Chauntecleer's bird nature itself conspires to supplement the fall: like his father's, and presumably every rooster's before him, Chauntecleer's endeavors to match his parent's singing necessitate the closing of the eyes. "Ah! beware of the betrayal through flattery," cries the Priest, and in an instant, Chauntecleer is caught by his natural enemy.

It is difficult to refrain from pointing up the skill of the rhetorical pattern of complaint beginning with line 3338, "O destinee, that mayst nat been eschewed!" and passing shortly to "O Venus, that art goddesse of plesaunce," then to "O Gaufred, deere maister sov-erayn," and finally to the capping mock heroics of lamentation in "O woful hennes, right so criden ye," the quadruple outburst drawing into fearful and wonderful juxtaposition comedy of situation with the inflated sublime of exclamatory closet tragedy. Whatever may be lacking in internal unifying factors is more than adequately compensated by the poetic effort to hold in delicate balance the humble matters of comedy with the elevated, the transporting, and the philosophical matters of tragedy.

The poem draws to its closing act in a burst of vividly detailed activity. All that has been restrained, controlled, elevated gives way in style and subject matter to the hectic demands of a chase. The serenity and moderated quietude of the poor widow's household is dissipated in a flash by the spirit of mobilized rescue spreading like wildfire to "many another man," and to the dogs, and in further hectic sympathy, to the hogs, cows, ducks and geese, and a swarm of bees. Then in a sudden move out of the excitement of the chase, the Nun's Priest closes in upon his moral goal in the colloquial and familiar tones of admonition: "Now, goode men, I prey yow herkneth alle" (l. 3402).

The reversal of Fortune by which Chauntecleer's native wit brings about his escape gives us some clue as to the relation of man's reasoned actions to the providential plan. The flattery by which he himself deceived his wife was superseded by that of the fox; now again, the laying on of flattery and praise for the sake of personal safety wins the cock his freedom; the fox's last attempt with unctuous and specious humility to win back his loss is deservedly unsuccessful, and Chauntecleer's answer to his enemy is a famous locus in Chaucerian moral statement:

> "Thou shalt namoore, thurgh thy flaterye,
> Do me to synge and wynke with myn ye;
> For he that wynketh, whan he sholde see,
> Al wilfully, God lat him nevere thee!"
>   "Nay," quod the fox, "but God yeve hym meschaunce,
> That is so undiscreet of governaunce
> That jangleth whan he sholde holde his pees."
>   Lo, swich it is for to be recchelees
> And necligent, and truste on flaterye.
> . . . .
> Taketh the moralite, goode men.   (ll. 3429–40)

Not only Chauntecleer, but the fox as well has come to a kind of wisdom that goes beyond the use of wit: both of them must observe a law of governance; both of them must come to rueful admissions of their failure to recognize the advantages of self-control. In the famous lines quoted above, both have learned through error.

The *Nun's Priest's Tale* thus raises the questions of human responsibility and destiny in the manner of tragedy or the moral romance but dismisses them, as a kind of impertinence, in favor of man's ability to learn from daily experience, in the manner of an ironic comedy. Its subject matter is a weighing of two sides of the ledger of man's serious and comic interests.

A host of questions is set in motion in contexts domestic and destinal. Insofar as the questions can be confronted, they challenge the facile view of tragedy set up by the Monk. The answers, insofar as they are given, are couched in the terms of ironic affirmation: man is responsible for errors in judgment; from the errors flows self-knowledge. And about chance, or love, or destiny, the least said the better.

One level of its meanings can be described by the word "quizzical." [7] They arise out of the complex picture of man seen as willful and self-loving, yet amiable and capable of loving others; created in the divine image but somehow all-too-human; responsible for his actions yet somehow controlled by forces beyond himself. To assert that man is free and at the same time that he is not is in effect to make us accept both assertions as true. To offer the view that love yields joy and then that it offers sorrow, or to hold in balance the philosophy of Boethius and Bradwardine with a world of laxatives and remedies for ague, is in essence to concentrate our gaze upon the disparities in the experience of fallen man and to confess to a certain helplessness in the human condition.

On another more accessible level of meaning we encounter the ironist's pronouncements to those who must pick their way through the obstacles of life: beware of flattery which destroys self-control, blinds us to what we should see, and loosens our tongues when we should be still. The lesson spoken at the close by cock and fox is securely anchored to the real world of expedience in which there are errors in judgment, flattery, negligence, lack of governance, and an uneasy acceptance of another. Whether the promulgator of those

---

[7] Two articles have opened up a new avenue of inquiry into the function of the fable as a literary type: Stephen Manning, "The Nun's Priest's Morality and the Medieval Attitude toward Fables," *JEGP*, LIX (1960), 403–16; and R. T. Lenaghan, "The Nun's Priest's Fable," *PMLA*, LXXVIII (1963), 300–307.

pedestrian truths is the inscrutable Sir John pronouncing so knowledgeably on life and love or Chaucer speaking through a mask, a sane
hope pervades them: the hope for rational creatures accepting the
appalling truth of their day-to-day responsibility within (it is de-
voutly wished) a rational universe.

The final plight of Chauntecleer demonstrates the relation of instinct to rational control, of thoughtless vanity to presence of mind,
of foolish pride to a just humility. The "happy" ending, with the
rivals standing hand in hand, so to speak, reciting what wisdom they
have achieved, reveals some truths in miniature, truths mundane and
pedestrian, but truths nonetheless.[8]

[8] Charles Muscatine, *Chaucer and the French Tradition* (University of California
Press, 1957), p. 242, offers salutary warning: "Unlike fable, the *Nun's Priest's Tale*
does not so much make true and solemn assertions about life as it tests truth and tries
out solemnities. If you are not careful, it will try out your solemnity too; it is here,
doubtless, trying out mine.... The shifting style and succession of topics never rest
long enough to serve a single view or a single doctrine or an unalterable judgment....
None of the targets of the poem's parodies are demolished, or even really hit at the
center. There are senses in which the solemnities of courtly love, science, marriage,
authority, eloquence, tragedy, the Monk, and the *Tale of Melibee* are funny, but the
Nun's Priest's Tale does not make us feel that they are always funny ... it offers no
conclusion but that sublunary values are comically unstable.... In the *Nun's Priest's
Tale*, as altogether in the mature Chaucer, we are compelled to respect the conservative conclusion because the question has been so superbly well confronted....
The Chaucerian mixed style illuminates the tale's microcosmic contradictions, just
as it expresses, in large, the great capaciousness of Chaucer's humane vision."
    D. W. Robertson, Jr., *A Preface to Chaucer*, p. 281, notes with insight that Chau-
cer's humor, "which is based on the confident acceptance of a Providential order
underlying the apparent irrationality of the world and its inhabitants, is sometimes
more profound and more persuasive than any 'highly serious' discourse couched in
the grand style can possibly be. True humor ... requires an intellectual approach
which permits a sense of detachment, not the detachment of the egoist or of the
self-styled sophisticate, but the detachment of a man whose faith is unshaken by the
shortcomings of society and whose love for his fellows enables him to regard both
their pettiness and his own with a certain equanimity."

THE WIFE OF BATH'S TALE

Allas! allas! that evere love was synne!

> *Bele iere e jenne e nice e fole,*
> *N'onc ne fui d'Amours a escole*
> *Ou l'en leust la theorique*
> *Mais je sai tout par la pratique:*
> *Esperiment m'en ont fait sage,*
> *Que j'ai hantez tout mon aage;*
> *Or en sai jusqu'a la bataille,*
> *Si n'est pas dreiz que je vous faille*
> *Des biens aprendre que je sai,*
> *Puis que tant esprouvez les ai.*
> *Bien fait qui jennes genz conseille.*
> *Senz faille, ce n'est pas merveille*
> *S'ous n'en savez quartier ne aune,*
> *Car vous avez trop le bec jaune.*
> *Mais tant a que je ne finai*
> *Que la science en la fin ai*
> *Don bien puis en chaiere lire.*
>
> *Roman de la Rose*

The demonstration of borrowings or adaptations from such sources as St. Jerome, Deschamps, Walter Map, and the *Romance of the Rose* in the *Wife of Bath's Prologue* cannot in any way prevent the impression that the creation of her character is invention of the first rank and that the so-called sources are but the basic ore out of which a brand-new coin is forged. Our appreciation of what Chaucer has done is considerably increased if we recall that the Wife's performance, as we have it, is not the first conception of her character. It represents an afterthought in which her personality has been vitalized and deepened by giving her a tale of the wish-fulfillment sort. This better afterthought is, we surmise, the refurbished prologue to her tale, with the change from what is now the *Shipman's Tale* to the more poetically suggestive account of the loathly lady made beautiful.[1]

[1] The assignment of the *Shipman's Tale* to the Wife of Bath has been a matter of considerable discussion. I am of the opinion so well expressed by J. S. P. Tatlock that

It is tempting to consider the possibility that the expanded performance of the Wife of Bath, in particular her long *Prologue*, was intended to reflect several of the points of view that pervade the *Romance of the Rose*, points of view which, although they are juxtaposed with attitudes drawn from antifeminist tracts or from religious treatises supporting virginity and single marriages, manage to give a kind of integrity to the Wife's whole defense.[2] I do not refer to the obvious relation that exists between La Vieille and Chaucer's creation in their debasing of love to the uses of sensuality and monetary gain, for this seems to me to be but a small part of the influence of Jean de Meun upon Chaucer's Wife of Bath. I refer rather to the philosophically defended principle of generation, opposing any code like that of courtly love or even that extreme position which makes chastity the supreme virtue and sees even in marriage only a concession to the frailty of the flesh.

One wonders, in the Wife's total performance, whether it is not this philosophical view of plenitude, continuity, and replenishment which is the support for the Wife's justification of the natural in-

---

"there cannot be the smallest doubt that the woman [for whom the *Shipman's Tale* was written] is the Wife of Bath."—*The Development and Chronology of Chaucer's Works*, Chaucer Society, 2d Series, No. 37 (London, 1907), pp. 205 ff. An interesting and highly provocative suggestion about the shifting of assignments and the amplification of the Wife of Bath's *Prologue* is that of Richard F. Jones, "A Conjecture on the Wife of Bath's *Prologue*," *JEGP*, XXIV (1925), 512–47, especially the discussion on pp. 521 ff. Much of the whole problem has been soundly and decisively re-examined by W. W. Lawrence, "Chaucer's *Shipman's Tale*," *Speculum*, XXXIII (1958), 56–68.

The Wife's *Prologue* and the tale represent separate acts of creation. The decision to articulate them is itself a bold and creative act, since it takes into account what looks to be an indomitable recalcitrance and a wistful longing for a charitable cooperation in love. The *Prologue*, like Old Comedy, offers a two-part structure composed of a theory and a series of demonstrations in which it is possible to see a progress towards toleration. Her tale, taken after her *Prologue*, allows us to see a fairly typical pattern of romance, the reward for loving well in the light of new values.

[2] One of the vaster, but most interesting excursions in the history of ideas is that of tracing out the intermingling of Platonic and Aristotelian ideas of plenitude and continuity with those of the Hebrew-Christian world with respect to the replenishment of the earth. A. O. Lovejoy's *The Great Chain of Being* (Harvard University Press, 1936) is a work of immeasurable value. C. S. Lewis' *Allegory of Love: A Study in Medieval Tradition* (Oxford University Press, 1936) and E. C. Knowlton's essays, "The Allegorical Figure Genius," *CP*, XV (1920), 280–84, "The Goddess Nature in Early Periods," *JEGP*, XIX (1920), 224–53, and "Nature in Old French," *MP*, XX (1923), 303–29, will throw considerable light upon the uses to which the doctrines can be put in literature. A book of extraordinary interest for all students of literature of the Middle Ages, particularly the *Romance of the Rose* and Chaucer's thought, is that of Alan M. F. Gunn, *The Mirror of Love: A Reinterpretation of "The Romance of the Rose"* (Texas Tech Press, Lubbock, Texas, 1952), especially Chapter XI, "The Philosophy of Plenitude," pp. 205–27.

stincts, and whether her experience which she opposes to the dicta of conventional theology does not have underlying it an intellectual tradition antipathetic to that of the older Christian writers. The beliefs that the generative process is sacred, that chastity may be offensive to God, that the organs of generation may be honestly defended even at the risk of being offensive to fastidious audiences, have the respectable authority of writers of the School of Chartres to support them. The vigorous defense of the physical side of love may be seen psychologically as an expression of a deep-seated and recalcitrant coarseness in the Wife of Bath, or even as an overflow of the antifeminist literature and bias of the times. Nonetheless it is a point of view which has a history and a tradition of its own. It is familiar as one aspect of a conflict within the medieval mind which could with conviction defend the world as good in all its phases while at the same time reaching for another world attainable only by denying the pleasures of this one; or to put it another way, as one aspect of the rationale which seeks through the amatory instincts the clue to the higher love of God.

The point of view which the Wife adopts is of course comic, and not all the premises of the Platonizing school are here. She does not go so far as to insist that chastity and abstinence are sins against God; on the contrary, she defends virginity and continence for those who would be perfect. But she does know that the purpose of love and marriage, its sacred aim, is to replenish the earth; this she defends spiritedly provided it is not divorced from the pleasures which are the joyful part of the conjugal debt. She does not go so far as to state that by fulfilling the law of love, by replenishing the earth, men participate in the creative power of the Deity—this would be too rare for an earthbound creature. She only can affirm with vigor that the generative organs have both a physical function and a pleasurable use ("for office, and for ese / Of engendrure, ther we nat God displese") which, within marriage, she will extravagantly exploit, as is her right within God's law.

It is obvious that the Wife of Bath knows much about the right uses of marriage and is as clear about the conjugal debt as is her literary cousin the Merchant, or her counterpart in the *Shipman's Tale*.[3] But she is not as much interested, so far as we can tell, in

[3] D. W. Robertson, Jr., *A Preface to Chaucer*, p. 327, finds the Wife "firmly among the evil who are in the Church but not of it." But the interpretation which he offers

"engendrure" as she is in sexuality itself. Her sensuality, her sexual desire, is the mark of Venus upon her, a force which has driven her into relationships that fall far short of love. With considerable pathos, she evinces a desire to be wanted: she could not withhold her Venus-chamber from any good fellow, nor make distinctions between her lovers, so long as they cared for her (ll. 625–26). Chaucer does not praise or blame her for being what she is. He obviously understands intimately the view that she brings to life, even writes with consider-able relish of her lustiness, but he also knows the melancholy that is a part of her response to the passage of time and the loss of beauty and vigor. This attitude he allows to stand side by side with her un-abashed joy in having had the world in her time. Despite the sensual and material motives (material values have guided her through three of her marriages), there shines through the shameless exuberance and the defiance of wishing to be right on her own terms, a vigorous love of life untouched by contempt or hatred. She reaches out, in-deed, for more of life, more of the world's experience, with the hope of attaining happiness in it and by means of it. From her eager looking forward to her sixth husband, whenever he will come forth, we can assume that in her opinion the more love there is in the world, the better a place it is. And if we find her argument convincing, it is not merely that there is an elevated tradition behind her (as we can see, it is but a fragment of the tradition), but that she corroborates our own instinctive feeling for life and defends our human nature, however perversely, with an almost wholehearted conviction.

The Wife of Bath is a teacher with considerably more experience in the ways of men than most women have had opportunity to acquire.[4] As she approaches her middle years and admits with regret the loss of the hectic passions of her youth, she is yet ready to enjoy another husband wherever he may be, and in the meanwhile bestow upon us the fruits of her schooling. What she gives us is not so much an art of love as it is an account of the battle between herself and her husbands for the upper hand, a battle in which sex becomes a part of the whole

---

is moralistic, one which I am not sure Professor Robertson intends. It results, it seems to me, from a too-close imposition of a theory upon a complex literary fact, which implies a "something more" than theory can explain.

[4] The fullest treatment of the degrees by which the Wife of Bath developed is that of Robert A. Pratt, "The Development of the Wife of Bath," in *Studies in Medieval Literature in Honor of Professor Albert Croll Baugh,* ed. MacEdward Leach (University of Pennsylvania Press, 1961), pp. 45–79. See also Richard F. Jones, in *JEGP,* XXIV, 512–47.

arsenal of feminine tricks; yet it is a battle from which much has been learned that can be of permanent value to all women who will sit at the foot of her professorial chair.

There is a more or less theoretical part to her *Prologue* in which the ground is cleared of some confusions (ll. 1–192) and in which sexual passion is given justification as a necessary part of engendering. Thereafter follows a tabulation of her husbands, with generously interspersed passages of poignant reminiscence and of wisdom which she has learned along the way. Forewarned is forearmed, according to the Wife. Accordingly, she lists the charges jealous men are apt to bring against their wives, so that thus forearmed the hitherto untutored wife may with wit, a nagging tongue, or her sexual allure attack before she is herself charged by her husband (ll. 226–450). It must have seemed a fine stroke to Chaucer, in an age when celibate theory preached the subjection of women to men in marriage as the relation of the lower to the higher reason, and when the literature of the aristocrats advocated the knight's faithful and humble service to his lady as an ideal of social behavior, to demonstrate marriage as a kind of free-for-all in which the wife wrests the upper hand from her husband and dupes him out of money and lands. Domestic comedy casts a practical and occasionally a jaundiced eye upon the ideals of other literary modes.

Needless to say, although the Wife of Bath, in the opposition of her experience to the authority of Scripture, rigorously opposes the ideal of St. Jerome that single marriage alone is countenanced by the Bible, and with abandon defends the uses of sex in marriage, much of what she actually says in the words imputed to the jealous husband indicates a violation of the law of charity and mutual forbearance, the *sine qua non* of all social relationships. Implied too in the perversion of marriage to private ends is the view reiterated in Chaucerian fabliaux that youth and age cannot marry successfully. By marrying three old men in succession, the Wife of Bath has violated not only the law of common sense but even the law of Nature, who would bring together those of comparable age. It is a curious matter that she despises the three "good" husbands while the two "bad" husbands, the ones who gave her real trouble, by a strange quirk of feminine nature, she admires:

> "We wommen han, if that I shal nat lye,
> In this matere a queynte fantasye;
> Wayte what thyng we may nat lightly have,

> Therafter wol we crie al day and crave.
> Forbede us thyng, and that desiren we;
> Preesse on us faste, and thanne wol we fle.
> With daunger oute we al oure chaffare;
> Great prees at market maketh deere ware,
> And to greet cheep is holde at litel prys:
> This knoweth every womman that is wys."   (ll. 515–24)

I do not believe that it is possible to demonstrate in the review of the Wife's five husbands any *steady* progress in moral attitude or intention, or any clearly marked path towards the marital harmony achieved ultimately both in the *Prologue* and in the tale. Yet, taking the three old, rich, "good" husbands as a unit, and comparing them with what follows, we can note a remarkable change in the relationship between the fourth husband and the Wife, a movement towards the relationship of like to like: a passionate, reckless, adulterous husband with the capacity to arouse jealousy and anger in his headstrong wife; a man who, needless to say, has met his match in Alice. Of him she can cry out with a momentarily rekindled rancor:

> "... in his owene grece I made hym frye
> For angre, and for verray jalousye.
> By God! in erthe I was his purgatorie,"   (ll. 487–89)

and in another mood,

> "For which I hope his soule be in glorie.
>
> .   .   .   .
>
> He deyde whan I cam fro Jerusalem,
> And lith ygrave under the roode beem,
>
> .   .   .   .
>
> Lat hym fare wel, God yeve his soul reste!"   (ll. 490–501)

One senses here respect and an affectionate regard for one who put up a good fight.

It is, too, the jolliness of that time of her life that stimulates in her the mingled delight and sadness of remembering the past:

> "But, Lord Crist! whan that it remembreth me
> Upon my yowthe, and on my jolitee,
> It tikleth me aboute myn herte roote.
> Unto this day it dooth myn herte boote
> That I have had my world as in my tyme.
> But age, allas! that al wole envenyme,
> Hath me biraft my beautee and my pith.
> Lat go, farewel! the devel go therwith!

> The flour is goon, ther is namoore to telle;
> The bren, as I best kan, now moste I selle." (ll. 469–78)

This relationship (ll. 453–502), had Chaucer chosen to expand upon it, would have given still another twist to the domestic fanfare of her life and would have made a fine fabliau in itself. He chose, however, to move on to the more fully developed comic episode, running in excess of three hundred lines, evolving out of the reading habits and sadistic turn of mind of the clerk Jenkin.

With her fifth husband, Alice makes the mistake of giving over all her "lond and fee / That evere was me yeven therbifoore" (l. 631). But before Chaucer is through with this last phase of the Wife's account, a self-contained anecdote ending upon a happier note than anything we have encountered before, the Wife has regained control of house and land and apparently has achieved all the mastery, all the sovereignty. The relationship with Jenkin the clerk is perhaps the most memorable episode of the *Prologue*. Chaucer devotes to it more than one-third of the lines of the piece (ll. 502–828). It is a comedy played with all the skill we associate with Chaucer at his comic best: irony in the mixture of the bookish and the domestic, a calculated sweetness in handling the subject of domestic reconciliation, a forthright good-natured coarseness, and the most generous attitudes toward normal sexual appetite held within bounds:

> "Of Phasipha, that was the queene of Crete,
> For shrewednesse, hym thoughte the tale swete;
> Fy! spek namoore—it is a grisly thyng—
> Of hire horrible lust and hir likyng." (ll. 733–36)

The bookish antifeminism running approximately 150 lines (640–790), while of a quieter condemnatory tone than the charges brought by the jealous husband (ll. 235–380), is yet a rhetorical balance to it. The charges of the jealous husband, we remember, were tolerable as coming from areas of comic and satiric thought, and aroused our approbation because of their origin not merely in literary sources, but, we feel instinctively, in the popularly accepted common knowledge: women are precisely as the jealous husband describes them; their wit and general cunning serve to accommodate them better to the world that would use them badly, and men must ruefully acquiesce to the truth that the women of low domestic comedy can be no other way than this chiding, scolding, money-grasping variety.

The recitation of perfidious wives by Jenkin, on the other hand, is a book-learned cloistered reading of feminine nature, which gains much of its strength from the authorities supporting the expressed views. The steady recital of women's "wikkednesse," beginning with the Biblical examples of Eve and Delilah and progressing rapidly through a variety of ancient betrayals, rancors, and acts of lust, reaches a climax of sadistic, macabre bitterness in the tale of Latumius and Arrius, who when told that his friend's three wives had hanged themselves on a tree in the garden said,

> " 'O leeve brother,' . . .
> 'Yif me a plante of thilke blissed tree,
> And in my gardyn planted shal it bee.' "   (ll. 762–64)

It proceeds bludgeon by bludgeon to recite the cold reminiscences of the temple of Mars in the *Knight's Tale:*

> ". . . somme han slayn hir housbondes in hir bed,
> And lete hir lechour dighte hire al the nyght,
> Whan that the corps lay in the floor upright.
> And somme han dryve nayles in hir brayn,
> Whil that they slepte, and thus they had hem slayn.
> Somme han hem yeve poysoun in hire drynke."   (ll. 766–71)

And it ends with the final blows of four proverbs:

> " 'Bet is,' quod he, 'thyn habitacioun
> Be with a leon or a foul dragoun,
> Than with a womman usynge for to chyde.'
> 'Bet is,' quod he, 'hye in the roof abyde,
> Than with an angry wyf doun in the hous;
> They been so wikked and contrarious,
> They haten that hir housbondes loven ay.'
> He seyde, 'a womman cast hir shame away,
> Whan she cast of hir smok;' and forthermo,
> 'A fair womman, but she be chaast also,
> Is lyk a gold ryng in a sowes nose.' "   (ll. 775–85)

One can sympathize with the good Wife, who at forty seems to have lost none of her vigor, for being subjected to the literary restraints of the twenty-year-old Jenkin, even though we sense something of the poetic justice inherent in their situation (we remember her own haranguing of the first three husbands, whom she outwitted by sheer strength and a shrewd and lively intelligence). Even clerk Jenkin is tricked into yielding "governaunce" into her hands, as we see, but not before we have noted a kind of internal balance or redressment in meaning as well as in rhetorical statement in Jenkin's learned reading in the ways of wicked wives.

Chaucer manifests his usual good sense in ending upon a happy note of reconciliation while at the same time preserving the integrity of the Wife's personality: sovereignty is what she wanted, and up to a point sovereignty is what she achieves by her trickery. But the earlier coarse statement familiar to students, beginning with the heartfelt cry, "Allas! Allas! that evere love was synne!" (l. 614), with its avowal of libertinism, gives way to the larger statement of a contractual relationship better than anything she has had heretofore. To Jenkin's words

> "... 'Myn owene trewe wyf,
> Do as thee lust the terme of al thy lyf;
> Keep thyn honour, and keep eek myn estaat' "— (ll. 819–21)

she provides the narrative response:

> "After that day we hadden never debaat.
> God helpe me so, I was to hym as kynde
> As any wyf from Denmark unto Ynde,
> And also trewe, and so was he to me." (ll. 822–25)

It is as good as she can get, and she has waited a long time for it. Did Chaucer intend us to see in the Wife's advancement into age the acquisition of a special kind of wisdom superior to merely instinctive knowledge or to that purely practical wit which has served her throughout her life? When one has read the tale finally assigned her, one is tempted to answer in the affirmative, to say that Chaucer has amplified that lyrical strain that appears from time to time in the *Prologue* and provided a deeper moral impulse than we have seen up to this point. Chaucer has, to be sure, made the story as suitable as possible, in all its details, to her nature. Yet, by giving her a feeling for the beautiful and the enchanted, in allowing her to relate a tale of internal as well as external, of masculine as well as feminine, transformation, a tale of right-mindeness in love, Chaucer has gone beyond any mere amplification of hints laid down in the Wife's *Prologue* and has brought into consideration a perpetually provocative dimension of her character and personality. We do her total performance an injustice if we see it merely as a realistic and sophisticated depiction of one kind of love in the world, a mere foil for the performance of the

Clerk. For the Wife of Bath marriage would never be a mere metaphor for something else, thank heaven; in her tale, however romantic,
the agents are rational and responsible, and however mysteriously, a
long lesson in gentilesse becomes a necessary part of the comic
resolution.

We need not seek too far afield for an explanation of the shift from
the *Shipman's Tale* to that of the loathly lady as suitable for the Wife
of Bath. The strong emphasis upon sexuality, from rape to the pleas-
anter foray of the marriage bed, is sufficiently close to the fabliau
tone, if not intention, of her *Prologue* to qualify the happier, less
cynical story for the Wife of Bath. As a teacher, she does not relin-
quish her professorial cap and gown, although the subject and atmosphere of her tale grow a little rarer. Also, the plot moves rapidly
enough to a thoroughly satisfying conclusion on a *quid pro quo* note
suited to the character displayed by the Wife in her *Prologue*. The
citation of learned authorities and use of illustrative *exempla* are again
what we noted of the Wife there, a determined and rampant garrulity
which includes some rather surprising sources. Furthermore, the
Wife is still an advocate, in the debate between men and women, of
the ascendancy of women. The dialogue in her tale may be, by comparison with the Prologue, less hectic, less polemical, but what she has
to say is itself less hectic and less polemical. However unusual the
names of Dante, Seneca, Christ, and Juvenal may sound on the lips of
an enchanted lady, they are cited without flamboyance or rhetorical
extravagance in support of a quiet and thoughtful solution to the
problem at hand.

The opening remarks of the *Shipman's Tale* dealing with the perils
of maintaining a wife and a large house would have made that tale
suitable enough for the Wife of Bath, but Chaucer chose, for the sake
of dilating her character, to give her much more substantial philosophical utterances bearing upon moral excellence; this material has
been skillfully oriented to exploring the basis of the marriage relationship, and in my view, the poet has finally given the better part of
wisdom in this matter to Alice. If this added dimension makes her a
shade inscrutable, it at least points to the deep well of charity from
which much of Chaucerian art flows. In this sense too, the *Wife of
Bath's Tale* must be seen not as an anticlimax after her brilliantly lit
up *Prologue*, but rather as a further exploration of her inner heart,

and we feel in complete agreement with B. J. Whiting's remark that there is "no better proof of Chaucer's overwhelming literary power and artistry than that to be found in the refurbishing of the *Wife of Bath's Tale* to make it accord with his own complex interior design for the soul of the Wife of Bath." [5]

Her story opens with a healthily nostalgic return to the good old days of King Arthur when the elf-queen and her entourage danced in the green meadows, a time when their apparently benign influence had not been extirpated by the meddling, snooping hypocrites who, in the Wife's scathing view, haunted the very nooks and crannies of Christendom. It was a time, if not of innocence, at least of strict law and quick punishment, unlike the present, when women are in danger of assault from the ubiquitous friars:

> Wommen may go now saufly up and doun.
> In every bussh or under every tree
> Ther is noon oother incubus but he,
> And he ne wol doon hem but dishonour. (ll. 878–81)

So coarse an innuendo serves several obvious purposes: that of keeping the tale well within the range of the Wife's character, that of requiting the Friar of the pilgrimage for his laugh at her expense; but more important in terms of knitting her little introduction to the tale itself, the elaborately sarcastic reference to dishonour as a very real possibility in the world leads quite naturally into the rape with which the story opens, and indicates a steady pressure from the vitally alive character of the Wife of the *Prologue* upon the materials Chaucer manipulates within the limits of her personality. In a sense, the world of irony and of the comically ugly or debased threatens to pull apart from, but ultimately strengthens, the romantic ideal towards which she strives.

But even a lusty bachelor-knight cannot, after his day of exercise, casually rape the maiden he encounters. [6] Arthur's law demands the loss of his head. The queen's action offers us another example in Chaucer's work of feminine influence mitigating the austerities of

---

[5] *Sources and Analogues of Chaucer's Canterbury Tales*, ed. W. F. Bryan and Germaine Dempster (University of Chicago Press, 1941), p. 224.

[6] Bernard F. Huppé, "Rape and Woman's Sovereignty in the *Wife of Bath's Tale*," *MLN*, LXIII (1948), 378–81, gives a plausible explanation of the social status of the maiden and the degree of crime involved. But see the sharply dissenting view of Gordon H. Gerould, *Chaucerian Essays* (Princeton University Press, 1952), p. 75, and that of Kemp Malone, "The *Wife of Bath's Tale*," *MLR*, LVII (1962), 487.

power; the positive law of the land is set aside so that the queen may herself decide "wheither she wolde hym save or spille." There is something like this in the *Knight's Tale* (ll. 1749 ff.) and in the *Prologue* to the *Legend of Good Women* (G 317 ff.), where the pleas of women are persuasive enough to convert the hearts of princes and tyrants and gods. In a sense whenever Chaucer resorts to the sentiment "Pitee renneth soone in gentil herte" as an attribute of both masculine and feminine hearts (the word "pity," or adjectival and adverbial forms derived from it, occurs with amazing prodigality in Chaucer's work), we are faced with the larger pattern of Chaucer's thought, the law of love and its mysterious operation in human institutions. Used in a variety of contexts, it appears most obviously in the exploration of sovereignty, in the relation of husbands and wives, in the relation of subjects and rulers, and in the relation of rational creatures and the Deity. As a reflection of the debate between authority and subjection, between two kinds of law, between pure power and humane and gentled judgment, between the sexes, all involving some aspect of love as a solution, it appears with great frequency as a kind of ground note to Chaucer's thought.

Here at the outset of the *Wife of Bath's Tale* it serves quite casually to contain *in parvo*, and to point toward, the resolution of the story. Within this association of ideas, the loathly lady of the tale and Prudence in the *Tale of Melibee* have a kinship based not merely upon the wisdom which it is their task to inculcate, but also upon ability to convert men's hearts and to reconcile their minds to courses of action rooted in moral law. In a more sardonically comic context, the *pietosa donna* of the *Merchant's Tale*, conscienceless May, provides an illustration both of the pitiful heart (l. 1986) and of a divinely inspired (albeit the divinities are pagan) persuasiveness by which the game is won.

The tantalizing question for which the knight must find the answer within the year and a day is what Chaucer himself, in another place, calls an "impossible." Comically it is a piece of daring ingenuity, generating a kind of gleeful superiority in audiences of all grades of innocence or experience, an anticipation of an epiphanous truth. Here, from the mouth of the Wife of Bath, it becomes an unerringly apt device of a professor of Feminine Wiles making way for ultimate truths. The recitation of opinions, lesser truths, so to speak, compared to the one for which we wait, serves as a substitute for the passage of time; these opinions in one way or another we have encountered in the Wife's own *Prologue* in the familiar charges attributed to jealous husbands:

> Somme seyde wommen loven best richesse,
> Somme seyde honour, somme seyde jolynesse,
> Somme riche array, somme seyden lust abedde,
> And oftetyme to be wydwe and wedde.   (ll. 925–28)

The wife cannot herself resist the narrator's personal involvement; she speaks for women everywhere:

> Somme seyde that oure hertes been most esed
> Whan that we ben yflatered and yplesed.
> He gooth ful ny the sothe, I wol nat lye.
> A man shal wynne us best with flaterye;
> And with attendance, and with bisynesse,
> Been we ylymed, bothe moore and lesse.   (ll. 929–34)

This is, she admits, pretty close to the truth; she is willing to admit, too, the general veracity of the statement that all women desire to be free and exempt from masculine charges and reproaches.

> ... be we never so vicious withinne,
> We wol been holden wise and clene of synne.   (ll. 943–44)

Those who maintain that women like most to be held discreet of tongue are far from the obvious truth, amply attested by Ovid (made over for her purposes), that women cannot keep a secret, a fact which apparently even women will not deny. This opinion, she avers, is "nat worth a rake-stele." We have, obviously, come no closer to the answer to the question; equally obviously the answer is not within the realm of common knowledge.

The tone of these adduced and dismissed opinions, as everyone notes, is perfectly suited to the speaker, an overflow, as it were, of that same exuberance and wit which is everywhere remarkable in her *Prologue*. Plain speaking must, however, give way to narration, to the laying out of the slim lines of the plot on which to set the weightier burden of the old hag's didactic preachment. Now, the opinions of common knowledge which are the stock equipment of low domestic comedy will find their counterparts in knowledge of a totally different sort, the practical wisdom of the Wife of the *Prologue* giving way to the unanticipated moral pronouncements of the old hag. In effect we see the gradually widening scope of comedy encompassing even materials of the most serious sort, in the end setting up a dichotomy, one side of which contains the incident of rape and common opinion, and the other wisdom and the mutually agreeable marital contract.

The circumstances under which the knight achieves the answer to the question remind us that the tale is one of the olden days of enchantments; the four and twenty ladies dancing in the forest, their disappearance as he approaches "in hope that some wysdom sholde he lerne," the presence of no other creature than that foul old lady, the faintly ironical suggestion of the dialogue (ll. 1001–4), and the casual persuasiveness of the lady are data handled with economy. Swiftly the terms of the bargain are set: she will give the answer to the riddle, provided he will pledge himself to perform whatever she requests. Upon his acquiescence, she whispers "a pistel in his ere" (l. 1021), although surely there is no one around for many miles to hear what she says. (We may note here, in the saving of the young man's life, the role she performs of a woman providing a man with the key to a final mystery, the foreshadowing of the role she will perform at greater length and with greater meaning in the education of the young man's heart.) That we do not know at this point what will constitute "the nexte thyng that I requere thee" (l. 1010) is but one indication of the greater subtlety of Chaucer's version over that of Gower's much more elaborated, more fully explained account, in which, at this point, the knight agrees to marry the old hag in exchange for the answer to the riddle.

When the knight finally gives his answer, he makes his speech before a full consistory of women: wives, maidens, and widows (these last "for that they been wise"), with the queen presiding as judge, a situation suggestive of the actual courts of love of Eleanor of Aquitaine and perfectly in keeping with the Wife's sometimes wistful, sometimes determined talk of domination by women.[7] Before such a consistory, and in a manly voice audible to the entire court, he speaks the answer given him by the old lady, now waiting for her opportunity to claim her reward.

---

[7] See George R. Coffman, "Chaucer and Courtly Love Once More—The Wife of Bath's Tale," *Speculum*, XX (1945), 43–50, an article which, among other matters, raises the important and perplexing question of the kind of comic spirit to be found in Chaucer.

"Wommen desiren to have sovereynetee
As wel over hir housbond as hir love,
And for to been in maistrie hym above.
This is youre mooste desir, thogh ye me kille."   (ll. 1038–41)

Immediately upon the granting of his life, the knight's triumph is supplanted by that of the old lady as she demands marriage in return for her successful aid, a desire to be his wife and his love as well. It is she who calls attention to the fact that she is "foul, and oold, and poore" (l. 1063),[8] which, with the knight's charge of low lineage, becomes the subject of her long rebuttal. The young knight's expression, twice, of his distaste for the relationship, his dismay at the unseemliness of such a request—"For Goddes love . . . / Taak al my good, and lat my body go" (ll. 1059–60)—is as much abhorrence at the unsuitable relationship of youth to age as it is dismay that one of his birth and station should be so foully disparaged.

"I nolde for al the metal, ne for oore,
That under erthe is grave, or lith above,
But if thy wyf I were, and eek thy love."
  "My love?" quod he, "nay, my dampnacioun!
Allas! that any of my nacioun
Sholde evere so foule disparaged be!"   (ll. 1064–69)

With this utterance we have arrived at the very center of the story, and it must ever be a joke of the most delicate irony, so illustrative of Chaucerian wit, that the heavier didactic and spiritual burden of the remaining half of the tale, the moral re-education of the hero, should take place abed, with the knight wallowing and turning to and fro

---

[8] The student may assess for himself Gower's greater explicitness and whether Chaucer has done better or worse by his omission of detail in the following description of the loathly lady from the *Tale of Florent:*

This olde wyht him hath awaited   Hangende doun unto the chin;
In place wher as he hire lefte: Hire Lippes schrunken ben for age,
Florent his wofull heved uplefte   Ther was no grace in the visage,
And syh this vecke wher sche sat,   Hir front was nargh, hir lockes hore,
Which was the lothlieste what   Sche loketh forth as doth a More,
That evere man caste on his yhe: Hire Necke is schort, hir schuldres courbe,
Hire Nase bass, hire browes hyhe,   That myhte a mannes lust destourbe,
Hire yhen smale and depe set,   Hire body gret and nothing smal,
Hire chekes ben with teres wet,   And schortly to descrive hire al,
And rivelen as an emty skyn   Sche hath no lith withoute a lak.

Sources and Analogues, p. 231, ll. 1672–91

while the old hag lies there smiling "evermo." Again the more serious
concern of Chaucer invites attention and comparison with Gower's
Tale of Florent, in which the knight, abed with his haggish wife, is
subjected to no moral preachment at all. He merely,

> . . . as it were a man in trance
> . . . torneth him al sodeinly,
> And syh a lady lay him by
> Of eyhtetiene wynter age,
> Which was the faireste of visage
> That evere in al this world he syh.

It is not only artfulness, we note, that Chaucer's work has, but a
seriousness of intention deep enough to risk violence to the depiction
of the Wife of Bath for the sake of utterances for which he apparently had an intellectual predisposition. And again, by comparison
with Gower's careful arrangement that all should be explained (the
hag is really the daughter of the king of Sicily under a stepmother's
spell) we see something of the greater artist's willingness to remold the
form for the sake of the meaning the form must support, abandoning
conventional and somewhat static clichés of romance for the higher
artifice.

After the charges of the knight (ll. 1099 ff.) that she is loathly, old,
and of low birth, spoken by him with honesty if some callousness, we
are launched into the hag's vigorous statement of the character and
sources of true nobility of heart. One by one, the hag examines the
charges lodged against her: to be sure she does not come of elevated
or moneyed lineage, but then, does aristocratic birth insure nobility?
The possession of wealth is far from being the source of nobility, and
we have not only the supreme example of Christ as the true source of
gentilesse, but the lesser authority of Dante himself, who assures us
that nobility cannot be transmitted by the parent to his offspring.
The temporal gifts of inheritance are the source of the hurtful harms
of this world, as experience shows us over and over again:

> "For, God it woot, men may wel often fynde
> A lordes sone do shame and vileynye;
> And he that wole han pris of his gentrye,
> For he was boren of a gentil hous,
> And hadde his eldres noble and vertuous,

> And nel hymselven do no gentil dedis,
> Ne folwen his gentil auncestre that deed is,
> He nys nat gentil, be he duc or erl;
> For vileyns synful dedes make a cherl.
> For gentillesse nys but renomee
> Of thyne auncestres, for hire heigh bountee,
> Which is a strange thyng to thy persone.
> Thy gentillesse cometh fro God allone.
> Thanne comth oure verray gentillesse of grace;
> It was no thyng biquethe us with oure place." (ll. 1150–64)

The source of such nobility as we should seek is the grace of God. Thus she expands upon her theme, intermingling Christian and pagan materials to form one elevated and humane point of view: all the authorities that she can muster agree that in the end nobility consists of performing gracious deeds, and these, she implies, can be done as well by a poor man as a wealthy one. Poverty, she insists in support of her main argument, has the sanction of God himself who chose to live, as Christ, in "wilful poverte."

The sermonette flows fluently out of the mouth of the narrator, in the main in an elevated strain, but verging, in the section on poverty, upon a certain aridity, a certain flatness of delivery, consisting for the most part of definitions of poverty and its benefits. Although it forms a part of the total response, it is not really an essential part of the theme of gentilesse, but rather an appendix to it inasmuch as the matter of riches and gentilesse has already been disposed of. One may complain, unnecessarily, that the Wife of Bath is indeed a learned lady who now leans heavily upon authority; yet within the story itself, the wisdom of the loathly lady is suitable enough, even if we marvel at the range of reading attributed to fairy folk. In either case, for the sake of consistency we may assume that the Wife has profited from her association with her learned husband, and that Chaucer refrains from sacrificing her meaning to the mere demands of verisimilitude.

The sermonette is not quite finished; she comes now to practical matters:

> "Now ther ye seye that I am foul and old,
> Than drede you noght to been a cokewold;
> For filthe and eelde, also moot I thee,
> Been grete wardeyns upon chastitee." (ll. 1213–16)

She is willing to admit, if only in a veiled way, that she is old enough to be his mother, and this should elicit some respect from the knight; but the test must be pushed to the ultimately unpalatable in the relationship of youth to age:

> "But nathelees, syn I knowe youre delit,
> I shal fulfille youre worldly appetit."   (ll. 1217–18)

At this point the correctives have all been applied; the impossible choice she now offers of an old and faithful wife as opposed to a young and unfaithful one is the ground out of which will grow the wise and healthy comic solution:

> "My lady and my love, and wyf so deere,
> I put me in youre wise governance;
> Cheseth youreself which may be moost plesance,
> And moost honour to yow and me also.
> I do no fors the wheither of the two;
> For as yow liketh, it suffiseth me."   (ll. 1230–35)

The knight is resigned; his endurance, his sufferance of the intolerable may be taken to be the visible sign of his spiritual advance.[9] The grace which his resignation merits is the marriage of youth to youth, a miracle which has its final, surprising element, not in the hag's triumphant statement of sovereignty (ll. 1236–38), but paradoxically in her hints of surrender and obedience to his control.

It should not surprise us that the conclusion of the tale has been dimly describable in the Wife's own marriage to Jenkin (ll. 817–28); indeed in the passage from rape to a robust and healthy sexuality, in the interplay of pagan law and Christian amendment, in the delicate balance between authority and experience we recognize the familiar voice of the Wife of the *Prologue*.

In retrospect the story is a gem of a special sort. In it sexuality plays a piquant counterpoint against a serious didacticism; both of these harmonize in the end in a view of marital bliss, which, if we may judge from the hag's sermon, is founded upon spiritual values. The latent materialism of the Wife of Bath, her this-for-that attitude, has yielded another bargain and this one the best she can imagine. The gentilesse of which she speaks, by its very nature, excludes mastery; the marital contract which it produces is both sane and felicitous, and

---

[9] See, for example, Joseph P. Roppolo, "The Converted Knight in Chaucer's *Wife of Bath's Tale*," *CE*, XII (1951), 263–69.

if we cannot imagine the Wife as having attained the level of morality reached by the sermon of the old lady, we are forced at least to see it as a wistful hope of which she is capable, and this more than any other factor has redeemed her for posterity.

THE CLERK'S TALE

As it is written, There is none righteous, no, not one.

ROMANS 3:10

Only if the husband represents a supernatural power, as in the earliest versions of the tale, is Griselde's behaviour logically justified. The Wife of Bath had enough sense not to make a god of a husband.

RAYMOND PRESTON, *Chaucer*

The *Clerk's Tale* is one of Chaucer's translations. One of his best, it is a version of a story he found ready to hand in Petrarch and in the anonymous French *Le Livre Grisildis*. These, in turn, were based upon an account in Boccaccio's *Decameron*, to which Chaucer seems not to have had access. The prose originals Chaucer chose to recast into rhyme royal, and throughout the translation from prose to poetry we can detect those necessary acts of accommodation, dilation, and contraction that make the work his own. He also goes beyond the labor of adaptation by making some actual additions which serve to increase the humanity of the heroine, decrease the humanity of her husband, and condemn the vacillating populace.[1]

Very little of the moral meaning of the tale is Chaucer's own. Boccaccio's version, for example, stated its conclusions quite simply:

[1] The work to which all must sooner or later refer in any study of the *Clerk's Tale* is that of J. Burke Severs, *The Literary Relationships of Chaucer's Clerkes Tale*, Yale Studies in English, XCVI (Yale University Press, 1942). It contains, on facing pages, Petrarch's Latin text and that of the anonymous French translator. Robert Dudley French, *A Chaucer Handbook* (New York, 1927), translates the Petrarchan text, pp. 291–311. John Speirs, *Chaucer the Maker*, pp. 151–55; Raymond Preston, *Chaucer* (London and New York, 1952), pp. 250–57; Charles Muscatine, *Chaucer and the French Tradition*, pp. 190–97; and E. Talbot Donaldson, *Chaucer's Poetry* (New York, 1958), pp. 917–20, all offer various shades of brilliant and sane critical insight into technique and meaning of the *Clerk's Tale*. James Sledd, "The Clerk's Tale: the Monsters and the Critics," *MP*, LI (1953), 73–82, is noteworthy not only for its clearheaded assessment of much that is misleading in scholarship dealing with the tale, but for its just appraisal of the narrative line.

divine spirits are found even in poor cottages; swinish lords are found in palaces. Petrarch's concluding sentiments are even more explicit: we should render to God the same patient service as Griselda rendered to her husband; we are tried that we may come to know our own frailty. These sentiments are translated by Chaucer in such a way as merely to corroborate them. If there is some kind of moral statement that is Chaucer's own, it may perhaps be described in his expansion of the Job theme. By and large, however, his immediate purpose has been to render the tale faithfully. Intact, it serves his larger purpose, which is to provide the Clerk with a response to the Wife of Bath on the nature of sovereignty in marriage.

The description of the Clerk in the *General Prologue* is short, but as many have observed, it is a consistent bit of portrayal, emphasizing in the Clerk's character the strains of self-denial, poverty, selflessness, devotion to duty and to study. Something of the spareness of his character is reflected in his speech, which he pares down to the fullest good sense and to pithy moral statement. He is, according to Chaucer, the perennial student and teacher. Recognizing and acknowledging the scholarly bent in the Clerk, the Host urges him to tell a merry tale in the plain style, one that will be neither boring nor excessively moral. Chaucer corroborates immediately what we know of the Clerk's intellectual and moral bent: He acquiesces "as fer as reson axeth" to tell a tale which he heard from Petrarch. His moral bent makes Petrarch's death the subject for a brief statement of mutability, while his intellectuality leads him to pass judgment upon Petrarch's introduction as an unnecessary frill.

Coming from the mouth of a man given to speaking in terms of moral virtue, and ending as it does upon a note of reconciliation and happiness, his tale falls into a spiritualized view of Christian experience best expressed by Dante, and reflected in vastly less systematized ways by Boccaccio and Chaucer. The structure of reality, in this view, is comic, played out in this life and the next in accordance with the right or wrong uses of the will. The law governing the universe is the law of love; vested in every rational creature, it entails both an obligatory sense of human responsibility and a profound trust in the abstract justice and mercy emanating from the mind of God. If certain matters are inscrutable, the Christian must yet keep hope that this life and the next are implicated inevitably and meaningfully with each other. The burdens and trials of this life are best borne by trusting in supreme Providence, which provides for all in accordance with His law. This beautifully organized complex of a communion of man with his creator is an essential part of Chaucer's religious belief. We do not have to look far to find its influence in the tender sentiment he lavishes upon those agents who suffer as wives, mothers, innocent children. Suffering, in this view, takes on a special significance, not only because Christ suffered as a man, but because suffering, through Christ, is a necessary part of the total experience leading to salvation. It is within this pattern of the progress of the soul that the tale of Griselda takes on its most suggestive meaning, and our response to the tale depends in part upon our ability to recover something of the vocabulary of religious belief.[2]

As a matter of fact the responses that the tale elicits fall simply into those categories suggested by two readers of Petrarch's version of the tale.[3] We are either overwhelmed by pity and find ourselves scarcely able to continue with it, or we insulate ourselves against it, maintaining that while the subject certainly excites pity and the style is adapted to call forth tears, it yet remains nothing but a poetical invention, a fiction. Many a casual reader of the tale since Petrarch's time, taking the second position, finds the literal recital of the tale simply intolerable, feeling that the virtuous Griselda, like Constance, exists far out beyond his power of identification; or that there is something revolting about great suffering on the part of persons so excessively good, and something even more revolting about assuming that Walter is lovable himself or has any right to mete out Griselda's trials. Some sense of artistic propriety makes the reader demand that there be in Griselda some element of guilt, some flaw which will make her suffering merited, some assurance that her virtue is not tried so sorely without cause. The fact of a happy ending in what must be considered an aspect of Divine Comedy, does not entirely wipe out the sense of injustice, nor the feeling that Griselda has been made the victim of Walter's caprice.

Chaucer was conscious of such responses; within the context of the story itself, he utters comments which provide distance between himself and these unbearable austerities of the tale. These enable him to

---

[2] A useful study of the relation between comedy and allegory is that of Nevill Coghill, "The Basis of Shakespearean Comedy," *Essays and Studies* (London, 1950), pp. 1–29.

[3] Albert Stanburrough Cook, "The First Two Readers of Petrarch's Tale of Griselda," *MP*, XV (1918), 633–43.

side with the objecting audience (ll. 456–62 and 621–23). But while he sides with us in our objections, he does all he can to enhance the story's fragile credibility by means of a purified style, virtually devoid of images, a tone of austerity, and an interior burden of moral suggestion. In the process of expanding and repressing his sources, and in making his subtle changes in the text without tampering with the quiet narrative movement, Chaucer has held in abeyance much of that habitual ironical cast of mind which assumes a disproportion between the way agents act and the way they speak and which makes its point through a free admixture of styles. The plain style which he employs is a reflection of the unalloyed motivation of the tale itself. Its prime purpose is to exalt and glorify the virtue of a woman, and by the very absence of metaphors which would dictate the directions of the imagination, to focus the mind upon its unmistakable higher meaning.

The level of meaning towards which we are irresistibly impelled is the highest level of allegorical interpretation. Walter's recognition of lowly Griselda's worth, after his reluctance to marry, the difficult terms of the marital contract, Griselda's saintly deportment and acceptance of the terms, the steady iteration of her totally sacrificed will (ll. 361, 505 ff., 659 ff.), her increase in virtue after marriage (ll. 407 ff.), Walter's desire to test her steadfastness, Griselda's refusal to look back upon the privation of her first child, her steadfast acceptance of the loss of her second child, Chaucer's and Petrarch's own exoneration of her willingness to let the children go (ll. 687 ff.), Griselda's acceptance of the third trial, the comparison of Griselda's lot with that of Job, the final reconciliation of Griselda and Walter and the restoration of her lost children—all move us in the direction of a level of meaning so closely tied in with the mystery of the soul's trial by God for His own reasons and for the soul's good, that we must call it anagogical.

Like the heroine of the *Man of Law's Tale*, the central figure reacts virtuously to all the kinds of experience to which she is subjected. That the figures are subtly different from each other in their larger implications is chiefly owing to the range of experience in which their virtue flourishes. For Constance, we recall, the vicissitudes are many and varied, involving travels over the sea, marriages and obstacles to marriage, separations from parents and spouse, and ultimately reunion and reconciliation. As her name suggests, she defines certain attitudes of constancy amidst the trials and storms of life. The storms and trials to which she is subjected within the destinal order can be overcome only by miracles and suspensions of the laws of nature. Even the long passage of years in the chronicle of her perils lends the impression of a vast pageant of history in which something greater than a mere individual, an institution perhaps, survives by the ultimate resources of divine aid.

For Griselda in the *Clerk's Tale* the total pattern of experience is severely restricted, consisting of marriage and the consequences of vows which are a necessary part of the contract. A time lapse of twelve years hardly obtrudes into the story, so intent are we upon the trials within marriage to which Griselda is subjected. But the restriction of the poetic vision to a single pattern of experience, instead of limiting the implications of the tale, makes rather for a concentration of thought upon certain irresoluble mysteries in the spiritual life of man.

As a matter of fact the whole question of theodicy rises quite spontaneously out of the successive religious infusions which are present in the Petrarchan and Chaucerian versions. Allowing Griselda to suggest symbolically suffering humanity in much the same way that Job does, and allowing Walter to suggest the seemingly capricious hand of God visiting oppression upon one of the faithful, help to supply the justifications for which so many readers strain. If God has reasons in the Book of Job, they may be adduced as reasons for the testing of Griselda. That early reader of Petrarch's version may have wept with good reason at the profoundly moving depiction of one put to test when to all external appearances she merited only praise. The point may be sharpened somewhat by reiterating the view of Hebrew-Christian history with regard to the relation of the soul to God, that man is guilty. If he is innocent, then God is unthinkable, capricious, a mere manipulator of his creatures, as Caliban imagined him to be. To rephrase the problem in the form of a question: Can mortal man be righteous before God, can a man be pure before his maker? (Job 4:17) Sovereignty, which is the theme of the tale, is never so unswervingly defined as when we move in the direction of anagogy, and see the political and particularly the marital levels of lordship as reflections of God's sovereignty in a universe in which all that is not God is subservient to Him.

There are, no doubt, those like Petrarch's other reader for whom the tale is but an invention, and for whom interpretation on this level is as intolerable as the literal acceptance of the events which comprise the story. Yet when we consider Walter's strength and Griselda's weakness, Walter's exalted station and Griselda's humble one, Walter's seemingly capricious will (even Chaucer shrinks from it on the literal level), and her compliant one, their relationship suggests a mystery beyond the surface meaning, which even at the end of the tale is not quite dissipated.

The inherited pattern of the story, based ultimately upon a relationship between a mortal wife and an other-world spouse, suggests, if nothing else, the vast gulf that exists between the Deity and his mortal creatures. Furthermore it raises the perplexing questions concerning the means by which the Creator makes his creation more lovable, more tractable, and in the end, salvageable. The testing of the human agent by the divine becomes in this view the proper subject to which is appended the familiar moral, and the allegorical equations that are suggested in it tend to redeem much that is difficult in the rare relationship of Griselda and Walter. Compare Chaucer's version with that of Petrarch, as shown on page 222.

No doubt most of the changes which Chaucer has wrought in his original are due to the demands of the metre and the stanza form. Nevertheless it is Chaucer who suggests that the testing is a part of reasonable creation, and that such "governaunce" is "for oure best." In this sentiment Chaucer is closer to St. James's view, that all that comes from God is good, than Petrarch is, who contents himself with setting the terms of the equation (we should be to God as Griselda was to her mortal husband). As clerkish opinion would have it, God tests us not that we should fall, for this would be leading us into evil, but that we may learn to submit ourselves to Him. In terms of the story, this means knowing that that God whom we thought we knew in our prosperity, makes himself apparent as well in adversity.

If the bond of Griselda to Walter within marriage demands her total obedience and patience under trial, and we accept the persistent allegorical drift, then we may accept Walter's dictates as those made by love to determine the strength of Griselda's love for him. In this complex of higher meaning involving the subjection of poor mortality to the richness of God, there is nothing of Chaucer's ironical cast of mind to divert attention by witty observation from the sense. On the contrary there is an affecting poignancy and the mystery of

This storie is seyd, nat for that wyves sholde
Folwen Grisilde as in humylitee,
For it were inportable, though they wolde;
But for that every wight, in his degree,
Sholde be constant in adversitee
As was Grisilde; therfore Petrak writeth
This storie, which with heigh stile he enditeth.

For, sith a womman was so pacient
Unto a mortal man, wel moore us oghte
Receyven al in gree that God us sent;
For greet skile is, he preeve that he wroghte.
But he ne tempteth no man that he boghte,
As seith Seint Jame, if ye his pistel rede;
He preeveth folk al day, it is no drede,

And suffreth us, as for oure excercise,
With sharpe scourges of adversitee
Ful ofte to be bete in sondry wise;
Nat for to knowe oure wyl, for certes he,
Er we were born, knew al oure freletee;
And for oure best is al his governaunce.
Lat us thanne lyve in vertuous suffraunce.

Chaucer, *The Clerk's Tale*, ll. 1142–62

This story it has seemed good to weave anew, in another tongue, not so much that it might stir the matrons of our time to imitate the patience of this wife—who seems to me scarcely imitable—as that it might stir all those who read it to imitate this woman's steadfastness, at least; so that they may have the resolution to perform for God what this woman performed for her husband. For He cannot be tempted with evil, as saith James the Apostle, and He himself tempts no man. Nevertheless, He often proves us and suffers us to be vexed with many a grievous scourge; not that He may know our spirit, for that He knew ere we were made, but that our own frailty may be made known to us through notable private signs. Therefore I would assuredly enter on the list of steadfast men the name of anyone who endured for his God, without a murmur, what this obscure peasant woman endured for her mortal husband.

Petrarch, *De Obedientia ac Fide Uxoria Mythologia*, trans. R. D. French, *Chaucer Handbook*, pp. 310–11

an increasingly apprehensible vision. The more we examine the emotions depicted, particularly in Griselda's yielding of her children and the denials of any will of her own, the more it seems that Chaucer has known how to preserve the best of his sources and to prevent any distortion of the delicate art necessary to bring their meaning into existence.

Whatever we may feel about the meaning that is brought into existence on the level of allegory, the Clerk, in responding to the Wife of Bath, has demonstrated something on the literal level which is completely opposed to the view of the lively Alice, and as impractical for successful marriage. She had, we recall, supported her view with some moral didacticism of her own in the tale of the transformed hag; and the Clerk, in telling his story, has known how to recapitulate some parts of her thesis in a general context, for example in the words of the spokesman to Walter:

> "Boweth youre nekke under that blisful yok
> Of soveraynetee, noght of servyse,
> Which that men clepe spousaille or wedlock;" (ll. 113–15)

and in Walter's response:

> "For God it woot, that children ofte been
> Unlyk hir worthy eldres hem bifore;
> Bountee comth al of God, nat of the streen
> Of which they been engendred and ybore." (ll. 155–58)

But he has been given a tale the literal point of which is as "inportable" as hers. On at least one higher level, however, it may be shown to have some justification (although the Wife would surely think, if Walter is merely an earthly lover, that Griselda is a fool). The Clerk's common sense asserts itself both in the close of the tale (feminine nature is now unfortunately alloyed with brass) and in the famous Envoy where he usurps the Wife's own kind of argument to demonstrate how wretched marriages are made. That he should sarcastically advance the very point of the Wife of Bath, while admitting that Griseldas no longer exist, is in effect to admit that marriage of the sort that he has demonstrated is no longer possible; is, in fact, an unattainable ideal.

The Clerk does not go so far as to define the ideal that *is* attainable in this mortal state. His task on pilgrimage is that of opposing to the Wife's point of view another one arising as surely from his own religious and moral inclinations as the Wife's from her recalcitrant and wayward humor. The purity of his view is preserved throughout the recounting of the tale, with no intrusions from the low-comic domestic world of nagging shrews. The Wife, by contrast, freely mixes into her comic defenses theological matters which vindicate her human appetites. The shadow of herself is everywhere in her prologue and her tale; the plain and clear personality of the Clerk by comparison remains submerged until his outwardly bland support of woman's sovereignty in the Envoy, a return through satire to the extravagant, quarrelsome world of domestic comedy. Indeed the return through polished comic verse to the realistic world of pilgrimage is an artistic necessity arising out of the antagonism existing between the unremittingly secular argument of the Wife and the unremittingly theological argument of the Clerk with regard to the right uses of marriage, as well as between the literary types which their views tend to generate.

Chaucer thus solves problems on the various levels of his creation. What he has accomplished for the pilgrimage by extravagant and facile claims on behalf of providential control in the *Man of Law's Tale* he now restates by the simpler, profounder demonstration of sovereignty in the *Clerk's Tale*. By its affinity with religious myth or with the original folk tale of the immortal lover it makes in its own way a religious statement vastly more austere than the prodigally disposed sonorities of the *Man of Law's Tale*.

But Chaucer salvages our sensibilities as readers. Griselda's unbearably pathetic situation draws from us a self-protective irritation at her spinelessness, a reaction which serves to indicate the degree of theological rigor the tale retains. He himself sides with us when in a personal intrusion into the tale he condemns Walter's desire to condemn his wife (ll. 460 ff.). But nowhere is his control so complete as when he restores us to a world of sane laughter by means of the time-tested comic types of shrewish wives and henpecked husbands. These surround us with less rarefied values and afford a refuge from the fatiguing, ultimate mystery. Indeed, when we consider the tale alone,[4] without its Envoy, we are as close to mystery yielding mean-

---

[4] There is a wide range of opinion about the purely literary value of the *Clerk's Tale*, ranging from the assertion by Donald C. Baker, "Chaucer's Clerk and the Wife of Bath on the Subject of Gentillesse," *SP*, LIX (1962), 633, that the tale "is not, of course, one of the great poems of the *Canterbury Tales*, and no amount of closer reading will make it so," to the view that it is a tale of "fragile purity" and

ing as we will ever be in the *Canterbury Tales*, on a level of poetical statement dealing with the highest and most insoluble matters. With the Envoy, however, we are back in the larger ironies of the social group on its way to repentance, being exposed to a point of view in which the question of marriage, offered first as a means of raising issues about contractual obligations in the supernatural order, is deflated to the practical level on which the pilgrims live.

"a triumph of Chaucer's conventional style."—Muscatine, *Chaucer and the French Tradition*, pp. 196-97.

On the grounds of intention the tale continues to breed disagreement, best exemplified by the discussion in Bertrand H. Bronson, *In Search of Chaucer*, pp. 103-14. Bronson's view, tentatively offered, is that Chaucer has rendered the story inacceptable "not only to us but possibly even to himself." Walter may be, he asserts, tantamount to the Deity in Griselda's eyes, but does not become so either for the narrator or for us. Walter puts his wife in the wrong by forcing her "to accept his savagery to herself and to her children, not *as though* it were just and right but *as true* justice, with glad and trusting grace; or else be derelict from her vows. In shunning a fault, she is betrayed into profounder wrong, a deeper infidelity to motherhood and to the light of truth. The poet does not blame her: this perversion of values is inherent in the story. But in praising her, he involuntarily falls into the same trap and assents to the evil. His moral judgment is suborned by the pathos of her lot. We cannot but feel that ultimately the ironic Envoy answers more than the dramatic needs of the occasion vis-a-vis the Wife of Bath, and serves as a genuine, though unconscious, repudiation of the false morality that the poet was forced by the story to espouse." This view is shared by Donald H. Reiman, "The Real *Clerk's Tale*; or, Patient Griselda Exposed," *TSLL*, V (1963), 372; Griselda is guilty of sin for failing to recognize the priority of the contract with God over a purely human one.

The other view is best exemplified by D. W. Robertson, Jr., *A Preface to Chaucer*, p. 376: "The Clerk systematically restores the order inverted by the wife [of Bath], calling attention specifically to the duties of the Christian soul as it is tested by its Spouse...and in the *Merchant's Tale* the fool's paradise advocated by the wife in her tale is fully exposed for what it is when an old man seeks to make of marriage a lecherous paradise on earth."

Perhaps the difficulty lies in the fact that, far from being bad poetry, it is so good of its kind, as to become, in Muscatine's phrase (p. 191), "a connoisseur's poem" beyond the capacity of "the untutored or the extravagant taste."

Chaucer himself toys delicately with the borrowed tale in the capacity of the narrator, but not in his own person as poet. The two styles represented by the tale and the Envoy are evidence of a close appreciation of the modes of experience each opposes to the other. The values of the tale are, obviously, rare, and the allegorical temper risks the literal for the sake of any other level of meaning. It is a mistake, I feel, to dismiss the literal level on the ground that it is illogical or repulsive when the literal statement exists to bring into being a meaning of a more abstract sort. The moral which came to be attached to the poem only partly explains the meaning in the most accessible moral way; a still higher level of meaning is possible through the allegorical method, by means of which the themes of obedience, marriage, sovereignty, contracts, sacrifice, and gentilesse are made to yield a statement suited to a Christian poem, by a Christian poet, in a Christian society. In this way the article of S. K. Heninger, Jr., "The Concept of Order in Chaucer's *Clerk's Tale*," *JEGP*, LVI (1957), 382-95, and that of Donald C. Baker, cited above, are making a substantial contribution to an interpretation of the poem.

THE FRANKLIN'S TALE

È gentilezza dovunque è virtute
Ma non virtute ov' ella.

DANTE, *Canzoniere*

O wonder,
How many goodly creatures are there here!
How beauteous mankind is!

SHAKESPEARE, *The Tempest*

In the *Franklin's Tale,* the view of marriage which has in a sense been dismembered is reconstituted in terms of a balance between service and dominance, between human weakness and strength of character, between respect for self and respect for others. The contract of mutual fidelity, put to a test by a tempter, is finally vindicated through the agency of a liberating love extending out of a domestic situation into other spheres of the social world. Whereas the ironical point of the *Merchant's Tale* has to do with the vengeance of the world outside of marriage upon an untenable situation within it, the moral point of the *Franklin's Tale* has to do with the extension of personal integrity, and the protection of that of others, out of the compass of marriage into other human relations.[1]

[1] Of great value is the succinct statement by D. W. Robertson, Jr., *A Preface to Chaucer,* pp. 374–77, on the thematic use of the marriage question in the *Canterbury Tales.* Of interest here too is his discussion of gardens, pp. 386–88. Although Professor Robertson now rejects his earlier article on "The Doctrine of Charity in Mediaeval Literary Gardens," *Speculum,* XXVI (1951), 24–49, as misleading in some respects, it still has great value for the student of the *topos.*

There is an increasing tendency to read the character, and hence the tale of the Franklin as a subtle exercise in the depiction of the Epicurean man, the term "epicurean" being limited here to an excessive delight in life apart from higher values and not, as in Dante, including the denial of the existence of the soul or a life after death. The term is based upon the familiar locus of the *General Prologue* which names the Franklin "Epicurus owene sone," and the treatment of him as an Epicurean tends to avoid the complicating statement by Chaucer that he was "Seint Julian ... in his contree," the Christian implications being perhaps unassimilable to the argument.

John Edwin Wells's statement, in *A Manual of the Writings in Middle English,* p. 735, still has a valid pertinence: "... while seeming not to protest against the

The issues which are raised concerning personal integrity can be solved only by the assumption of responsibility by the human agents, and the choice afforded Dorigen, the central character, between death and dishonor, like the larger question of evil in the universe, bears finally upon the moral freedom of rational creatures in it. Unable to face the consequences of her commitment, Dorigen is advised by her husband of the inescapable burden of her obligation, the keeping of her word. In the paradox of an optimistic romance, Arveragus, by acting generously for the sake of preserving his wife's good word, salvages the honor of his marriage and sets in motion a widening circle of charitable action outside of it.

Thematically the *Franklin's Tale* caps the purely social interpretations of sovereignty in the discussions of marriage throughout the *Canterbury Tales*. It affirms from one point of view the responsibilities inherent in contractual relationships, and from another, the

---

Host's scorn for *gentilesse* the Franklin quietly tells a tale in which *gentilesse* is the motive of almost every vital act of each of the principals." Robertson, *Preface*, pp. 276 and 471-72, finds that the Franklin's conception of "gentilesse" is consistent with the "entirely superficial nobility of a wealthy man of the middle class who is 'Epicurus owene sone' and is hence, like the summoner in the friar's Tale, blind to anything beneath surface appearance." He is, furthermore, akin to January and the Wife of Bath in manifesting a particular Epicureanism, namely "marriage which avoids the image of the sacrament." "Chaucer," Robertson writes, "had no way of knowing that the spiritual descendants of the Franklin would one day rule the world" in the modernity of these attitudes.

It is too easy to overstate the Franklin's Epicureanism, and too easy to read this Epicureanism downward into sensuality. When we observe the text we discover that "ease" is but one factor in marriage; there is bliss, there is "solas," there is "joye," there is "prosperitee," there is "suffraunce," there is "temperaunce," and there is the cherishing of the other. As a matter of fact, marriage has always been a lawful remedy for concupiscence in the Christian-Hebrew tradition, and Chaucer and his Parson knew this well enough (*Parson's Tale*, ll. 915-45). And in an age when marriage for political reasons or for the sake of family advancement was not uncommon, it is an unusually honest, truthful picture which Chaucer presents. Marriage is both a contract and a sacrament: insofar as it is a contract it is based upon human realities which St. Paul openly recognized; insofar as it is a sacrament it is based upon the law of love, a harmony of interests, including children and the fruits of the spirit, being achieved by two persons learning to make the best of their human natures. I feel there is no reason for us to deny the existence of both elements in the *Franklin's Tale* or to argue a subtle implication about the Franklin's character from the absence of either. In any event there is no reason to suppose that "ease" in marriage was the exclusive prerogative of Epicureans; I dare say that pious Christians have always felt it to be one of their inalienable rights.

Cf. the discussions of Raymond Preston, *Chaucer*, pp. 275-76; of John Speirs, *Chaucer the Maker*, pp. 164-67; of Hugh C. Holman, "Courtly Love in the Merchant's and Franklin's Tales," *ELH*, XVIII (1951), 241-52; see too the review of Robertson's *Preface* by Robert E. Kaske, "Chaucer and Medieval Allegory," *ELH*, XXX (1963), 188-90.

necessity of charitable dealings in all difficult ones. By extending its meaning to include even the world of business, its gaze looks outward to the whole community of men.

As in the *Merchant's Tale*, a symbolically suggestive garden serves the needs of the genre. The temptation in the garden was for Damian successful, and the Tree of Knowledge bore for the audience bitter fruit beyond the savoring of old January. The temptation for Aurelius is unsuccessful, and the fruit borne is the vindication of "franchise and alle gentillesse." [2] Not only the audience, but the principal agents themselves, enjoy the knowledge brought forth.

The tale assigned the Franklin by his creator is aptly suited to a man of good will. In the words of Walter Morris Hart, it is designed to illustrate the contagious influence of good.[3] The generous action of Arveragus' powerful but humble personality is indeed communicated to the sentimentalized squire and in turn to the hardheaded businessman-magician, who will not be outdone in noble action. This burden which the tale supports comes after much else: the musing upon the nature of mutual tolerance as a sane basis of human relations and in particular of marriage; the discussion of evil and the relative freedom of created things in potential collision in a "good" or divinely ordained universe; the consideration of the preservation of honor in the face of tricky bargain entered into in a moment of half-serious banter; the difference between appearance and reality; the subtle distinction between moral and merely physical chastity— matters which go far beyond the view of Hart. It is not difficult, however, for us to fail to connect the opening sermonette on mutual forbearance with the more ample demonstration of this forbearance in the action of Arveragus, then of Aurelius, and finally of the magician, a gentilesse which springs from the golden rule of good manners, and which disseminates its influence beyond the marriage to dissipate the threat of adultery and eventually of severe financial embarrassment.

[2] Kenneth Kee, "Two Chaucerian Gardens," *MS*, XXIII (1961), 162, writes: "By having the squire Aurelius renounce his rights to the lady before the garden is reached, Chaucer effectively suppresses the implications which the tradition of the garden carries with it. Thus the shadow cast by both the love-garden and the Garden of Eden are lifted. Courtly love and the Fall are held in abeyance, and Dorigen returns to her husband Arveragus as innocent in body and heart as when she left him."

[3] "*The Franklin's Tale*," *Haverford Essays* (Haverford, Pa., 1909), pp. 185–234.

Even if we discount the Franklin's pretense of rhetorical indifference ("Colours of rethoryk been to me queynte; / My spirit feeleth noght of swich mateere.") and assume the truth of scholarly judgment that the *Franklin's Tale* is replete with figures, its narrative virtue nonetheless lies not so much in its embellishments—indeed the *exempla* daunt the new reader—as in a certain clean charm and freshness in the depiction of likable agents, in the wedding of philosophical statement [4] with situation and character, in the reaching out for truth beyond illusion, and in a happy moral demonstration vastly different from the sardonic irony of the previous *Merchant's Tale*.

The opening of the tale describes the relations of Arveragus and Dorigen in terms familiar to any reader of medieval love poetry. These terms are romantic and courtly: a lover serves his lady, they are both of high estate, the lover suffers pain and distress for his lady. She is inspired with pity to love him, but not in the special way of *amour courtois:* these lovers marry and in marrying define the terms of their mutually held contract; that is, he will never assume mastery against her will nor play the jealous lover. He will, nevertheless, pledge his obedience. She, for her part, responds with equally generous terms. He will have no cause for quarreling with her: as a counter to his obedience she pledges humility and fidelity. The husband wishes only to retain the appearance, the name or reputation, of mastery; "the name of soveraynetee, / That wolde he have for shame of his degree." And with this sly comment Chaucer makes an immediate line in our minds with the previous exploration of the mastery theme.

His unusual sanity now offers a common-sense solution to the bitter extremes posed by the Wife of Bath's *Prologue* and by the *Clerk's Tale*. The relationship of lovers in the matrimonial bond is that of mutually tolerant, trusting friends, neither of whom acquires mastery over the other:

> Love wol nat been constreyned by maistrye.
> Whan maistrie comth, the God of Love anon
> Beteth his wynges, and farewel, he is gon!   (ll. 764–66)

Patience, endurance, temperance, self-control, discretion, self-knowledge are infinitely to be preferred to highhandedness in human

[4] Edwin B. Benjamin, "The Concept of Order in the *Franklin's Tale*," *PQ*, XXXVIII (1959), 119–24, addresses himself specifically to this neglected aspect of the tale.

relations, as Arveragus the wise man knows. The result is a marriage
of the ideal sort, described in terms of a delicate mixture and balance
of service and lordship, a marriage in which Dorigen is both the beloved of courtly tradition and the wife of acceptable theological doctrine. In Chaucer's terms,

> Thus hath she take hir servant and hir lord,—
> Servant in love, and lord in mariage,
> Thanne was he both in lordshipe and servage.
> Servage? nay, but in lordshipe above,
> Sith he hath bothe his lady and his love;
> His lady, certes, and his wyf also,
> The which that lawe of love acordeth to.   (ll. 792–98)

This attitude marks a considerable advance over any purely courtly
love tradition inasmuch as it reconciles the role of women in the
courtly love code with their role in marriage, presenting to Chaucer's
sophisticated audience a truly Christian relationship justifiable on the
grounds of mature common sense, and perhaps more importantly, on
the grounds of that higher love which Boethius celebrates in the *Consolatio* at the close of the second book. It is a paradox that the law of
love, while a guise for a kind of necessity that rules the universe, yet
assures to man his freedom throughout the moral realm. If our practical common sense demurs that marriage surely brings with it restriction and limitation, this story nevertheless insists upon the terrible
burden of freedom, which takes precedence over even the terms of
the contract. And love, while it liberates, carries with it grave responsibilities not only of being free, but of assuring, nay guaranteeing, the
freedom of one's contractual partner. Thus, while the friends in marriage are debtors, as the Wife of Bath and the old knight January
would have us remember, their relationship is the delicate one of a
rewarding liberty, a relationship conducive to virtue both ethically in
the relation of friends and neighbors and morally in clarifying the
relation of creature to creator.

When Arveragus departs from his castle home at Penmarch, em-
barking upon his quest for fame and reputation, he leaves behind a
loving wife vulnerable to fears. Her ceaseless weeping gives grave
concern to friends, who persuade her eventually to come disport with
them. But her fears persist, and these are given philosophical and
appealing utterance in one of the few Chaucerian loci to deal with the
problem of evil (ll. 865–94). Her prayer is Boethian in tone and

asserts much the same basic premises that are to be found in the *Consolatio*, namely that the world is governed ultimately by the providence of God; that nothing in it was made without a use or function. But the black rocks on which her husband may founder, she opines, seem to be anything but the beautiful and useful parts of a good creation, especially since they have been a means of man's destruction. Is it possible that a good creator has wrought such means to destroy man, who is created in God's image?

The extravagance of her outburst is a measure of the distress underlying her longing for her husband. But this speech is something more than the expression of an overwrought mind or the indication of a poignantly feminine perturbation. It is more too than a mere indication of the range of interests attributable to the teller of the tale, although this does add a cubit to his stature.

What this "more" is becomes discernible as the larger landscape of God's world with its problems of conflicting freedoms and functions gives way to the smaller, man-made pleasure garden with its inevitable, gentle tempter, where the problem of evil, of personal freedom and responsibility will be put to the test.

The Franklin's middle class morality notwithstanding,[5] we are back in the milieu and intellectual ambience of a courtly love code, with its subtle attack on the integrity of marriage, a code consciously opposed to the ideal clearly stated in the *Merchant's Tale* as "that hooly boond / With which that first God man and womman bond" (ll. 1261–62). And just as we may suppose Arveragus acted in his courting days—but with the goal of marriage—so now we see Aurelius enduring the role of the romantic, suffering lover: despairing of the goal, hinting at his love in poetry, looking meaningfully at Dorigen in social gatherings, and finally by a gradual process revealing his affection for her.

Dorigen is faithful to her husband, swearing by God that she will never by word or deed betray him; in the next breath, in jest, she makes way for the trap in which she is subsequently ensnared, setting the terms of an "impossible," the removal of those rocks along the coast. In a sense she offers an impossible for an impossible: I will love you best if by the removal of the rocks you allow the man I love best to return to me. A delicate irony! In short, she requires a miracle, the only solution to the problem of evil as stated in her long exclamation about the relative functions—and freedoms—of created things. Indeed

[5] Hart, *Haverford Essays*, p. 186.

the only way in which the collision of freedoms may be prevented is
by a suspension of the laws of the universe so that one freedom may
prevail. This miracle may be performed only by God—or by magical
illusion, wherein only the surface appearance of nature and life, not
its essential reality, is affected.

And so out of the garden has come the first assault upon the marriage, one which opposes the ideal of adulterous persuasion to the
ideal of marital fidelity. Aurelius has his good features; the conventions he lives by are as valid for his actions as those by which Dorigen
and Arveragus abide. The lines which assure us of Dorigen's scorn
must indeed have sounded, as Hart reminds us, very strange in his
ears:

> "What deyntee sholde a man han in his lyf
> For to go love another mannes wyf,
> That hath hir body whan so that hym liketh?"   (ll. 1003–5)

But they serve their purpose in widening the difference in convention
and attitude between them and assuring us of Dorigen's fidelity in the
"paradox of married lovers." Moreover, when Aurelius has successfully brought about the illusion of removed rocks, Dorigen's extravagant complaint rings in our ears both as the natural demonstration of
her character and femininity and as a further exploration of the theme
of freedom. First stated on the larger scale in the bitter contemplation
of the black rocks, it is now reduced to the purely human consideration of possible moral choices arising out of the garden in which
Dorigen, however jestingly, toyed with the impossible.

Aurelius in his dismay appeals to the pagan gods for the miracle of
the sustained opposition of sun and moon so that the rocks will in
actuality be submerged for a period of two years. He recognizes that
only a miracle will accomplish the goal; in his heartfelt prayer addressed to the pagan gods (Apollo to intercede on his behalf with
Lucina) Chaucer opposes conventions once again: the courtly lover
prays to gods; Dorigen appeals to the one God. And as we later see,
Aurelius uses the offices of magic, in a sense an emulation of God's
power, to which the Franklin will oppose the tradition and weight of
Holy Church. At any rate, for the price of a thousand pounds, he has
his sham miracle, not for two years as he hoped, but for a week or
two.

When Dorigen is confronted in a temple with the unforeseen

threat of the loss of honor—Aurelius is still the gentle, amiable lover as he presents her with the consequences of her joking bargain—she sees the choice before her as one between death and dishonor, maintaining that she would rather die than be a faithless wife sullying her reputation. In her long outbursts she cites instances of many women, both wives and virgins, who chose death over dishonor; and, running out of such examples as chose self-slaughter, she cites others who, when their husbands died, refused second marriages and so constitute exemplars of uxorial chastity and fidelity.[6]

The whole complaint does give the impression of an emotionally distressed woman contemplating the choice of death or dishonor, dwelling upon certain of the examples among those who made the fatal choice, then widening the range of association and self-reproach to examples of continent and faithful wifehood, which she seems on the verge of violating. The gradually increased tempo, the variety of rhetorical pattern, and toward the end, the cramming of illustrations into few lines, manage to say, whether or not the list is precisely apt, that these wives provide models of chastity such as Dorigen would emulate if she could. Chaucer has felt no need to reiterate Jerome's view here that the virtue of women is purity. In the light of the sanity and good-natured seriousness of the first sixty lines of the tale, none of us can doubt that gentilesse as the bond of perfection precludes any active moral defection in Dorigen. But love has made her free, and it is this terrible freedom to choose between dishonor and life with truth that the complaint spells out and foreshadows for the remainder of the tale.

It would be ridiculous for us to entertain even for a moment the possibility of either death or dishonor as the solution to the problem. The sanguine nature of the teller of the tale prevents it, the literary type opposes it, the intellectual tone precludes anything but a witty conclusion or answer to the riddle it has posed. We cannot say even that the solution grows out of the character of the agents, though there are some who would see the triple generosity as an outgrowth of the character of Arveragus. But the plot seems rather situational

---

[6] The dynamics of the complaint have been evaluated by Germaine Dempster, "Chaucer at Work on the Complaint in the *Franklin's Tale*," *MLN*, LII (1937), 16–23, and "A Further Note on Dorigen's Exempla," *MLN*, LIV (1939), 137–38, and by James Sledd, "Dorigen's Complaint," *SP*, XLV (1947), 36–45. More recently the subject has been reopened by Donald C. Baker, "A Crux in Chaucer's *Franklin's Tale*: Dorigen's Complaint," *JEGP*, LX (1960), 56–64.

than an expression or outgrowth of character, and all of the male agents must exemplify in one way or another the principles of honor and generosity. Their willingness to conform to the principles, or at the very least to emulate at whatever personal cost a precedent action, lends to the tale its note of moral romance and the tone of a Christian comedy.

Dorigen must keep her word since in Arveragus' opinion, "Trouthe is the hyeste thyng that man may kepe" (l. 1479), an irony no less than the irony of being trapped by a sham miracle as a consequence of what was thought to be a sham bargain in the first place. For the reader asks, what of the obligations of the marital contract wherein alone the convention of *amour courtois* and that of Christian marriage have been accommodated to each other? But firmly Dorigen is sent out to take the consequences of her promise; and Aurelius releases her from her bargain rather than commit a dishonor "agayns franchise and alle gentillesse" (l. 1524), commending the love of man and wife and hailing her as the truest and best wife he has ever seen. In his turn the magician, seeing in Aurelius honor and in Arveragus true nobility, releases the squire from his indebtedness.

The two acts of generosity succeeding that of Arveragus are slowly developed by Chaucer. He will make his point, but by demonstration as much as by overt statement; for although the reader thinks the story has reached its proper close in the restoration of the wife to her husband and of the stability of the marriage to its original state, Chaucer has yet to dispose of the bargain between his cheated squire and the almost cheated magician. Far from being a blemish upon the structure of the tale, the elaboration of magnanimity in Aurelius and the magician, cycles of generosity set in motion by Arveragus' devotion to an ideal of behavior, seems the necessary demonstration of the theme in as concrete a way as possible. Is this a weakness in execution? [7] Or is it rather concern with the working out of the plot even at the risk of psychological credibility? A concern for demonstrating rather than merely stating the theme? It is, to my mind, in the successive acts of charity and mutual forbearance that one point, perhaps *the* point, of the tale is made in an inevitable idealistic solution to the plot. It is, too, this repeated action of generosity which rouses in us a sense of approbation, of mellow feeling, of almost-laughter touched by reflection.

[7] See Hart, *Haverford Essays*, p. 201.

Tatlock has written most persuasively of the character and performance of the magician in the tale; he has noted that the magician is
"the most subtly interesting person of the tale," that he has sagacity
and tact, that he is proficient in business as well as in his science, that
he is humorously sympathetic toward Aurelius, in short that he is a
"business-like man of science who is a gentleman as well." [8]

The complexity of his character is, we may note further, a clue to
the supernatural, to the final poetic meaning of the story. It is, after
all, the illusion he creates which supplies the answer to the demand
for a miracle implicit in the lament of Dorigen. The setting side by
side of Dorigen's plea to God, which only a miracle can solve, with
the plea uttered by Aurelius to the magician implies a sly metaphorical
rapprochement between the magician and God Himself. The mixture of aloofness with kindness, the pleasantly masculine evocation of
a springtime world of hunting and hawking and jousting in the midst
of December, his anticipation of the needs of the young squire ("I
knowe the cause of youre comyng"), his judicious dissipation of the
obligation at the close of the story—all stir the imagination. He seems
more than the businessman-magician; he verges upon the creator-poet
shaping the stuff of dreams and mere appearance to create a reality.
Although he lacks what Dante, in speaking of the virtuous heathen
calls the "good of the intellect," he is capable of the warmer traits of
humanity; more noteworthy, and crucial in the tale, the illusion of
reality which he creates sets in motion the widening circles of selfless
charity, the last act of which he himself performs, participating so to
speak in the miracle which his "poetry" has been enabled to imitate.

> "But God forbede, for his blisful myght,
> But if a clerk koude doon a gentil dede
> As wel as any of yow, it is no drede!"   (ll. 1610–12)

We can consider then in this state of mind how much Chaucer has
risked for the sake of so delicate and poignant a theme: an Arveragus, who seems at first glance—and sometimes at second—a fool to
risk so much for an ideal of truth; a promise made by a distraught
wife in a moment of jest, a promise which is as binding as a contract; a
miracle which is only an illusion; a deliberate collision between conventions; a magician with a shrewd sense of business who gives up his
claim to a thousand pounds. The risk is eminently worthwhile. If we

[8] J. S. P. Tatlock, "Astrology and Magic in Chaucer's Franklin's Tale," *Anniversary
Papers* [for] *George Lyman Kittredge* (Boston, 1913), pp. 340–41.

have had for the moment to suspend our disbelief, poetic faith has led inevitably to another kind of faith.

Seen in the light of the spiritual revolution which Christianity effected in the history of the world, what we witness is the inevitable impingement of the spiritual order upon the sensual nature of man and upon the social and mundane spheres. It is not strange that the Fall in the Garden should become for Chaucer the basis for commentary upon a subsequent fall in a garden both here and in the *Merchant's Tale*. It seems worth noting that in the Merchant's garden, with its temptations and its resultant fall, the emphasis rests upon a kind of successful evil, an insistence upon the attraction of youth to youth as a retaliation for the blind lust of a duped old man. But here and in the other marriage tales, the relationship of equal to equal becomes, if not sacramental, at least symbolic of larger meaning spreading beyond the social unit of marriage into other spheres. The garden here produces only a semblance of a fall, and out of the semblance arises a generous vindication of the rule of love.[9]

In terms of the problem of evil and of the necessity of making choices, a Christian rather than a purely Boethian construction casts a good deal of light. The departure from the Garden imposed upon our first parents the necessity of using the will forever to make moral choices, a new way of accommodating creature to Creator. The soliloquy uttered by Dorigen voicing the frightening possibility of collision between the freedoms of created things is in a sense a lamentation that the departure from the Garden deprived men of a continuously miraculous life in which no conflicts or catastrophes could exist, a cooperation with God. But man wished to be free, and he must accept the consequences of being free, working out as best he can, in the sight of a watchful God, his own destiny. Dorigen in her subsequent complaint suggests fallen humanity under the painful necessity of making choices, while Arveragus' restraint from disturbing Dorigen's freedom reflects, at however distant a remove, the restraint of God from interfering in men's choices. Arveragus' condi-

---

[9] Cf. Malcolm Mackenzie Ross, *Poetry and Dogma* (Rutgers University Press, 1954), p. 196. "The grace of charity is the lifeblood of the Mystical Body, the living energy of the Christ symbol. It is Love who bids the tortured George Herbert to sit and taste His meat. It is the same Christian charity that in Chaucer's *Franklin's Tale* transcends the logic of courtly love dissolving in a single mercy the plight of the wife and the sensuality of the lover."

tion as a purely human agent is profoundly affecting.[10] In even a faintly allegorical light, however, we understand the function he performs of focusing attention on primal obligations.

Dorigen may not know the difference between illusion and reality, may be ignorant of magic, but more important for Chaucer's moral purpose, she does not realize the enormities to which love has liberated her in the delicate balance between self-control and obedience. She must bear the consequences of her freedom, and out of this exploration of her freedom grows the consummate artistry of the tale. From it flows the translation of gentilesse out of the abstract regard for truth into pity, and finally into generous action.

Any attempt to answer the final question of the tale clarifies its poetical bearings: worldly attitudes distress and strain its intentions. From the point of view of any possessive husband, Arveragus is a fool for setting aside his prior marital rights for the sake of his wife's integrity and "franchise." From the point of view of the callous amatory man, the squire is a fool, amiable though he be, for not taking Dorigen against her will and against any law of love. From the point of view of the practical man of the business world, the magician is a fool for not insisting upon the obligations of the bargain Aurelius has made with him. The absurdity of straining for what the literary type cannot countenance makes it equally obvious that Chaucer intends a balanced *jeu* in which any of the candidates may be defended as generous beyond all others. Indeed the posing of the question at all forces us to set against each other the practical considerations of selfish action against those more charitable actions which the story has presented to us. In fine the tale seems a vindication by the higher imagination of a poetically realized comic, Christian truth opposing the "practical" facts of a lower mode of comic statement. Weighing the one against the other, we tend to see in the opposition of the *Merchant's Tale* to the *Franklin's Tale* the same antithesis that exists between the bitterly, unassailably true, and that more harmonious and optimistic vision which qualifies as a higher kind of truth.

[10] Percy Van Dyke Shelly, *The Living Chaucer*, p. 283: "...Chaucer, or the Franklin,...is giving his views on the subject of human relationships in general, stressing the necessity of patience and tolerance and of our recognizing that at one time or another we are all guilty of offence."

CODA TO THE ROMANCES

In the first coda I tried to make some statement about the thematic range of the tales designated as forms of comedy and irony. They were obviously not all the same kind of irony, and they all displayed a wide range from serious to non-serious. Each of them functioned within the larger pattern of pilgrimage, the more bawdy tales being given the justification by the persona that he was being truthful to the stuff of life and that he felt in the main only an artist's responsibility towards his materials.

Needless to say, such a defense of poetry functions as a part of the whole structure, and gives way at the close to a wholeheartedly moral stance in which artists no less than ordinary human beings are subject to a higher judgment. They are in fact as much responsible for their artistic creations as for other human acts. We can see in retrospect that only by means of such an opening gambit as this defense of poetry could such tales come to function significantly within the framework of pilgrimage. Chaucer as ironist knows with Pandarus that a thing is made clear by its contrary. Comedy and irony, with their coarseness and cruelty, are a part of the attitudes, aesthetic and moral, to which Chaucer like Dante adhered and which they managed to incorporate even into "serious" forms of literature.

It is not merely in Aristotle's terms that there is a delight in beholding painful objects; there is, in Christian terms, an intellectual pleasure and profit to be derived from them. In the *Canterbury Tales* the ugly and the ridiculous, the presumptuous and the arrogant have great contrastive value with other aspects of the world on pilgrimage. The infernal world of the self-willing, the self-gratifying, the self-deceiving impostors opposes in its vices that other purgatorial world in which the heroes become undeceived, tutored, resigned, and in which the acquisition of even some pedestrian truth makes clear once and for all the difference between men as worse than they are and men as better than they are, or at least as they ought to be. The difference is in short that which is set forth for us in the *Parson's Tale,* where the vices and the virtues, seen as the by-products of the active conscience and the will-in-action, set forth for us the two provinces both of life and of art.

Chaucer makes capital of the devices of romance as he inherited it from the Continent and observed it practiced in his own country. In the most conventional terms it meant for him tales of chivalry, of love, and of religion; it meant tales, moreover, in which the protagonists emerged from their situations somehow changed for the better. Its central focus was that of a protagonist engaging in a quest or enduring an ordeal of some sort, facing the possibilities of choice, and shown, if not in the actual process of struggling with choice, at least as having made the choice. In such tales the role of women is significant and hence raises the subject of marriage both as literal contract and anagogically as any other contractual relationship in which mankind can be bound.

Chaucer knew the range of chivalric romance and in one way or another exploited the form as it suited his purpose. While his heroes are knights and squires (and royal rooster), he suppresses as irrelevant the familiar clichés of romance: the spell placed upon a maiden by a wicked stepmother in other versions of the *Wife of Bath's Tale.* Testing agents from classes other than the nobility intrude into the aristocratic milieu: an old hag, a businessman-magician, a fox of doubtful station. It should not come as a surprise that knightly adventures as such are not his métier; they exist in the *Knight's Tale* but are subordinated to the larger considerations of love and virtue. What we might have had from the *Squire's Tale,* were it finished, we cannot say; *Sir Thopas* implies grave criticism of a form without meaning. It is safe to say that in the others in this genre, including the pietistic romances, the fact of God's providence and the moral law is a ground note to the thematic meaning and raises the question of the accommodation of the human will to the Supreme Will; the agents in the tales are seen from one point of view or another questioning it, adjusting themselves to it, or "losing" themselves in it. Even when the agents are perplexed, like Chauntecleer they act as if they were free, and the obligation to act "as if" becomes a social as much as a spiritual obligation.

The rarest flight into romantic statement is to be found in those tales dealing with saints or saintly persons. The *Prioress's Tale*, the *Second Nun's Tale*, the *Man of Law's Tale*, and the *Clerk's Tale* are pious romances of one sort or another. They have in common a quality of extravagance and improbability, a central dedicated figure subjected to grave injustices and transcending our common experience, and a stanza pattern reserved by Chaucer for his religious pieces as "fittest for grave discourse." Each is an adaptation from an original. The tales are consistent in their attitudes: humility before the divine, credulity about the miraculous. Their art is perfectly attuned to the pathetic, the sweet, the lyrical in domestic relationships. The tales of the two nuns offer themselves less as experience than as objects for contemplation, literal and allegorical levels of meaning coalescing with no strain upon the reader. What we believe, how we should act, where salvation lies, become obviously the substance of their meaning. What they have to say is obviously stated in terms of the demonstrated rapport between the transfigured soul and providential power.

This is simply to say that Christian belief, from its most simple to its most sophisticated levels of acceptance, forms the background for all the tales. The very harmony of their collective statement as to the overcoming of difficulties by divine aid and the triumph of good may give the uneasy feeling that Chaucer is not his usual self, that his writing lacks a characteristic tartness. The truth is that the literary type demands a demonstration of pure virtue, of happy cooperation between God and His creatures, and so prevents the operation of a sardonic fortune which is not the providence of God but merely caprice and malign fate.

In the *Man of Law's Tale* and that of the Clerk, Christian ideals flourish under fantastic circumstances. Both place a strain not only upon the reader but upon the persona-poet as well. In the *Man of Law's Tale*, Chaucer's main effort is directed at making the character of Constance moving and appealing, at presenting the frankly incredible with rhetorical flourishes and an openly stated didacticism sufficient to overshadow the unbelievable. When she acts, she is deliberately limited merely to suffering the fate doled out to her as an exemplar of constancy. Serenely certain of God's protection, her life is that of a dedicated and providentially guided soul, a vessel of purity amidst the wickedness and oppressions of the world.

The *Clerk's Tale*, by comparison with the bravura style of the *Man of Law's* is an overwhelmingly simple, yet profound demonstration of the subjection of human to divine will. By virtue of its affinity with religious myth or with the folk tale of the immortal lover to which religious significance came to be attached, it makes a religious statement vastly more affecting than the prodigally disposed sonorities of the Man of Law. Griselda as the epitome of patient suffering offers that paradox of acting which is nothing but willing endurance, and her motto would seem to be Job's "Though he slay me, yet will I trust in him" (Job 13:15). If the audience cannot, by analogy with Walter, call God cruelly sporting or capricious, it is forced to admit before His ineffable majesty and power that we are all nothing; our part is to suffer, to persevere, and to hope with patience.

The grave serenity of these tales, their odor of sanctity, their insistence that this life is ineluctably implicated with another, their opposition of personal purity to worldly accommodations of the flesh offers us, as the prose *Parson's Tale* cannot do, the apex of wish-fulfillment romantic statement in the *Canterbury Tales*. They oppose a quiet otherworldliness to the mundane preoccupations of the comic and ironic tales; and against a concern with matter and personal gratification in it, they oppose a concern with salvation, God's justification, the saint's glory. The difference between the life of Truth to which the saintly ones are awakened and the blinding dream in which the others are imprisoned marks out for the reader the highest reaches of pure mind and body opposing the vigorous lusts of earth and offering a way of life which is, however rare, a valid ideal beyond concessions to the flesh. It is, needless to say, a conservative set of imperatives containing the threat of a certain inertness which Chaucer's art manages to make interesting and even lively by his sympathy with domestic relationships and his skill in depicting the pathetic.

It behooves us not to see these tales as isolated statement, however. They serve their function of providing us with a range of meaning in the pilgrimage far beyond the merely social and ethical sphere of man's activities. Chaucer does not allow them to remain divorced in statement from tales of profaner or more secular interest. Thus the rarefied mystery of the *Clerk's Tale* closes with a broadly satiric plea for women to become nagging shrews. The mystery of the tale itself is not lost by adducing the comic attitude; it is rather placed in high relief. Yet Chaucer's habitual irony has asserted itself, and within the context of the purgatorial journey the whole truth becomes for the moment a set of data involving both redeemed and fallen man.

The *Knight's Tale*, the *Wife of Bath's Tale*, the *Nun's Priest's Tale*, and that of the Franklin all deal in one way or another with the accommodation of the protagonist to a situation which demands resignation and a degree of self-knowledge. All of them raise in one way or another the question of human responsibility and the will, all of them have principal agents involved in love, all of them contain a trial by ordeal; in all of them an old recalcitrance gives way to acceptance of a truth. Each carries a heavy weight of the speculative and the philosophical, without being primarily moralizing or didactic. The body of wisdom which they carry is largely concerned with bringing into existence the terms on which a social good may be given a higher dimension, and in particular with relating a social good to some higher law. The meanings which are brought into existence in these tales depend to a great extent upon our assessment of the function of matters other than plot; indeed each of these tales attests in its own way to the special relationship which, in Chaucer's hands, the type romance bears to moral statement.

The *Knight's Tale*, for example, is chivalric, its agents are above the common run of humanity, the problem of love which it poses is serious, and its ending is happy in only a much qualified sense of the word. Irony perplexes and distresses any simple meaning. Arcite wins a tournament but loses his life; his tragic death is seen as a triumph of escape from the threat of age and a waning reputation and makes way for the marriage of his friend and his sweetheart. There is a *demande d'amour*, and the noble protagonists are subject to proofs of strength, but the question of love is subsumed under the larger questions of fate or destiny and the definition of an essentially inscrutable Providence. These larger questions themselves stimulate consideration of the problem of responsibility. The fate of the agents is resignation to their place in the grand scheme which love has set in order. Freedom for them becomes, in the Boethian rationale, freedom to fulfill the law of necessity.[1] The concept of earthly love is stripped of its

---

[1] Cf. the view of John Speirs, *Chaucer the Maker*, p. 123. After the initial complaints of the heroes, the Boethian views are delivered by a narrator's voice and applied to the various situations as an articulating choral commentary; these increase the distance between the audience and story and invite the long philosophical view. The final explanation of the way of Providence with his creation is delivered by

courtly disguise, of any merely erotic tone, and marriage is seen ironically as the social goal, as well as the fulfillment of the law, with the new concept of love as its basis at a vast remove from mere appetite.

Irony exists on the mythological as well as the philosophical level. Providence, however much it may seem to be capricious, exists as order which man interprets only in a limited way. This order Chaucer manages to convey precisely by the symmetry and balance of the tale, and its meaning, however badly each of us will verbalize it, must arise out of an essential irony in the human condition in which each man endeavors with anguish and suffering to bring about a *rapprochement* between himself as a sentient, rational being, willful, passionate, and the divine order in which, by means of his very anguish and suffering, he may be brought to participate. It is not quite the same thing as the *Clerk's Tale* where we have a closer and longer look at resignation and the finally oblated will, but it is kin to it.

Thus what the *Knight's Tale* has to say is very serious, and the more so for being placed at the head of the *Canterbury Tales*. Kane's view that it is all show, that it awakens little emotion, and that the bright pictures which it leaves in the memory are cold, and Root's judgment that it is a tale arousing our thought about "the terrible reality of the mystery of life, its tragedy and its pathos," may be seen as the latitude of opinion the tale has aroused.[2]

By fleshing out the meaning of chivalric romance with Boethian commentary Chaucer realizes the highest potential of the form beyond the level of the Boccaccian original and invests a high seriousness in it. As an artist as well as a moral man he makes a positive statement here, as later in *Sir Thopas* he makes a negative one, about a literary type which can too easily abrogate its responsibility towards "the truth of the human heart."

The other tales in this category (the Wife of Bath's, the Nun's Priest's, the Franklin's) more easily span the range between romantic and comic, partly because they are freed from the heavy task of justifying Providence. They carry, to be sure, varying degrees of

---

the tale's one realist who is given the task not only of pleading in Boethian terms for resignation on the part of the hero to the higher law of necessity, but of correlating that law with marriage, which is seen in the light of making the best of things.

[2] George Kane, *Middle English Literature: A Critical Study of the Romances, the Religious Lyrics, Piers Plowman*, p. 88; Robert Kilburn Root, *The Poetry of Chaucer*, p. 172.

speculative matter but are not primarily didactic. The social good
which they define, as comic or social romances, is raised into relief
against a backdrop of theological and ethical questions. Their meaning thus arises largely out of matters other than plot by which theme
may be enriched: overt statement by the narrator, the use of *exempla*,
imagery, philosophical disquisition, and the like. In them we see something of the achieved balance between literary form and theme, between narrative and textural richness for which Chaucer seems,
among his other goals, to have been striving.

Here his great artistic powers become the instruments of a rich and
generous humanity. Human recalcitrance is corrected against a background of the theological and moral values of his time. Social comic
romance is made to yield a more than merely social meaning. Indeed
the whole range of Chaucerian vision is here: romantic wish-
fulfillment of the *Wife of Bath's Tale*, for example, where what was
in origin a sentimental, more conventional example of the genre is
given a stringent novelty first by adducing attitudes from the fabliaux
and then by deepening its tone with high *sententiae*; the encompassing irony of the *Nun's Priest's Tale* where the answer to the
Monk's definition of tragedy produces a blend of tragic and comic
values; the innocent wisdom of the *Franklin's Tale* where something
close to the theological virtue of charity rises like an illumination
upon the scene.

Practical considerations dominate these tales. The realities of marriage become the bases, so to speak, the ground of morality in the
education of the hero. In fact, the values on which marriage may
securely stand, as well as the prerogatives assumed in it, are the subject of the Wife of Bath and the Franklin, and form the background
of much of the argument between Chauntecleer and Pertelote in the
Nun's Priest's Tale. In short, their philosophical speculations do not
divert their meaning from practical considerations for life prudentially lived. In their range of interests they look persistently—and
with a qualified optimism—towards this life. The pious tales, by comparison, have otherworldly interests; in them marriage is more clearly
a suggestive of a higher union or is even set aside as preventing the
realization of a higher contract. Yet between them they clarify whatever theological and moral values inform the Chaucerian romance,
providing a note of hope and, in the chivalric tales, corroborating our
inner convictions about man's adaptability.

To be sure these tales do not have the severe economy of the *Reeve's Tale* or the incomparable balance of the *Friar's Tale*. Yet we cannot complain about the extended list of *exempla* and the philosophical excursion of the *Nun's Priest's Tale*, about the little sermon on old age, poverty, and family lineage in the *Wife of Bath's Tale*, about the laments of Dorigen in the *Franklin's Tale*. To do so is to strike out at the very complexity of Chaucerian vision. Precisely by virtue of their presence within the forms do these tales, along with the *Merchant's Tale* (a kind of parody of romance values) rank as the richer and more suggestive statements of the Canterbury pilgrimage. How successful they are may be assessed by setting them in the perspective of the Physician's and Manciple's tales where the more or less didactic utterances are imperfectly integrated into the narrative or constitute an excessive response to it.

All of this discussion raises a final point: Chaucerian romance, like Chaucerian comedy, cannot easily be systematized. The attitudes in both modes may vary from playful to serious. Both manage to raise in one way or another the subject of evil, of suffering, of the difference between what men want and what they get. These notions underlie, even dictate the ironic tone of much that Chaucer says.

The form of the chivalric romance in particular he freely exploits to suit his own purposes, keeping the meanings humanistically down in the world where men are seen as capable of growth in knowledge, of developing new relationships with others. A philosophical irony plays over the sheer facts of the human condition, replacing any extravagant emotional response by bemusement before the problems of a fallen humanity making its way out of its dilemmas. The pious romances naturally corroborate religious beliefs: God's mystery, His beneficence, His order give value and perspective to the somewhat suprahuman actions depicted in the tales. The agents of such tales, while beyond our common humanity, are shown as exemplars of virtuous cooperation with a Destiny which God himself has ordained.

The recalcitrance and incorrigibility of the comic and ironic tales give way to various grades of resignation and the acceptance of others: in the *Knight's Tale*, the realization of one's role in the order of things; in the *Wife of Bath's Tale*, the acceptance of another on new terms; in the *Nun's Priest's Tale*, a saving self-knowledge assuming priority over cosmic uncertainties; in the *Franklin's Tale*, the acceptance of responsibility and the consequences of one's actions.

But it is a *canny* acceptance that we feel in the *Wife's Tale*, a *mundane* self-knowledge in the *Nun's Priest's Tale*, an *imposed* necessity in the *Knight's Tale*, in a typical Chaucerian distancing from any loftily stated solution to human problems, and it is here that we measure the degree to which Chaucer declines the high sublime.

In the pious romances Christian norms are confirmed by the actions depicted. In the others Christian morality functions as part of the texture, but the solutions depend less upon any facile solution drawn from religion than upon an all-pervasive prudence with regard to them. This is only to say that whatever Chaucer's own beliefs, he was writing about life, not philosophy, about specific situations, not Christian Truth. This is his sanity, this capacity for clearing the air so that men can be seen as they are, part of a larger order, yet sharply individual, themselves.

CONCLUSION

W e note, towards the end of the Canterbury pilgrimage, predominantly sober and grave attitudes dictated first by expedience in the tale assigned the Manciple [1] and then by moral prudence in the tale assigned the Priest. This is not to deny the comic balance provided by the links, but simply to call attention to the method by which the larger plan—the metaphor, if you will—of pilgrimage is

[1] The plea for governance and self-control may be taken to be Chaucer's most often reiterated precept, emerging with fairly insistent regularity in the pilgrimage, but always with the special cast of mind and personality of the pilgrim entrusted with the statement. We recall the description of the Knight, that of the Clerk, the performance of the Monk and the Nun's Priest, which in a variety of contexts make use of the lesson of the guarded tongue and of self-control. Apart from the satiric and admonitory elements of the *Manciple's Tale* the narrative itself bears a relationship to other parts of the pilgrimage. Its comment upon freedom in marriage calls to mind a similar situation in the *Miller's Tale;* it calls to mind the arguments of the Wife of Bath in favor of women's freedom; it calls to mind the situation of the *Merchant's Tale* where jealousy and cuckoldry go hand in hand to produce sardonic comedy; it calls to mind the larger and more charitable statement of the *Franklin's Tale* with its commentary upon the paradox of liberty in love.

The wide range of Chaucerian commonplaces, the frankly admonitory and moral passages, the free admixture of styles, and the sharp dichotomy of tones between the prologue to the tale and the tale itself have caused more than a little doubt about the artistic values of the performance. The question of genre, of style, of suitability to narrator, of focus, all perplex the unwary reader. It has generally been assumed that in this tale about Apollo, "the Greek setting, the rather learned rhetorical development, and the moral disquisition are completely incongruous with the dishonest Manciple," in the apt statement by J. R. Hulbert, "*The Canterbury Tales* and their Narrators," *SP,* XLV (1948), 576.

With regard to the morality of the tale, Wordsworth's note to Mr. Quillinan carries great weight: "The formal prosing at the end and the selfishness that pervades it flows from the genius of Chaucer, mainly as characteristic of the narrator whom he describes in the Prologue as eminent for shrewdness and clever prudence. The main lesson, and the most important one, is inculcated as a Poet ought chiefly to inculcate his lessons, not formally, but by implication.... How could the mischief of telling truth, merely because it *is* truth, be more feelingly exemplified. The Manciple himself is not, in his understanding, conscious of this; but his heart dictates what was natural to be felt, and the moral without being intended forces itself more or less upon every Reader. Then how vividly is impressed the mischief of jealous vigilance and how truly and touchingly in contrast with the world's judgments are the transgressions of a woman in low rank of life and one in high

provided with that natural coda which Chaucer's humane and Christian comedy demands. It is a method by which the social stresses of the interacting pilgrims of the links are somehow brought to resolution within the broad compass of the closing sermon; a subtle integration by which the dramatic and realistic level of the frame and the fictive level of the tales are made finally to coalesce in a single moral

---

estate placed on the same level, treated."—Markham L. Peacock, Jr., *The Critical Opinions of William Wordsworth* (The Johns Hopkins Press, 1950), p. 214.

J. Burke Severs, "Is the *Manciple's Tale* a Success?" *JEGP*, LI (1952), 1–16, raises the crucial question implied by the title and answers it affirmatively on the assumption that it is a moral tale. Wayne Shumaker, "Chaucer's *Manciple's Tale* as Part of the Canterbury Group," *UTQ*, XXII (1953), 147–56, finds tonal correspondences between the performances of the Manciple and the Parson, opening the way to our considering the two fragments as part of a continuous structure, even though in so doing we pass over the discrepancies in details of place and time. Morton Donner, in "The Unity of Chaucer's Manciple Fragment," *MLN*, LXX (1955), 245–49, takes issue with the view that the *Prologue* to the *Manciple's Tale* is a superior effort while the tale itself is hack-work, offering the opinion that the tale is closely linked with its prologue by virtue of being an illustration of a point made in it. Earle Birney, "Chaucer's 'Gentil' Manciple and his 'Gentil' Tale," *NM*, LXI (1960), 257–67, finds the tale perfectly suited to the character of the Manciple and to the ironic comedy Chaucer is in the process of weaving. Most recently Richard Hazelton, in "The Manciple's Tale: Parody and Critique," *JEGP*, LXII (1963), 1–31, attempts to prevent repeated misreadings of the tale by presenting it as a parody in the manner of the comic writers in the Latin and French traditions. The tale is "a creative transformation of literary flotsam into rich and strange comic art ... to emphasize at the expense of the artistry the element of critique that parody bears with it (the temptation and fall of moralistic criticism) is to 'maken ernest of game'; it is to assume that the piece is a tract and not a work of comic art. The *Manciple's Tale*, with its parodic mockery of the immoral 'moral Tale' as well as of courtly masquerade seems to invite such emphasis, and the evidence I have offered to suggest Chaucer's participation in the poem could encourage it. What we must remember, however, is that comedy traditionally bears its morality lightly, and Chaucer's is no exception. While it assumes moral doctrines —generally obvious and conventional moral doctrines—it does not promulgate them. ... I have tried to keep the emphasis where it belongs—on Chaucer's parodic methods and on his artistic accomplishment" (p. 31).

On the *Prologue* to the tale there is less disagreement. It is a jewel of a very rough kind, in its coarse garrulity illustrating better than almost any other link the hold exerted upon Chaucer's imagination by the bourgeois tradition of low realistic comedy, a mode of experience so attuned to his temperament and to his ear for the voice of England that posterity regards the results as Chaucer's typical level of utterance.

In its coarseness, its bitterness, its patent cruelty, it is not divorced from the concept of comedy to which Chaucer instinctively adheres. We are reminded of Aristotle's remark that there is delight derived from beholding imitations even of painful objects, a delight which we may assume is to be found not only in the terrifying death and destruction of tragedy, but in the ugly distortions of comedy, and that there is an intellectual pleasure to be derived from them. Attention to the ugly and the cruel has great value here as the last emphasis in the links upon human folly and recalcitrance before the sober tone of the Parson's "merry" tale on repentance, vice, and virtue.

statement general enough for all the pilgrims and specific enough to elicit from Chaucer himself the prayer for salvation in the Retraction. The levelling off, so to speak, into didactic preachment makes clearer the drift of Chaucer's moral intention for the design as a whole, while at the same time implying grave criticisms of some poetic modes.

The quarrel of the Cook and Manciple, the intercession of the Host, is one last version of the bickering which has been the heart of the pilgrimage, a pattern of quarrel with the restoration of festivity. Bacchus here is the harmonizing influence, the medicine which dissolves the rancors of society. Into the particular wrangling of Cook and Manciple the Host intrudes in order to turn "ernest into game." To this we may contrast the general situation of a society at variance with itself, with the Parson turning the game finally "into ernest," dissipating the mood of festivity once and for all and putting an end to the bickering. His sermon is the final harmonizing factor in the Canterbury pilgrimage, a call to virtue and to the sanctified life. It is delivered with sufficient asperity and sincerity to reach into the creative life of the author himself, moving him to the great renunciation of the Retraction.

The defects of the Cook and the Manciple are necessities in the principle of contrast; they have been means to an end in the larger structure of the framework: their contemptible antisocial actions with the specious appearance of harmony give way to the larger promised accommodations, if not harmonies, of the penitential way, existing on the one level between the artist-creator (whom we have seen manipulating his material toward a certain goal) and his material, and on the other level between the artist as creature and his Creator. Here the Host gives way as the bluff and hearty arbitrator of social actions to the greater conciliator of the moral and spiritual life, the priest of God.

In the closing chapter of the journey, the Host has lost his patronizing and derisive attitude towards the Priest, and all the other voices of the pilgrimage are silent. It is to instruction that the Host and his charges now yield themselves in this final performance. This last link of the *Canterbury Tales*, more than any other, has the capacity to stir in us considerations as to the form which Chaucer was imposing upon his somewhat amorphous materials. The vagueness of the setting (". . . we were entryng at a thropes ende"), the lengthening shadows as the sun descends in the sky, the inevitable sense of choice of the ideal priest, whose only interest is the salvation of souls, to tell the last summing-up tale ("Thou sholdest knytte up wel a greet mateere"), the rejection of fables, indeed of poetry of the alliterative sort in favor of "plesaunce leefful," a sense of the brevity of time and the admonition of the need for haste, the general air of entertainment giving place to edification as though much of the pilgrimage and the time of life has been expended upon trifles—all point up the metaphorical relationship between "this viage" and "the wey . . . Of thilke parfit glorious pilgrymage / That highte Jerusalem celestial." What the *Knight's Tale*, by virtue of its philosophical additions, was able to tell us about the pilgrimage of this life, the *Parson's Tale* will far exceed by virtue of doctrine pure and unadorned. It will, furthermore, replace the stoical resignation of the *Knight's Tale* with an active, purposeful prescription by means of which man through knowledge may overcome vice with virtue, and more important, through penance, set himself once more upon "the righte wey of Jerusalem celestial."

When we look forward to the long "merry" tale of the Parson and backward to the weightiness of his obligation and intention

> "To shewe yow the wey, in this viage,
> Of thilke parfit glorious pilgrymage
> That highte Jerusalem celestial,"   (ll. 49–51)

the injunction to be fruitful and brief is humor delicately suspended between two worlds, and for the sake of the relationship between them, the priest disregards the injunction to be brief; the matters of "virtuous sentence" to be discussed are too important, too serious for him or for Chaucer to pay attention to the mere demands of verisimilitude and the brevity of time. Donaldson writes with considerable power and persuasiveness:

Over the fictional pilgrimage, which has for many years been the reflection of his own mind and which now becomes its reflection in a more personal sense, there comes something of the chill and urgency of late afternoon. There is hardly time for the telling of one more tale. The shadows are lengthening and the sun has but twenty-nine degrees to sink before darkness falls on the nine-and-twenty pilgrims. Libra, the Scales that symbolize God's justice, is ascending the skies. Already a kind of darkness that makes recognition difficult seems to have come over the pilgrims. Where are they? At the end of a little nameless village that is surely neither on the road to Canterbury nor on the road back, but on a road that leads to a city far from England. The Host speaks to the parson as if he had never seen him before, recognizing only the priest and knowing nothing of the man. In this suddenly alien and lonely world we must hurry to get in the last, virtuous tale. Why is it the last? Not because the grand plan that Chaucer devised has been brought close to completion, but because a grander one of a greater Creator is hurrying to its end.[2]

And so the Parson begins with the great statement of rectification from Jeremiah: Stand ye and look; ask of the old ways which is the good way; walk therein and you will find refreshment for your souls.

The metaphorical drift is noteworthy, but more noteworthy is the fact that the attitude expressed should encompass and include that rejection of "fables and swich wrecchednesse" which is given final utterance in the Retraction. All that splendid vision which is possible through the work of the imagination is now ruled out in favor of the overtly, purposely didactic, that more direct commentary upon the human condition and its relation to the Divine. This alone is the lawful pleasure that the man of the cloth can, within the limits of his character, offer; this is the last act of the drama which Chaucer can tolerate for his audience and for the literary form that he is constructing. By its uncompromising separation of theology (and the moral philosophy it generates along the way) from poetry, indeed, by virtue of what it is, it becomes markedly different in subject matter, scope, and treatment from anything else in the *Canterbury Tales*.

Many a student has discovered from examining the catalog of sins that many passages afford a commentary upon certain of the pilgrims and upon certain ideas which bind the stories together; for example, the long statement dealing with the uses of marriage, which manages to throw a good deal of light upon the norms from which the marriage group diverges; in a variety of contexts we can see aspects of the character of the Squire, the Merchant, the Franklin, the Monk, the Wife of Bath, the Miller, the Reeve, the Pardoner, and others. As a matter of fact, the question has arisen from time to time whether Chaucer meant the tales, when he was in the process of developing them, to conform in some way to the scheme of the deadly sins. The classical attempt to see the tales as an illustration of the sins is that of Frederick Tupper, who presented a stimulating and spirited essay which received an equally spirited and stimulating reply from John L. Lowes.[3] It is, from my point of view, a totally unfounded assumption

---

[2] E. Talbot Donaldson, *Chaucer's Poetry* (New York, 1958), pp. 948–49.

[3] Frederick Tupper, "Chaucer and the Seven Deadly Sins," *PMLA*, XXIX (1914), 93–128, and "Chaucer's Sinners and Sins," *JEGP*, XV (1916), 56–106. John L. Lowes, "Chaucer and the Seven Deadly Sins," *PMLA*, XXX (1915), 237–371.

to maintain that Chaucer meant to cast over the entire work the enveloping scheme of the capital sins, or that he intended us to look back from the *Parson's Tale* and see in anything but a general sense that the tales have their final commentary in the various parts of the sermon. There is a certain antipathy between art and the codification of morals, however much morality may enter into art. As a matter of fact, if Chaucer at any time felt that his tales illustrate point by point the moral catalog, we have no indication of it. He was more concerned to depict men in comparatively few basic associations and to explore with what looks like infinite variety their actions and reactions. This is not to deny an easy conversance with the sins: they appear, for example, in the *Pardoner's Tale;* but he avoids a rigid schematism in favor of that more subtle pattern that may appear when men act—their actions being viewed by the poet without revulsion—and when by their very independence and individuality they assert and define the infinite variety of character and creation.

Out of the multilevelled view of experience which is the "middle" of the *Canterbury Tales,* with its variety of literary types and wide range of meaning, emerges one central theme: the very core of Chaucer's artistic vision is that ceaseless debate, which ultimately produces the contemplative ironist, between the concept of destiny and divine Providence and the fatiguing promise of moral responsibility and the freedom of the will, between the persistent claims of the appetites of the natural man and the higher claims of the spiritual man, indeed between the pressures from our wish-fulfillment selves and those of the realistic day-to-day world. These are present everywhere in the *Troilus* in a subtle intermixture; in the *Canterbury Tales,* however, this *sic et non* of the medieval *conflictus* is more obviously present in the very alternation of the tales and in the varying persuasions of the speaking pilgrims. The delicate balance between man as God-created yet self-asserting, as God-seeking yet self-loving illuminates the antagonism implicit between the goal of Canterbury and the desire to reach the goal on terms personally and willfully defined. In short, Chaucer's view of humanity produces the whole range of comic and romantic experience, a range so comprehensive as to make tragedy a mere episode and so inclusive as to admit the presence even of the vile Pardoner and the intrusion of the Canon's Yeoman, trembling on the brink of momentous conviction.

It seems not to have been his attitude towards the spiritual that changed as Chaucer grew in artistic maturity. What is new is his increasing sympathy for and interest in human actions which are mainly secular and profane. This interest his reading corroborated, so far as we may judge. Whenever he read the *Romance of the Rose*, the *Consolation of Philosophy*, the *Wretched Engendering of Mankind*, Boccaccio, Dante, or the French models for his fabliaux, each writer could easily have confirmed his proclivity for irony and realism which are thereafter engrafted upon an existing romantic, didactic, sententious tradition of moral literature.

The flowing together of attitudes romantic and religious with those that are comic and ironic, is, we have suggested, the special mark of Chaucerian wonder and the means by which he evinces a certain inability to define more precisely the terms of his perplexity. Even more subtly projected in the *Troilus* than in the *Canterbury Tales*, this perplexity lies at the very root of their meaning. In the varying plights of Troilus, Criseyde, and Pandarus, Chaucer has demonstrated some modes of experience. In the terms in which each has been presented, no one of these modes has been found to be satisfactory. Within the range of the poetic form, the dilemmas remain unresolved: man is morally responsible, yet mysteriously the victim of fate or destiny; he is obliged to obey the law of Love, yet human love is found to be unstable. The palinode as a capstone to the questions raised does not entirely dissipate either the moral or experiential confusion. On the contrary, by opposing its "new" law of love to the "old" law of the poem, it distresses by proposing that the reader set aside sympathies which have been hard won during the course of the poem.

We may spell this out more precisely: Between them Troilus and Pandarus divide the stores of romantic innocence and satirical wisdom. Troilus' erotic idealism, his paralysis of will, his slavish submission to love and Pandarus' active shaping of experience to suit the moment, his refusal to be ruled by merely wistful hopes, stand on either side of Criseyde's complex participation in life. A mixture of innocence with resourcefulness, of easy mendacity with a concern for fidelity in others, of yielding surrender with expedient self-sufficiency, she is troubled by philosophical limitations on her freedom, yet acts as if she were free without enervating deliberation. Even the repeated pattern of her affair with Diomedes, while it appears to be a destinal pattern of history which her character invites, carries with it the overtone of the necessary accommodation of herself to the grim facts of life.

Her weakness, from the point of view of romance, in compliance to a new lover, insofar as she is free to choose, must be seen as her strength from the point of view of Chaucerian comic realism. If we feel that by comparison with her (and Pandarus) Troilus is not nearly so interesting, it is because her more complex worldliness and complicity with life overwhelms that world of arms, love, and virtue in which he has his existence.

Within the range of the *Troilus*, then, Criseyde tests the opposing attitudes of romantic tragedy and those of ironical comedy. She serves as the mirror through which man beholds the divine law, exciting virtue in the lover; but she is also the self-exonerating, surviving woman, sister to the resourceful doxies of the fabliaux. Her unsuccessful participation in both realms of experience is an admission of the insoluble complexity of existence and a comment upon the fragility of any one view of it. This it seems to me is the point which the palinode spells out in the contrast of pagan and Christian terms. That is to say, the closing statement not only provides a new point of vantage from which to review the foregoing form, but in so doing, makes the views of experience expressed in it morally unstable.

This debate between two laws, this counterpoising of attitudes towards experience which Chaucer crystallizes in a new way at the very end of *Troilus*, is carried on from the very outset of the *Canterbury Tales* in terms of human instinct and religious convention. This inner argument is thereafter modulated throughout the great middle of the structure and given a final lucid statement in the performance of the Parson.

The *Canterbury Tales* and the *Troilus* are obviously not the same kind of structure. Their methods of presenting experience differ. In addition to the commingling of attitudes within the individual tales, Chaucer's journey poem demands the device of comparison and contrast, of debate and quarrel among persons of varying station and point of view. Indeed, alongside the logical inner movement of the *Troilus*, the episodic tales seem diffuse and unfocused. Both, however, explore reality in contexts secular and spiritual. Both end with a statement which resolves the issues raised by the tactic of rejection and a spiritual affirmation. Both state, overtly or by unmistakable implication, the dangers of loving the world too much on any terms, even the world which art defines. Both endings are surprisingly personal.

The penitential statement with which the *Canterbury Tales* comes to a close rejects specifically all those poems in which the instinctual life is praised, a rejection which becomes obligatory in the light of the sacramental view of life superimposed upon pilgrimage by the Parson. It makes its point by its position of emphasis and is intended finally to focus our sensibilities upon the moral bearings of the poem. As in the *Troilus* the solutions are not those of a new moral awareness expressed by the central agent. Chaucer himself adduces the moral for his audience, calling attention in what seems a final ironical statement to the plight of the rational creature endeavoring to understand the mysterious relationship between the eternally permanent and the humanly transient. For Troilus death brings a sudden illumination, but we must interpret it ourselves. For the audience of the *Canterbury Tales*, there is the utterance of the Parson, an admonition and an exhortation, but the audience must learn to see its meaning in context. This is not to say that a knowledge of good and evil has not been coming into view. Social goods and social evils have been paraded before us for our contemplation, in a variety of secular tales. In the background of these and in the tales of the more religious members of the pilgrimage there has been a theological matrix which has lain, so to speak, beneath the total structure as an ultimate criterion.

In the balancing of the two worlds one sentiment gradually emerges: there is no knowledge which this world offers which adequately comprehends the multiformity of human experience. Yet, the literary form must come to an end, support some conclusion. The essentially romantic form of the *Canterbury Tales* no less than *Troilus* demands an emphasis not merely upon action and conflict and adventure, and upon love in all its range from secular to divine, but upon virtue as the highest goal of the spiritual man. It is in this central phase of divine comedy that the *Canterbury Tales* draws to a close. *Troilus'* conclusion leans heavily upon Boccaccio's

> Ed ogni cosa da nulla stimare
> A rispetto del ciel.

This Chaucer expands to

> ... [he] held al vanite
> To respect of the pleyn felicite
> That is in hevene above; ...   (V, 1817–19)

and proceeds to a condemnation and an admonition:

> [He] dampned al oure werk that foloweth so
> The blynde lust, the which that may nat laste,
> And sholden al oure herte on heven caste. (V, 1823–25)

The point of the close of the *Canterbury Tales* is not different from this.

That Chaucer should have been a poet of love-after-the-Fall does not come as a surprise to us; neither should we be surprised at the quieter tones of melancholy that lie at the heart of his delight in a world eagerly embraced.[4] What is bequeathed to us after the Golden Age, Chaucer seems to say, is a world in which man must continue to live, but always with the ideal uses of the law beyond the grasp of his fallen nature. Love is the most meaningful face of Law, a necessary part of the universe, its principle of order. For human beings it provides the model of behavior for charitable and just action between lord and subject, parents and children, husband and wife, friend and friend, profession and profession, class and class. But without that primal, natural innocence, participation in the law is faulty. Man after the fall translates love downward into a variety of lesser loves with their power subtly to divert from the higher good. Such loves inevitably corrupt unless they become more conformable to nature as vicar of God and unless participants in them assume responsibility for observing, along with morality, good sense and decorum: in marriage, for example, the suitability of union between those like each other in birth, age, disposition. Within the mutable world the disordered relation of man to neighbor bears the sterile fruit of spiritual death itself and yields the futile questions: "What is this world? What asketh men to have?"

However, for the tutored soul there is a wisdom that grows out of the human condition and the passage of time: a bearing of the fruits of

---

[4] Cf. Charles Muscatine, *Chaucer and the French Tradition* (University of California Press, 1957), p. 132: "...to present secular idealism as a beautiful but flawed thing, and to present practical wisdom as an admirable but incomplete thing, to present them, indeed, as antithetical and incongruous to each other, is by implication to present a third view, higher and more complete than either. This philosophical third view hovers over every important sequence in the *Troilus*, and is made explicit in the epilogue."

For Chaucer as for Dante, the focus of even a perplexed world vision is the law of love. The student would do well to consult the perceptive treatment of love's law in J. A. W. Bennett, *The Parlement of Foules: An Interpretation* (Oxford: Clarendon Press, 1957), pp. 186–93, for "...a view of the place of love in human life which is balanced, harmonious, and satisfying, yet which does not ignore the paradoxes and dilemmas that are as old as human society."

charity, resignation, a tempered joy in the natural order, and a final recognition of the relation of the goods of this world to the Highest Good; in fine, a continuous negotiation of the contract that redeemed man makes, however mysteriously, with God through the intermediary Logos.

This is the underlying *argumentum* of the *Canterbury Tales*. What emerges from the juxtapositions, within the great middle, of the varieties of truth, is a continuing sense of the mystery, a sense of charity towards the human beings involved in it. At the end of the *Tales*, after the double visions of man as fallen and redeemed have been set forth for us to see in the Parson's sermon, Chaucer makes his own confession. He is, so to speak, in the vestibule of the Most High. To arrive there with him we must re-examine the divided commitments of the tales themselves.

INDEX